The Grissim Ratings Guide to Manufactured Homes

by John Grissim

Rainshadow Publications • Sequim, Washington

Published by:
Rainshadow Publications,
a division of Rainshadow Ventures, LLC
7456 Old Olympic Highway
Sequim, WA 98382
Phone 360/683-1458   Fax 360/683-1108
Email: publisher@grissimguides.com
Web site: www.grissimguides.com
This book may be purchased on-line at the above web site or by calling toll-free 800-304-6650 or by ordering from book stores

Copyright ©2007 by Rainshadow Ventures, LLC

All rights reserved, including the right of reproduction in whole or in part in any form, except in the case of brief quotations embodied in critical articles and reviews.

NOTE: This printing contains minor corrections and revisions. For listing updates and news, please visit our web site and click on "Updates."

While every effort has been made to ensure the information in this guide is accurate and the recommendations have wide applicability, the reader is advised that the strategies and recommendations offered in this guide are subject to local and state laws and regulations. Nothing in this book should be construed as a substitute for competent legal or financial advice. The reader is urged to obtain the advice of an attorney on any matter relating to points of law.

Cover illustration is derived from a cutaway home image courtesy of Patriot Homes, Inc.

ISBN   0-9725436-1-9

Printed in the United States of America by McNaughton & Gunn
Cover design: Deidra Stierle, ThreeSixty Graphics

FIRST EDITION   SIXTH PRINTING

6 7 8

Contents

Acknowledgements	iv
Introduction	v
How to use this guide	8
A primer on manufactured homes and other factory building systems	11
Index of current HUD-code manufacturers in the U.S.	12
Index of brands and series and their manufacturers	13
Manufactured home construction features & comparison table	16
Notes on the MH Construction features & comparison table	19
Glossary of MH terms, abbreviations used in this guide	20
Builders of manufactured homes in the U.S.	22

Acknowledgements

I am grateful to the many manufactured home professionals who share my belief that a guide of this nature can benefit both the industry and its consumers. Two in particular, Grover Tarlton, VP of Champion Enterprises, and Chris Nicely, VP of Clayton Homes, Inc.—both in charge of marketing for these sprawling corporations, went out of their way to facilitate access to knowledgeable people. Thanks also to Erv Bontrager, VP of Commodore Homes, for sharing his perspective and historical knowledge of the industry. Commodore's Carol Herbon, Champion Homes' Shelly Detwiler and Giles Industries' Felix Valdes were uncommonly helpful in answering many questions for their brands' listings. Rob Loomis, sales manager for Golden West homes (CA plant), generously shared his thorough grasp of the historically quirky California marketplace. My sincere thanks to you all.

The Consumers Union Southwest Regional Office in Austin, Texas, contributed helpful feedback and support, as did Bill White, former inspector supervisor for the Arkansas Manufactured Home Commission and author of the National Consumer Law Center's very helpful *Guide to Mobile Homes*. In addition to his code enforcement background, Bill has extensive experience as an expert witness on behalf of consumers in cases involving faulty construction and installation His formidable knowledge of the builders in the Southeast was enormously helpful. I am most grateful.

I'm indebted to MH consultant Steve Hullibarger, principal of The Home Team and author of the highly-regarded book *Developing with Manufactured Homes*, for sharing his considerable expertise while critiquing the MH Construction Features Table in these pages. Fred Townsend, regional manager for Clayton Homes (Louisiana), and Doug Gorman, owner of Home Mart (Tulsa, OK) fielded my many questions and provided important background information, as did noted sales trainer John Underwood, principal of The Selling Edge. Thank you all. Among the state MH associations, thanks are due to director-presidents Bill Trottier (Arizona), and Ron Dunlap (Virginia) as well as Robert Leclaire, director of Maine's State Administrative Agency. Herb Teider, publisher of the trade magazine *Manufactured Home Merchandiser*, and editor Chris Olvera, were very supportive of this project, as was David Oxhandler, the indefatigable owner/webmaster of mobilehome.com. Thank you all. Thanks, too, to the many sales center professionals who provided information, in particular those in the Northwest region, notably Tom Martin, Del DeTray, owner of DeTray's Quality Homes, Gary Stoskopf, owner of Housing Mart and Vella Tudor and Dick Vetter of Golden Homes.

Finally, I offer profound thanks to my wife Susan Robinson, without whose unwavering support, patience, good humor and numerous contributions (including the concept for the book's cover) this guide would not have been possible.

Introduction

This book is the direct outgrowth of my first consumer guide to manufactured housing, published in 2003, now in its second printing under the slightly revised title *The Grissim Buyer's Guide to Manufactured Homes and Land—How to find a reputable dealer and negotiate a fair price on the best kept secret in American housing*. Shortly after that book's release, I began receiving emails and phone calls from readers asking if there were any books available that provided ratings of all the builders. When I answered, no, often the reply was words to the effect "You should to write one. There's no way to tell who's who out here, let alone how good a house they build." I had to agree.

I knew from previous research that the venerable *Consumer Reports* magazine had once considered rating MH builders, but after it discovered there was a great diversity of homes from region to region, produced by dozens of builders promoting hundreds of brands, the magazine dropped the idea as unwieldy. Yet clearly a great need was there. As time passed and buyers of my book continued to urge me to tackle the task, I took a closer look at possibilities.

What quickly became apparent was that MH builders generally believe that when it comes to homes, consumers don't know, or don't care about, brands. There is some truth in this. After all, a home is not something that one buys regularly, like beer or cars, for which one develops loyalty. For the most part, brands are primarily used to enable manufacturers to distribute virtually the same home, with different brand names, to dealerships that compete against each other in the same market—a perfectly legitimate strategy called multiple marketing. Good for the builders, confusing for home shoppers.

In addition, larger MH builders, Palm Harbor and Champion Enterprises, for example, each with many plants around the U.S., typically allow their plants to create variations on standard home plans to reflect regional consumer tastes, dreaming up their own brand and model names for distribution. Again, a good idea, but one that contributes to more confusion.

As I continued my research, however, I discovered that few manufacturers build homes for every sector and price point; rather, they choose a market niche and carefully assemble a formula of construction features and specifications that together yield homes competitively priced for that niche, typically at two or three price points. When I began compiling lists of features and specs—leaving aside brand names for the time being—and plugged them into a universal table of construction features and specifications, arranged from one to ten in quality, the picture became much clearer—and much simpler. The process also lent itself to a numerical construction rating that seemed both fair and objective, and that could be enormously helpful to home buyers.

In the fall of 2004, now convinced that a ratings guide was feasible, I resolved to research and interview every HUD-code home builder in the U.S.—79 in all (now 83 with this printing)—to obtain not only detailed construction data, but additional information useful for home shoppers that would be presented in an at-a-glance directory format. I anticipated the task would involve at least a year of research and interviews, and would demand patience and bulletproof civility. It took all that and then some.

Having learned from my last book that this can be a secretive industry, wary of outside inquiries, I anticipated resistance from some manufacturers. Alas, I was not disappointed.

Some manufacturers behaved as if they thought I was with *Sixty Minutes*. Many seemed completely unprepared to deal with a media inquiry, let alone a consumer advocate who wanted to chat about construction minutiae such as the thickness of wall board and whether the electrical outlet boxes were nailed to the studs or attached to the walls with clips or wings.

Some manufacturers refused to respond, even when informed that their listings would be completed and published, with or without their assistance. In the interest of home shoppers, I mention this unresponsiveness in those companies' listings, leaving consumers to draw their own conclusions. But in fairness, I believe many manufacturers, while well-intentioned, are simply clueless—they have no idea how today's media operates, have no one assigned to handle media inquiries, and have little idea how these shortcomings may potentially affect consumer perceptions of their products.

The good news is the great majority of manufacturers responded wonderfully. True, it took an average of nearly three weeks of repeated phone calls, faxes and emails to obtain an interview with a knowledgeable spokesperson, but once they understood the nature of my inquiry, they willingly cooperated. I would add that during the long process of research, I became acquainted with some very bright, very conscientious and talented people who deeply care about the manufactured home industry, who fervently believe in its great potential, and who are working hard to repair an industry image tarnished by past abuses and excess.

A final note: Writing each listing involved gathering and sorting through a great deal of information, often requiring the exercise of personal judgment regarding both the content to be included and the determination of numerical ratings. The responsibility for both, as well as the accuracy of the information presented, is mine alone. Some difficult calls were made, but every effort was made to be fair. I realize that some manufacturers may be less than happy with their listings, but I hasten to add I have no axe to grind. If I have erred, I have done so on the side of the consumer.

And there you have it, the first comprehensive consumer ratings guide to every manufactured home builder. My sincere hope is that this book, used in conjunction with *The Grissim Buyer's Guide to Manufactured Homes and Land,* will help you become an informed, pro-active, confident, swindle-proof buyer. But if these books do nothing more than give you the peace of mind that comes from knowing you made the right decisions at each step on the path to acquiring your new home, their purpose will have been served.

Good luck!

John Grissim

Would you like some expert assistance at a modest cost?

Shopping for and buying a manufactured home, and purchasing or leasing the land that goes with it, can be a daunting process, especially for first-time buyers. There are many decisions to be made, everything from checking out dealerships, to selecting a home and options and negotiating a sales price, to finding reputable lenders with the best loan packages and working with contractors and sub-contractors.

If you would like some personal assistance, I'm here to help. With years of experience dealing with the manufactured home industry, and with a trusted network of experts and professionals I can call on, I can help guide you through the process, providing the no-nonsense advice and clear honest answers you need to help ensure a successful outcome at a significant savings in time, frustration and worry. In short, I'll be your personal consultant. The fee: $60 per hour.

Not sure if I can help in your particular situation? Feel free to call me toll-free (800-304-6650) during business hours (Pacific time) and I'll give you ten minutes at no charge to discuss possibilities. Or email me. I'll be happy to respond promptly. The address: john@grissimguides.com

Here's how it works:

Order one, two or three hours of my time—your choice. You can call direct to the office or order online—www.buyersguidetomh.com—click on the Home & Land Advisor tile. I'll put you on the clock each time I consult with you. You choose how best to spend your time, either a few minutes at a time as needed, or we can block out much longer blocks of time.

You set up a consultation schedule that works best for you. Should you desire a review and consultation of documents such as purchase contracts or construction bids, we'll arrange for you to provide them by fax, email or mail.

I will do my best to be available to you during crucial periods of the process to ensure you have access to my input and recommendations in a prompt, timely manner.

Once you have purchased assistance, you may take advantage of my services at any time for up to 12 months.

How to use this guide

This guide is designed primarily to be used as an essential companion resource for *The Grissim Buyers Guide to Manufactured Homes and Land*, written to help first-time manufactured home buyers understand how the manufactured home industry operates (insider secrets and all) and how to confidently deal with the many complex issues and potential pitfalls involved in the purchase and siting of a new manufactured home. More information about that book is on page 94. However, if you are already familiar with this industry and how manufactured homes are sold—and the shenanigans that unfortunately are still going on—this guide will serve you well as a stand-alone reference for up-to-date information on the companies and the products they build.

Note: the terms manufactured home and HUD-code home refer to the same product and are used interchangeably here. For a quick primer on the distinctions between the different types of homes built in factories, please see page 11.

In these pages you will find descriptions of the entire spectrum of what manufactured housing has to offer, from gorgeous high end dwellings indistinguishable from site-built homes to bare bones single section housing, from luxurious two-story Cape Cods costing $250,000 (exclusive of land) to $20,000 low-end entry level boxes you could probably kick your way out of. You will find no bias for or against any type of home, regardless of the quality of its construction (or lack of it). Even the most humble abode can represent the realization of the cherished American dream of home ownership, and its owner deservedly proud to call that home his or her castle.

Index of MH builders, pg. 12
Listed here are all 79 U.S. companies that build HUD-code homes. Some are subsidiaries of larger companies on the list—for example, Marlette Homes and Golden West Homes are subsidiary companies of Clayton Homes, Inc.. These companies are identified as such. For a full picture of that company, please be sure to read the listing of the larger company to which it belongs.

Index of brands, series and models—and their manufacturers, pgs. 13-15
Every brand, series and model mentioned in this guide is listed here alphabetically, with the name of the MH builder producing them. But there are literally thousands of model names, and builders regularly discontinue some names and add others. If you don't find here the name you're looking for, ask your retailer for the name of the builder responsible. That name *will* be on the list of MH builders. From there you can go directly to the manufacturer's listing.

Manufactured home construction features & specifications table, Pgs. 16-18
Take a few minutes to browse this table and the cut-away illustration on page 9 of a two section home. The accompanying notes (pgs. 19-20) and the glossary of terms (pgs. 20-21) provide commentary and definitions of terms, respectively. The table describes not only the principal construction features and specifications involved in the production an a home (I've chosen 56 in all), but presents them within a one-to-ten scale representing their comparative quality. I believe it's fair to say this is the most comprehensive, detailed table ever made available to MH buyers.

The table serves three main purposes:
1. Using the manufacturer's construction rating in this guide—say, for example, 7—you can

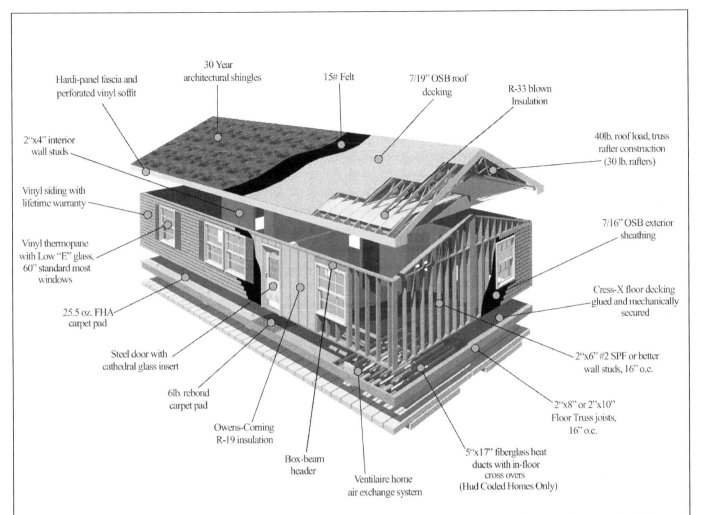

This cutaway is of Patriot Homes' Heritage American model, a well-built higher end home that retails in the low 70s. Shown are the principal construction components of a factory built home. This model features a number of desirable upgrades such as 30 year architectural shingles, Low E thermopane windows and 2"x6" exterior wall studs 16" on center. Illustration courtesy of Patriot Homes

examine the features and specs in the table that fall beneath that number to get a good idea of what likely goes into that builder's homes.

2. You can take the list of features and specs of a home you are considering and see where they line up in the table, thus enabling you to arrive at your own construction rating for that particular model, independent of what a sales center may claim.

3. You can see how construction features are measured, enabling you to ask knowledgeable questions. For example, if a sales person says a home has an "upgrade carpet and pad," you can ask "How many ounces?" for the carpet, and "How many pounds?" for the pad, and learn precisely how much of an "upgrade" you're dealing with.

About the construction ratings

Construction quality is a major consideration of any home purchase. You'll notice the ratings in these page vary considerably. In general, builders with the highest ratings are found in the northern tier of the U.S. where harsh winter weather mandates stronger, higher quality construction. Below average ratings abound in the southeast and the south central U.S. where Sun Belt weather is more forgiving of cheaper materials and lower quality construction, and where demongraphics suggest the need for affordable shelter more frequently trumps the desire for a home that has a site-builot appearance and which will hold its value and appreciate.

How the construction ratings in this guide were calculated

Product information was obtained, either directly from the manufacturer or from other sources, following which a determination was made regarding that builder's principal market niche, e.g. affordable housing for working families, high end homes for solvent retirees. In cases where the product offering is broad, a range of price points was selected. Next, a full list of standard construction features and specifications for the manufacturer's homes in that niche or range was examined. Available options and upgrades were also studied, particularly those that reportedly were ordered in a high percentage of home purchases (2"x6" ext. wall studs instead of 2"x4", for example), but the standard construction features were given the preponderant weight.

The list was then plugged into the construction table. Consideration was also given to less quantifiable elements: exterior and interior aesthetics and degree of customization offered. In addition, some construction features are regarded as more indicative of below average, or poor, quality than others and were given more weight. Examples:
- electrical outlet boxes attached to walls with wings or clips instead of nailed to studs
- carpet attached to floor w/ staples instead of tackless strips
- interior wall studs 2"x3" 24" On Center
- 5/16" wallboard

The resulting contruction rating number, therefore, is more a considered opinion than a stricly mathmatical calculation. While some may quibble about the rating number, the goal is to provide home shoppers with a useful reference number, a tool to help them quickly get up to speed on any MH builder in a matter of minutes and to enable meaningful comparisons of different manufacturers and their products.

Notes on the listings

Some descriptions of company backgrounds and histories are less robust than others, in large measure due to the absense of knowledgeable people with good institutional memories. As the introduction mentioned, MH builders generally are ill equipped to deal with outside media inquiries. Most have no marketing department at all. Their sales organizations are geared to sell to retail sales centers, whom they regard as their true customers, not actual home buyers.

Under "What distinguishes the brand from the competition," the information here largely derives from the builders' opinion of their products and how they see their competitive advantage in their marketplace. Your own observations may differ.

Web site ratings — Most manufacturers received poor ratings. This is an industry that on the whole has no clue about the Web or the power of the Internet to help their bottom line. But there are stand-out sites worth a look: Palm Harbor, Patriot, Pine Grove, Silvercrest, Jacobsen and Bonnavilla, for starters. Also, check out the dealer site, azchampion.com. Elsewhere, Fortune Homes' site provides a downloadable pdf Factory Tour (2.6MB) that is outstanding. Skyline's on-line factory tour is also highly recommended.

Other resources, new company listings since this guide was printed

For recent news of interest to home buyers, for example, mergers, acquisitions and court cases, please visit www.grissimguides.com, and click on News & Notes. For new company listings since this guide went to press, click on Updates on the home page.

An important reminder

A recent Roper survey revealed that 39% of home buyers reported major problems with their homes, only 22% of whom said they were satisfactorily corrected. Most problems can be traced to improper home set-up (or installation). Thus, in addition to construction quality, choosing a reputable dealer and a home builder with a strong track record of warranty service are two very important considerations in your purchase of a manufactured home.

A primer on manufactured homes and other factory building systems

If you're new to manufactured homes it's easy to be confused by the dfferent terms you will hear. Here's are some definitions to help you better understand what these homes are—and what they are not.

Factory built home
Any home that is constructed inside a factory and then brought to the site in big pieces, usually sections or modules, and assembled. There are four types of factory-built homes: modular, manufactured, pre-cut and panelized. See definitions below.

Site-built home
Any home that is built on the site, which the vast majority of homes are.

Off site built home
Another term for factory built, sometimes used to avoid having to use the term manufactured home with its connotation of mobile home.

Stick-built home
Same as a site-built home, although the term is inaccurate. Factory built homes are also stick-built; the "sticks" (lumber) are simply assembled inside a factory.

Manufactured Home
Simply defined, a manufactured home is a complete dwelling unit designed for year-around-living, and substantially constructed in a factory in conformance with a national building code developed in 1976 by the U.S. Department of Housing and Urban Development (HUD). The home can consist of one or more transportable sections, each constructed on an integral permanent steel chassis (frame) to which are attached axles, wheels, brakes and a hitch. Each complete section is then hitched to a tractor trailer and towed from the factory to a retail sales lot or to a home site. Once a home is placed on its site, usually on jack stands or blocks, the wheels and running gear are removed and recycled back to the factory. The home is then tied to the foundation (well, it's supposed to be but enforcement varies widely) and skirting is installed around the perimeter to enclose the space beneath the home.

The key distinction here is the home is towed to its site on its own wheels. A second distinction is "manufactured home," at least technically, refers to any such home constructed after June, 1976 when the Federal Manufactured Home Construction Safety Standards, called the HUD Code, went into effect. All such homes built prior to this date are officially called mobile homes.

HUD-Code home
Same as a manufactured home.

Mobile home
Technically, any manufactured home built prior to June, 1976 (see above). There are still hundreds of thousands of these antiques still around, many of them poorly engineered, and shoddily constructed with cheap materials before governmental regulators stepped in. Many others, built to a higher standard and well maintained, are still going strong. Alas, the term "manufactured home" has never really caught on with the public, and nearly everyone outside the industry still calls them mobile homes, even the *New York Times* and *the Wall Street Journal*. Some people still call mobile homes house trailers. As one industry wag once proclaimed, "We don't build house trailers any more, we build manufactured trailers."

Modular home
A factory built home constructed of prefabricated modules, entire rooms and larger, which are transported on flat-bed trucks to a home site and assembled using a crane. Sometimes the module is jacked up and the flat bed truck is then driven out from beneath it. Most modular homes are built in conformance with the UBC or IRC Codes, or other local code requirements, not the HUD code. With few exceptions mods are more costly than manufactured homes while offering savings over comparable site built homes (from which they are usually indistinguishable in appearance). Modular homes show great promise but in the ten years prior to 2007, annual production has remained flat at around 45,000 homes.

Pre-cut homes
Essentially kit homes in which all the lumber and other materials are measured and pre-cut at the factory, then transported to the site and assembled by the builder. Packages may include many more building materials such as pre-hung windows and plumbing. Homes in this category can be very high end. Also included here are log homes, A-frame homes and domes. All are built to local codes.

Panelized homes
Homes constructed of largely complete panel sections built in a factory. This process is also called a structural insulated panel system, or SIP. Example, a wall panel could consist of windows, a door, all the inside wiring, and insulation, its interior side covered with gypsum (drywall), its outside with exterior siding. The finished (closed) panels are then transported to the building site, together with floor and roof panels, and assembled with the help of a crane. An alternative system uses open panels in which the interior is left open for on-site installation of wiring, insulation, etc. Built to local codes. Note: The use of panelized sections is a growing trend among big home builders who develop large subdivisions of site-built homes. In essence these homes are hybrids: built on site using many large components (panel section, roof trusses, etc.) made in a factory.

Index of Manufactured Home Builders in the U.S.

Adrian Homes	22
Advantage Homes	27
BonnaVilla Homes	22
Buccaneer Homes	25
Burlington Homes of Maine	23
Cappaert Homes	24
Castle Homes of PA	27
Cavalier Homes, Inc	24
Cavco	25
Champion Enterprises Inc.	26
Champion Homes	28
Chariot Eagle	37
Chariot Eagle West	37
Clayton Homes	38
Commander Homes	32
Commodore Homes	47
Deer Valley	48
Destiny Industries, LLC	49
Dutch Housing	29
Eagle River Homes	50
Fairmont Homes	50
Falcon Luxury Homes	51
Fall Creek Homes	49
Fleetwood Homes	52
Fortune Homes Inc	29
Four Seasons Housing Inc.	54
Franklin Homes Inc.	55
Fuqua Homes of Missouri	56
Fuqua Homes of Oregon	56
Gateway Homes	27
General Manufactured Housing	57
Giles Industries	39
Golden West Homes	45
Guerdon Homes	57
Hallmark Southwest Corporation	58
Hart Housing Group	59
Highland Homes	30
Hi-Tech Housing	60
Holly Park Homes	61
Homark Company	62
Homebuilders Northwest	63
Homes of Merit	31
Horton Homes	63
Indies House	64
Jacobsen Homes	65
Karsten Homes	40
Kabco Homes	66
Kit Manufactured Homes	67
Laurel Creek Homes	67
Lexington Homes	68
Liberty Homes	69
Magnolia Homes	70
Manufactured Housing Enterprises	71
Marlette Homes	44
Moduline International	33
Modular One LLC	72
Norris Homes	41
Nashua Homes of Idaho	73
New Era Homes	33
Nobility Homes	74
Oak Creek Homes	75
Oakwood Homes	42
Palm Harbor Inc.	76
Patriot Homes	77
Pine Grove Homes	79
Platinum Homes	80
R-Anell Custom Homes	80
Redman Homes	31
Ritz-Craft Homes	81
River Birch Homes	82
Schult Homes	43
Scotbilt Homes	83
Shamrock Homes	84
Silver Creek	85
Silvercrest Homes	34
Skyline Homes	85
Solitaire Homes	87
Southern Energy Homes	46
Summit Crest Homes	35
Sunshine Homes	88
Superior Homes	89
Titan Homes	36
Town Homes	89
Valley Qualilty Homes	90
Virginia Homes Manufacturing	91
Waverlee Homes	92
Wick Building Systems Inc.	93

Index of brands, series and models—and their manufacturers

Industry-wide, there are about 250 brands and model series but thousands of model names, many created to distinguish slight variations in a single floor plan. Not only can this be confusing (even to sales people), but they're subject to change as builders adjust to market conditions. If a model you've seen is not on this list, the retailer will be able to tell you the series and and brand to which it belongs.

100 Series—Guerdon Homes
200 Series—Guerdon Homes
300 Series—Guerdon Homes
Acadian Series—Burlington Homes of Maine
Advantage Series—Champion Home Builders
Alamo Series—Patriot Homes
Anniversary homes—Homebuilders Northwest
Anniversary—Modular One LLC
Artcraft Homes—Wick Building Systems
Aspen series—Homebuilders Northwest
Astro Homes—Commodore Corp.
Atlantic Homes—Champion Enterprises
Augustan—Deer Valley Homes
Autumn Manor—Four Seasons Housing
Backyard Home Series—Silvercrest Homes
Badger Built—Liberty Homes
Badger—Liberty Homes
Barrington—Fleetwood Enterprises
Bay Manor—Homes of Merit
Baycrest—Karsten Company
Bayview—Fairmont Homes
Beacon Hill Homes—Fleetwood Enterprises
Benchmark—Franklin Homes
Blazer—Deer Valley Homes
Bluebonnet Series—Patriot Homes
BonnaVilla—BonnaVilla Homes
Brentwood II—Virginia Homes Manufacturing
Bristol—Virginia Homes Manufacturing Corp.
Brookwood Series—Sunshine Homes
Buccaneer—Buccaneer Homes
Buckeye—Palm Harbor Homes
Burlington Classic—Burlington Homes of Maine
Cabin Series—Guerdon Homes
Cabin Series—Summit Crest Homes
Canyon Crest—Marlette Homes
Cape Coral—ScotBilt Homes
Castle Cape Cod—Castle Homes of Pennsylvania
Castle Estate Series—Karsten Company
Castle Series—Castle Homes of Pennsylvania
Castle Series—Karsten Company
Casual Elegance home—Homebuilders Northwest
Cavco—Cavco Industries
Cedar Canyon Series—Kit Homebuilders West
Celebration—Fleetwood Enterprises
Celebration—Fuqua Homes of Missouri
Celebrity—Fairmont Homes
Century Homes—Fairmont Homes
Century Villa—Fairmont Homes

Champion—Champion Home Builders
Champion Homes of Indiana—Champion Ent.
Chancellor Series—Jacobsen Homes
Chanduleur Homes—Champion Enterprises
Chapparall—Skyline Corporation
Charleston—Deer Valley Homes
Charleston IV—Hallmark Southwest Corp.
Chateau Elan—Schult Homes
Choice—Fuqua Homes of Missouri
Classic—Highland Manufacturing
Classic Series—Jacobsen Homes
Classics—Golden West Homes
Clayton—Clayton Homes
Colonial Series—Manufactured Housing Ent.
Colony Factory Crafted Homes—Commodore
Columbia—Marlette Homes
Commodore Homes of Indiana—Commodore Corp.
Commodore Homes of Pennsylvania—Commodore
Commodore Homes of Virginia—Commodore
Coronado Series—Moduline International
Country Cabins—Magnolia Homes
Country Classic Series—Waverlee Homes
Country Cottage Series—Valley Manufactured
Country Manor—Golden West Homes
Country Manor—Homes of Merit
Country single wides—Homes of Merit
CountryPlace—Palm Harbor Homes
Cozy Cabin—Homark Company, Inc.
Crystal Park Series—Kit Homebuilders West
Crystal Valley—Patriot Homes
Custom Design Series—Summit Crest Homes
Custom Golden Estate Series—Golden West
Cypress—General Manufactured Housing
Desert Manor—Marlette Homes
Discovery—Palm Harbor Homes
Dynasty Homes—Horton Industries
Edgewood Series—Silvercrest Homes
Edison Series—Burlington Homes of Maine
Elation—Marlette Homes
Elegant Series—Magnolia Homes
Eleganza—General Manufactured Housing
Elite—Karsten Company
Elite Series—Waverlee Homes
Elite—Summit Crest Homes
Evergreen series—Homebuilders Northwest
Extra Value Series—Marlette Homes
Fairmont—Fairmont Homes
Fall Creek—The Fall Creek Home

Festival—Fleetwood Enterprises
First Edition—Marlette Homes
Floridian Series—Patriot Homes
Forest Manor—Homes of Merit
Foxglove—Hi-tech Housing
Foxwood—Fairmont Homes
Freedom Series—Oakwood Homes
Friendship—Fairmont Homes
Galaxy- Oak Creek Homes
Galaxy Super Value Series—Oak Creek Homes
Georgetown Series—Sunshine Homes
Giles—Giles Industries
Gold Medal Line—R-Anell Homes
Gold Medal Series—Champion Home Builders
Golden Estate Series—Golden West Homes
Golden Oaks—Golden West Homes
Golden Pacific—Golden West Homes
Golden State Series—Kit Homebuilders West
Golden Villa—BonnaVilla Homes
Golden West Exclusive—Golden West Homes
Good Neighbor Series—Silvercrest Homes
Grand Bay Series—Sunshine Homes
Greenbrier Ltd.—Skyline Corporation
Hallmark —Oak Creek Homes
Hart Housing—Hart Housing Group
Heritage American—Patriot Homes
Heritage American Wakefield Series—Patriot
Heritage II—Dutch Housing
Heritage—Modular One LLC
Heritage—ScotBilt Homes
Hide-Away Lodge—Homark Company, Inc.
Highland Homes Series—Highland Manufacturing
Holly Park Estates—Holly Park Homes
Holly Park—Holly Park Homes
Holly Park Single Sections —Holly Park Homes
Homes of Legend—Champion Enterprises
Horizon—Oak Creek Homes
Horton Homes—Horton Industries
Hudson Series—Eagle River Homes
Imperial Series—Solitaire Homes
Independence—Fairmont Homes
Independence—Patriot Homes
Indies—Indies House
Inglewood—Cavalier Home Builders
Innsbruck—Fairmont Homes
Kensington Park—Skyline Corporation
Keystone—Clayton Homes
Keystone—Palm Harbor Homes
Kingston Millennium—Golden West Homes
Kingswood—Nobility Homes
La Casa Homes—Homebuilders Northwest
La Grand—Marlette Homes
Lakeland Series—Marlette Homes
Lancer—Solitaire Homes
Landmark—Fuqua Homes of Missouri

Legacy—Schult Homes
Legacy—Summit Crest Homes
Legend—ScotBilt Homes
Lexington Park—Skyline Corporation
Lexington Series—Lexington Homes
Lexington—Skyline Corporation
Liberty—Liberty Homes
LifeStages Home—Fleetwood Enterprises
Limited—Four Seasons Housing
Lincoln Park Homes—Patriot Homes
Litchfield Limited—Cavco Industries
Lone Star Series—Silver Creek Homes
Lonestar Series—Patriot Homes
Longhorn Series—Patriot Homes
LXE II Sectionals -t—Ritz-Craft Homes
Manor Hill—Schult Homes
Manor Series—Silvercrest Homes
Manor Special—Nobility Homes
Marshfield Homes—Wick Building Systems
Mastserpiece—Palm Harbor Homes
McKenzie Double Section—Karsten Company
McKenzie Triple Section—Karsten Company
Meadow View—Marlette Homes
Meadowcreek—Summit Crest Homes
Medallion Gold—Superior Homes
Medallion Platinum—Superior Homes
Mega—General Manufactured Housing
Meridian—Oak Creek Homes
Mid-American—Fairmont Homes
Millennium—Dutch Housing
Mission Series—Patriot Homes
Mountain Retreat- Nashua Homes of Idaho
Mountain Retreat Plus—Nashua Homes Idaho
Nashua Classic 24- Nashua Homes of Idaho
New Cottage Series—Silvercrest Homes
New Moon—Redman Homes
Norris Homes—Norris Inc.
Nu-Hart 110—Hart Housing Group
Oak Creek Series—Oak Creek Homes
Oakwood Classic Series—Oakwood Homes
Oasis—Schult Homes
Palace Series—Castle Homes of Pennsylvania
Palm Harbor—Palm Harbor Homes
Park Ridge—Holly Park Homes
Performer Series—Golden West Homes
Petersburg—Virginia Homes Mfg. Corp.
Pine Grove—Pine Grove Homes
Pinnacle Homes—Patriot Homes
Platinum Series—Kabco Homes
Platinum Series—Platinum Homes
Pleasantview—Holly Park Homes
Pointe—General Manufactured Housing
Power House—Cavalier Home Builders
Prairie—Hi-tech Housing
Presidential—General Manufactured Housing
Presidential—Schult Homes

Primrose—Hi-tech Housing
R-Anell Series—R-Anell Homes
R-Series—Solitaire Homes
Radiant Series—Magnolia Homes
Regal—Schult Homes
Regency—Nobility Homes
Regency Park—Shamrock Homes
Residential—Shamrock Homes
Richwood—Nobility Homes
Ritz-Craft—Ritz-Craft Homes
River Bend—Palm Harbor Homes
River Crest—Marlette Homes
River Ridge—Commander Homes
Riverdale—Commander Homes
Rollohomes Homes—Wick Building Systems
Royal American—Homark Company, Inc.
Royal American Special Edition—Homark Co.
Royal Villa—Solitaire Homes
Sage—Hi-tech Housing
Santa Fe Series—Cavco Industries
Shamrock Single-Wides, tags—Shamrock Homes
Sierra Vista—Marlette Homes
Signature Series—Marlette Homes
Silver Creek II—Silver Creek Homes
Silvercrest Classic—Champion Homes
Silvercrest Discovery—Champion Homes
Sizzler—General Manufactured Housing
Skyview—Skyline Corporation
Solitaire—Solitaire Homes
Sonora—Schult Homes
Southern Energy of Texas—Southern Energy
Southern Energy—Southern Energy Homes
Southern Estates—Southern Energy Homes
Southern Homes—Southern Energy Homes
Southern Pines—Destiny Industries
Southern Star Limited—Oak Creek Homes
Southridge Homes—Patriot Homes
Sovereign Series—Champion Home Builders
Special Edition—Nobility Homes
Spectrum Series—New Era Building Systems
Spring Creek—Commander Homes
Spring Creek—Fuqua Homes of Missouri
Spring Manor—Nashua Homes of Idaho
Spring Manor Single Wide- Nashua Homes Idaho
Springdale—Four Seasons Housing
Springview—Skyline Corporation
Springwood—Nobility Homes
Springwood Special—Nobility Homes
Star Pointe Series—Fuqua Homes of Oregon
Starlight—Hi-tech Housing
Starview—Karsten Company
Statesman—Fairmont Homes
Stinger—General Manufactured Housing
Stonebirch—River Birch Homes
Stoneybrook—Highland Manufacturing
Summerbrook—Four Seasons Housing

Sun Park—General Manufactured Housing
Sun Villa Homes—Cavco Industries
Sunbuilt—Cavco Industries
Sunflower—Hi-tech Housing
Sunshine Series—Sunshine Homes
Super Triple Wide- Nashua Homes of Idaho
Super Value Series—Schult Homes
Texas 36 Wide—Oak Creek Homes
The Anniversary Home—Fleetwood Enterprises
The Big Foot—Cappaert Homes
The Boss—Horton Industries
The Chelsea—Hi-tech Housing
The Devon—Hi-tech Housing
The Entertainer Home—Fleetwood Enterprises
The Essex—Hi-tech Housing
The Excel—Karsten Company
The Greenbrier—Skyline Corporation
The Hampshire—Skyline Corporation
The Inspiration Home—Fleetwood Enterprises
The Ramada—Skyline Corporation
The Screamer—Cappaert Homes
The Silver Series—Skyline Corporation
The Terminator—Cappaert Homes
Town Home Series—Town Homes
Trillium—Hi-tech Housing
Tropic Isle Special—Nobility Homes
Twin Manor—Homes of Merit
Two-Story Townhouse Series—Silvercrest
Ultimate Value—Patriot Homes
Ultra—Fuqua Homes of Missouri
Valley Manor Series—Valley Mfrd. Homes
Valley Mansion Series—Valley Mfrd. Homes
Vantage—Cavco Industries
Victorian Series—Patriot Homes
Victory series—Adrian Homes
Villa 2000 Series—Karsten Company
Villa 2700 Series—Karsten Company
Villa Ridge—Patriot Homes
Villa Series- Nashua Homes of Idaho
Village Profile—Cavco Industries
Villager Homes—Cavco Industries
Vision Series—Cavco Industries
Waverlee—Liberty Homes
Westcourt Homes—Cavco Industries
Westfield—Fairmont Homes
Westwood Craftsman Series—Silvercrest
Westwood Series—Silvercrest Homes
Willow Model—Fuqua Homes of Oregon
Winchester IV—Hallmark Southwest Corp.
Windsor Homes—Palm Harbor Homes
WinRock Homes—Cavco Industries
Wintergreen—Dutch Housing
Wisconsin Badger—Liberty Homes
Woodfern- Hi-tech Housing
Woodland—General Manufactured Housing
Yorkshire—Commander Homes

Manufactured home construction features & specifications comparison table

Item	Mainstream site-built home and some high end manufactured homes		Manufactured home mid-range to high-end			Manufactured home low mid-range	Manufactured home entry level & low end	
Note: see comments to this table on pgs. 19-20	10 EXCELLENT	9 SUPERIOR	8 VERY GOOD	7 GOOD	6 ABOVE AVERAGE	5 AVERAGE	4 BELOW AVERAGE	3 POOR	1-2 VERY POOR
Aesthetics: Exterior	Attractive, indistinguishable from site-built		Attractive, comparable to site-built if w/ steeper roof slope, attached garage, etc.			Unmistakably identifiable as a manufactured home/"mobile home"			
Aesthetics: Interior	Excellent floor plan, pleasing sight-lines, high ceilings, superior fit & finish			Good floor plan with design accents (plant shelves, alcoves), good fit & finish			Utilitarian floor plan, small rooms, low ceilings, poor fit & finish		
Customization	Great flexibility, many options/upgrades. Can build to customer's plan, design engineers on staff			Quite flexible: flip/mirror plans, move walls, windows, increase roof pitch		Some, but limited	None		
Roof pitch (or slope)	4/12 to 12/12			4/12 to 7/12 (3/12 for triples)		3/12		2/12 only	
Roof sheathing	1/2" plywood or OSB					3/8" plywood or OSB			
Shingles/ roof under-layer	30-year architectural shingles 15 lb. felt			25-year shingles, 15 lb. felt		20-yr. shingles, 15 lb. felt	20-yr. shingles, 15 lb. felt (roofs less than 3/12 require 30 lb. or 2 layers of 15 lb. felt		
Eaves and extension	All sides, 12" to 16"			Front and ends, 8"-12"		Front /back, 8"	Front and back, 3"		None
Roof insulation R-value	R-38 or more			R-33			R-21		R-7
Sidewall insulation R-value	R-19 or more			R-13			R-11		R-7
Exterior wall studs	2"x 6" 16" O.C.					2"x 4" 16" O.C.	2"x 4" 16" O.C.		
Exterior sheathing	7/16" Plywood				7/16" OSB			3/8" Plywood	
Exterior siding	Fiber-cement siding, painted e.g. HardiPanel, HardiPlank			Quality vinyl siding (foam backed)		Economy grade vinyl siding or 4'x8' sheets of 1/2" dia. hardboard, manufactured wood or particleboard			
Exterior sidewall height	9-10 feet			8 feet		7-1/2 feet		7 feet	
Exterior house wrap	Yes (e.g. with Tyvek or equivalent)						No		
Interior wall studs	2"x 4" 16" O.C.			2"x 3" 16" O.C.		2"x 3" 16" O.C.		2"x 3" 24" O.C.	
Drywall or wallboard to-stud fastening	Screwed and glued			Nailed and glued			Stapled and glued		
Drywall or wallboard thickness/finish	1/2", bull nose corners tape & textured or tape & painted		Pre-finished/ pre-painted wood used	1/2", square corners, taped & textured/primed/painted		3/8" vinyl covered wallboard with battens at seams, corners	Vinyl covered wallboard	5/16" vinyl on wallboard	
Molding, interior finish	All molding, baseboards, jambs, sills, casings set, nailed, caulked, painted			Pre-finished wood, set and primed, customer to paint		Vinyl covered wood molding	Vinyl on particleboard	Paper on particleboard	

The Grissim Ratings Guide to Manufactured Homes 17

	Mainstream site-built home and some high end manufactured homes			Manufactured home mid- to high-end			Manufactured home low mid-range	Manufactured home entry level & low end		
Item	10 EXCELLENT	9 SUPERIOR	8 VERY GOOD	7 GOOD	6 ABOVE AVERAGE	5 AVERAGE	4 BELOW AVERAGE	3 POOR	1–2 VERY POOR
Floor decking	1-1/8"" plywood	3/4" Plywood or OSB	5/8" plywood	3/4" Cresdek or Novadek		5/8" Cresdek or Novadek	3/4" generic particleboard	5/8" generic particleboard	
Floor insulation R-rating		R-33		R-21			R-11		R-7
Decking fastened by	Glued, screwed		Glued and nailed					Glued and stapled	
Floor joists		2"x 8" 16" O.C. (2"x 6" OK for single-sections)				2"x 6" 16" O.C.		2"x 6" greater than 16" O.C.	
Carpet		32-50 oz.		26-31 oz.	22-25 oz.	19-21 oz.	16-18 oz.	15 oz. or less	
Fastened to floor	Installed over cushion w/ tackless strip using power stretcher or knee kicker					tackless strip and staples	Stapled only	Stapled, glued	
Carpet pad	6 lbs/cu.ft., 1/2" dia. bonded polyurethane ("rebond")						5 lb. rebond, 7/16" dia		3/8" foam
Vinyl covering	High quality tiles or rolled vinyl w/urethane wear layer			Heavy, quality rolled lineoleum with no seams, urethane wear layer		Middle grade lino	Economy grade vinyl lino		
Front door	36"x 80" 6-panel steel front door (insulated core) w/ dead bolt lock and peep hole					36x80 steel			
Rear door (to outside)	36"x80" steel, dead bolt, (doors to attached garages are 32" wide)			36"x80," dead bolt		steel, 32"x74," x 76" or 78"	Aluminum, 32" x74," 32"x 76" or 32" x 78"	Aluminum, 34" or 35" x 74," 76" or 78"	
Matching key locks			Yes					No	
Interior doors	30"x 80" solid wood, 6-panel		30"x 80" wood frame door, hollow core	30"x 80" paneled, hollow core		28"x 80" plain luan, foam core		26"x74" plain luan, hollow core	
Interior door hinges		3, full mortised: both door and casing				2, mortised to door or casing		2, surface mounted	
Windows	White vinyl vacuum sealed dual glazed w/ low-E,		White vinyl, dual glazed Low-E			White vinyl, dual glazed	Single pane, aluminum frame, w/ self-storing storm windows		
Water piping	Copper					Pex or CPVC			
Pipe fittings	Copper/brass			Brass				Plastic	
Water shut-off valves		At all fixtures					Main water shut-off only		
Outside faucets	2				1			None	

Floors, floor covering / Doors and windows

18 The Grissim Ratings Guide to Manufactured Homes

Item	10 EXCELLENT	9 SUPERIOR	8 VERY GOOD	7 GOOD	6 ABOVE AVERAGE	5 AVERAGE	4 BELOW AVERAGE	3 POOR	1–2 VERY POOR
	Mainstream site-built home and some high end manufactured homes		Manufactured home mid-range to high-end			Manufactured home low mid-range	Manufactured home entry level & low end		
HVAC									
HVAC register locations	Cool climate: perimeter (in toe kicks in kitchen/bath(s)/ Hot climates: ceiling						Middle of floor		
HVAC ducting	Sheet metal, caulked w/ mastic, wrapped w/ fiberglass insulation					Fiberglass, wrapped		Fiberglass, taped only	
Air return system	Through dedicated return air floor ducts			Through wall vents, ceiling vents on both sides of wall connected to attic ducting, openings beneath interior doors			Openings under doors only		
Electrical outlet boxes				Nailed to studs			Attached to wall w/ wings, clips, screws		
GFI outlets	Additional GFI outlets			20 amp outlets in kitchen and bathrooms - required by HUD code					
Phone/cable/Internet	Yes, Cat. 5 ready (home networking, security alarm)		2-3 phone jacks, cable ready boxes, customer or contractor to wire				No		
Kitchen									
Kitchen faucet	High quality brand name metal single lever			Single lever (metal)	Dual knob (metal) with sprayer	Dual knob (metal)	Dual knob (metal works, plastic shell)		
Kitchen sink	High quality cast iron, 8" deep	Corian 8" integrated with counter top	Full size, stainless or white enamel on metal (porcelain), 7" deep			Stainless 6" deep	Smaller, non-standard size, acrylic, 6" deep		
Counter tops/edging	25" wide, granite, w/ 4" hand-laid tile backsplash	25" wide, Corian, 4" ceramic tile backsplash	25" wide, laminate, edged w/ wood/tile, 4" ceramic backsplash	25" wide, Formica, beveled edge, ceramic or rounded edge, 2" tile backsplash		25" wide, Formica or post-form, self edged	24" wide, Formica, self-edged w/Formica backsplash (requires smaller, non-standard sink)		
Cabinets	Full-size: base ht. 36" (31" overhead ht.), stained wood, raised stiles, quality knobs or fingerpulls, Melamine interiors, hidden hinges			Full-size, stained hardwood face, raised stiles, plywood walls, hidden hinges		Full-size, MDF, vinyl-wrapped stiles, open hinges	Smaller size, MDF, no lining, exposed hinges, economy knobs, no toe-kicks, no bottom shelf in base cabinets		
Cabinet shelves	1/2" Melamine or equiv. fully adjustable			1/2" MDF adjustable			1/2" particleboard, not adjustable		
Drawers	Hardwood face, plywood, glued/screwed, 18" deep, 2-1/2" & 4"-plus ht.			Hardwood face, plywood, stapled/glued, 16" deep, 2-1/2" & 4"-plus ht.			Vinyl-wrapped face, 12" deep, stapled/glued, face serves as front of box		
Drawer guides/rollers	Metal/metal, full suspension		Metal/plastic, full extension		Metal/plastic w/ drawer stop		Plastic/plastic w/ drawer stop		
Bath									
Bath sinks/countertops	Vitreous china/ Corian		Vitreous china/ laminate w/ ceramic edging or both made of cultured marble				Acrylic, Formica self-edged		
Vanity sink(s) overflow			Yes				No		
Master bath tub/shower	60" 1-piece fiberglass				48" 1-piece fiberglass		48" 2-pc. plastic		54" 1-piece tub/shower
Toilets	Vitreous china, elongated			Vitreous china, round			Acrylic, round		
Water heater	50 gal.			40 gal.			30 gal.		20 gal. elec.
Refrigerator	20-25 cu. ft. FF, side-by-side w/ water/ice		18-22 cu. ft. FF, side-by-side			16-17 cu. ft.		14 cu. ft. over-under, auto-defrost	
Plumbed for ice maker/water			Yes				No		

Note: see comments to this table on pgs. 19-20

Notes on the manufactured home construction features & specifications comparison table

Aesthetics: Exterior & Interior Curb appeal is an important consideration for many home buyers, including those who would prefer their new home not have the appearance of a conventional manufactured home. MH interiors can be very attractive, fully comparable to site-built.

Roof pitch 4/12 is regarded as a minimum pitch for a residential appearance to a site-built home. A 5/12 roof will usually be hinged. Higher pitched roofs will all be hinged.

Eaves & extensions Eaves are often eliminated from the rear (i.e., back yard side) of an MH to avoid exceeding maximum highway width when in transit, or to cut costs. A home can look ugly without them, even missing on just one side. Consider having the eaves shipped loose and installed on site.

Roof insulation The higher the R number, the greater the insulation. R-values will vary depending on the region of the U.S. The legal minimum for HUD code is R-14/7/7 (for roof/ceiling, walls and floor. As a general rule, higher R values mean less energy is needed to heat and cool a home. Most manufacturers insulate the roof by blowing in cellulose; others use fiberglass battens identical to those in the sidewalls. Both work fine.

Exterior sheathing This may not be needed if the ext. siding is HardiPanel or some other 4'x8' wood or cement-fiber product.

Sidewall insulation R-value R-19 is insulation designed for a 2x6 sidewall. R-13 is a high-density insulation designed for 2x4 exterior sidewalls.

Exterior wall studs 2"x 6" 16" O.C. is the standard, for two reasons: It allows for more insulation (yielding lower energy costs) and adds needed strength to the home during transit (minimizing cracks in dry walls, for example). This feature, together with how the electrical outlet boxes are attached to the walls, can reliably indicate if a home falls into the category of less than average or poor construction quality.

Exterior sidewall height A site-built home will almost always have a minimum 8' side wall height, and usually a flat ceiling. Nine feet is becoming ubiquitous with site-built homes in many regions.

Interior walls studs Some manufacturers argue that 2"x 3" on 16" centers is fine for non-load-bearing interior walls. Probably true, but if on 24" centers, that merits a poor construction rating.

Dry wall or wallboard thickness/finish Also called gypsum (mostly in the east). If it's covered with vinyl or wall paper, it's called wallboard. Paper is no longer common. Hence vinyl on wallboard, or VOG. A home may also be delivered with its dry wall "blue nailed," i.e., unfinished and ready for the home buyer to finish, paint and/or texture.

Molding, interior finish There is far more emphasis on crown moldings, casing, and baseboard moldings in the Eastern US than the West, reflecting regional traditions and taste. For example, in the West, crown molding (where the sidewall meets the ceiling) is rarely found.

Floor joists Under "below average," "greater than 16" O.C." is a bit over 19 inches.

Carpets If possible avoid anything less than 16 oz. Low end carpeting carries disparaging nicknames such as Dog hair, fuzzy-side up and the ultra-cheap, Essence of carpet, not much more than a beach towel.

Carpet pad If possible, avoid 3/8" foam padding. It wears quickly, turning into granules.

Carpet fastened to floor Many plants in the Eastern US do a full installation of carpets; in the West, carpeting is installed in single-sections only, but shipped loose in sectionals, for a subcontractor to install.

Vinyl covering Whether as hand-laid tiles or "rolled goods," vinyl can be an amazingly high quality product. The difference is the wear layer. The thicker that layer, the higher the quality.

Interior doors The industry standard for mainstream site-built homes is a 30x80 wood frame door, hollow core.

Windows The phrases dual glazed and thermal pane (also thermo-pane) are synonymous.

Water piping Copper is considered best and is standard with site-built homes. PEX and CPVC are also excellent, proven, and virtually equivalent in quality and performance.

Outside faucets Make sure you have at least one if you plan on having porch plants.

HVAC register locations Registers in the middle of the floor are a hallmark of manufactured homes built to average (or less) construction quality.

HVAC ducting There is a third type of ducting: a round, flexible insulated duct made of a wire coil (for strength) and wrapped in plastic, widely used for crossover ducting between home sections. In smaller diameters, it's also used in attic areas for up-flow systems. All three types perform well (i.e. no leaks) if conscientiously assembled.

Air return system Dedicated return ducts are by far the best. Ceiling vents on either side of a room wall are less intrusive visually (Karsten does this).

Electrical outlet boxes If attached to walls, not nailed to the studs, this is a strong indicator of less than average/poor construction quality. It doesn't take too many yanks on the vacuum cleaner cord to eventually pull a wall-mounted outlet box out of the wall.

GFI outlets HUD code requires them over all drain

boards, sinks, anywhere an electrical appliance could contact water, as a safety measure. Some high end builders will add them elsewhere, e.g., utility room.
Phone/cable/Internet High end homes may be pre-wired to allow a wide range of consumer electronics, including Internet, home entertainment and security alarm systems. Mid-range homes may have wall boxes with cable/wire tubes down to the crawl space, ready for wiring.
Kitchen faucet Many builders boast of a single-lever kitchen faucet, but these vary widely in quality. Be sure to check specifics.

Kitchen sink Which is best, stainless or white enameled metal sinks, is a matter of taste, but Palm Harbor's stainless sinks have a sound-deadening coating on the bottom, a welcome touch.
Counter tops A 24"-width counter top is indicative of low quality construction, often requiring a smaller non-standard sink that can't be replaced by any sold at home improvement stores.
Master bath tub/shower The 54" 1-piece tub/shower is notoriously inadequate as a tub. The drain is in the middle and the tub is so shallow and confining that one must sit with knees bent nearly to one's chin.

Glossary of terms and abbreviations in the listings of U.S. MH manufacturers

Architectural shingles An upgrade from the standard, flat 3-tab shingles, having a thicker looking, more three-dimensional appearance that adds to a home's curb appeal (and hides the fold line of a hinged roof that can sometimes be seen otherwise).
Auto-defrost A de-frost cycle on less-expensive refrigerators that needs to be manually selected to activate.
Bull nose A rounded corner or edge, associated with a wall or countertop.
Cathedral ceilings Also called vaulted ceilings. Ceilings that slant up to the center ridge line, at roughly the same angle as the outside roof pitch, usually meeting at the ridge line in the center of the home.
Cape Cod A home with a steep roof (usually 8/12 or greater) and two or three dormer windows. With HUD code versions, typically the attic space is finished as a second story by the homebuyer after move-in.
Commode Toilet.
CPVC Chlorinated Polyvinyl Chloride, plastic piping approved for potable (drinkable) water, usually white in color. Can be connected with either threaded components or glued fitting
Cresdek The trade name of a brand of engineered particleboard, widely used as floor decking. See also, Novadek.
Corian The trade name of a high quality faux marble product. See cultured marble.
Cultured marble Also **cultured granite, cultured onyx**. A cast polymer product mixed with colorants to create "veining" and/or the appearance of genuine marble, granite or onyx, made with a high-gloss "gel coat" coating. The process yields an attractive, durable, rock-hard product, highly regarded.
Dormer, or dormer window A vertical window on a projecting structure built out from a sloped roof.

See also Cape Cod.
Dry wall sheets of gypsum, usually 4'x8' in varying thicknesses coated with paper or vinyl and attached to wall studs and/or ceilings. Also called wall board when covered with patterned vinyl or paper.
Double-wide A two-section home
FF Frost-free. Refrigerators that do not need to be de-frosted, typical of better quality refrigerators
Floor Industry jargon for a section, e.g., a double-wide consists of two floors; a factory can produce five floors a day.
Floor joists structural members placed perpendicular at regular intervals between floor beams to form the floor structure
Full-finish Dry wall that has been taped, prepped, primed and given at least one coat of paint.
GFI - Ground fault interrupt. Special wall plug outlets, usually in wet areas such as kitchens and bathrooms, that are built to instantly shut off in the event of a short circuit, to prevent electrical shock. Required by the HUD-code.
Gypsum see Dry wall
Hardiplank, Hardipanel Trade names for James Hardie siding, made from fiber cement, in many patterns and finishes, well regarded.
HUD code The building code established by the federal Department of Housing and Urban Development for the production of manufactured homes.
HVAC Heating, ventilation, air conditioning.
In-line registers Floor registers that are located in the middle of the floor (instead of along the perimeter or ceiling), typical of average or less construction quality
Interior storm windows Also called **self-storing storm windows**. These economy panes fit on the inside edge of a window casing, held in place by

clips. Found on low construction quality home.

Lavy Bathroom sink, also called a vanity sink

Low E glass Refers to low emittance. Window and skylight glass treated with a microscopically thin, invisible metal oxide significantly cut down on heat (or cooling) loss.

MDF Medium density fiberboard. An economy quality fiberboard used for cabinet doors and shelving.

Melamine The trade name of a high quality, high density fiberboard, usually painted white on both sides, widely used for cabinetry shelving.

MH Manufactured home

Mortise A shallow indentation made in a door or window casing (and on the edge of a door or window) into which a hinge plate can be placed and secured so that it is flush with the surface. Hinges are said to be mortised.

Novadek The trade name of a brand of engineered particleboard, widely used as floor decking. See also, Cresdek.

O.C. On center. Used to describe the intervals between studs. 16" O.C. means the centers of the wall studs are placed at 16" intervals in the wall.

OSB Oriented strand board. a very strong composite material comprised of thin strands of wood bonded with a strong adhesive, highly regarded.

Perimeter heat Floor registers mounted on the perimeter of a room, either in the floor or the wall (in contrast to registers in the center line of the room)

PEX Cross-linked Polyethylene, a flexible tubing with crimped-band fittings, tat connects to metal pipes and other plumbing. Widely used, well-regarded.

Pod See Tag.

Proud seams Edges of dry wall panels that buckle outward slightly as a result of a slight torquing or bending of the wall, often during transport or from poor installation

Prow porch A covered porch on the gabled front end of a home extending across the entire width of the home, with the roof and porch extending out in a shallow angle similar to the prow (or bow) of a ship. Popular with mountain retreats.

PVC Polyvinyl Chloride, a plastic pipe (usually black) used for wastewater drain and septic systems. Can be connected with either threaded components or glued fittings.

Rebond A rug cushion comprised of bits of polyurethane glued together, i.e. re-bonded. Usually green and white in appearance. Widely used.

Ring shank nail A nail, usually for anchoring roof decking, that has tiny rings around its length that give it a grip close to that of a screw, enabling roofing to remain in place in winds up to 145 mph.

Roof pitch A measure of roof slope, the number of inches the roof rises every 12 inches of lateral length.

RSO Retail sales order. An order taken at a retail sales center for a home to be built and delivered to the customer's site (as opposed to the sale of a home model already on the sales center lot).

Sectionals Homes comprised of two or more sections

Self-edged A square, 90 degree edge on a countertop.

Single-section A single section home, same as single-wide, also SW

Single-wide A single section home, also SW

Stiles Raised strips of wood used decoratively, usually on kitchen cabinets.

Studs Vertical lengths of wood at intervals in a wall.

T&G Tongue and groove

T/T Taped and textured throughout

t/o Throughout

Tag (or Tag-Along) Also called a pod. A small section, usually room- or porch-size, attached to a home. This small section tags along the highway behind the two bigger sections.

Toe-kick A recessed area abut two-inches deep at the base of counter and sink areas (typically kitchen and bath) that allows one to stand comfortably closer to the counter.

Top plate The hoz. structural member across the top of a wall nailed to the top of the wall studs.

Trapped entrance An entrance to a retail sales center configured to prevent visitors from access to lot models without first passing through an office or reception area controlled by the sales staff.

Turn-key A type of home sale transaction in which the seller, in this case the sales center, performs all the tasks associated with preparing the home for move-in—i.e., site preparation, permits, well, septic, utilities hook-up, home delivery, installation and trim out, garage and deck construction, landscaping—and then turns the door key over to the home buyer.

Vaulted ceiling See Cathedral ceiling.

Vanity sink A bathroom sink, also called a lavy .

Vinyl siding Exterior siding made of vinyl designed to look like wood lap siding or wood paneling, sometimes like cedar shingling. Popular in the Midwest/East, gaining a foothold in the West.

Vinyl-wrapped molding Molding (usually made of particleboard) wrapped with a vinyl cover printed with a wood grain pattern, typical of lower quality finish work.

Vitreous china Also called porcelain (which it isn't). The strong polished ceramic material widely used to cast toilets and sinks.

VOG Vinyl on gypsum, i.e., dry wall covered with a vinyl sheet, usually with a color and/or pattern. Also called wall board.

Wall board Dry wall/gypsum, usually 3/8" dia.) covered with a vinyl sheet. See VOG.

Builders of Manufactured Homes in the U.S.

Adrian Homes (privately held)
P.O. Box 266
Adrian, GA 31002
PH: (478) 668-3232 FX: (478) 668-4943
Web site: www.adrianhomesmfg.com
Brand name: Adrian Homes
Background: Privately held. Established in 1962, this relatively small, one-plant operation focused exclusively on modular structures: schools, apartment buildings day care centers, and homes in the low medium to medium price range. Since then Adrian has changed ownership four times. Current owner Alliance Homes, Inc. purchased company in 2000. Company entered the HUD-code home market in 1999, just as the MH industry crashed, with a line low-end entry level homes. Most of its production remains modulars (65%), including government contracts for guard stations, fire stations, and custom commercial buildings. Its line of modular homes shows promise.
States where sold: GA, FL, NC, SC
Principal market niche: Low end to low medium.
Retail price range before tax (includes transportation & set-up): $50,000 - $80,000
Principal market niche: buyers of entry level affordable housing, retirees
Competes against: Fleetwood, Clayton, Homes of Merit
Construction rating: 4
Description of a popular model: Victory Series, 28 x 60, two-section, 3 BR, 2BA, 1,640 sq. ft. 3/12 roof pitch, 20-year shingles, 2x4 exterior wall studs, wall board interior walls, in-line floor registers, 16 oz. carpet, white metal windows. Base price: approx. $50,000
What distinguishes brand from its competition: Nothing stands out. Company entered the HUD code home market only six years ago and has not yet achieved a strong brand identity, but its single-factory 130-employee work force has long experience in modulars and is capable of turning out a consistent, reliable product.
Number of dealerships — Company owned: none
Independents: 45
Percentage of HUD homes sold of total homes produced: 35%
In-house financing? No
In-house Insurance? No
Warranty structure and length: 1 year
Web site rating: A failure – Some links don't work, "news" is dated (2003), no features/specs provided for HUD homes.
Comment: Adrian is a small player in a crowded Southeast market and it's puzzling that it chose to enter the HUD affordable housing marketplace just as the industry was crashing in late 1999, especially with a product lacking stand-out features. After the devastating 2004-5 hurricane season, the company benefited from FEMA contracts for replacement homes. Those, plus the demand for affordable retirement homes, accounted for 50% of Adrian's business. Given Adrian homes' low construction rating, most customers may likely want to add up to $10,000 in options to bring homes up to better quality.

BonnaVilla Homes (privately held)
111 Grant Street, P.O. Box 127
Aurora, NB 68818
Ph. 402-694-5250 Fx. 402-694-5873
Web site: www.bonnavilla.chiefind.com
Background: Founded in 1970 with a single plant producing HUD-code homes, BonnaVilla is a division of the Nebraska-based Chief Industries, a flourishing diversified international corporation (farm products, steel buildings, ethanol fuels, RVs, intemodal chasses). In 1976 BonnaVilla added modular homes, which today account for 85% of its production. Nearly all its homes can be built to either HUD or IRC (Mod) specs.
States where sold: NE, ND, SD, IA, CO, KS, MO, MT, OK, MN
Principal market niche: mainstream homebuyers
Retail price range before tax (includes transportation & set-up): $105,000 to $125,000
Competes against: site builders, Magnolia, Summit Crest
Construction rating: 9
Description of a popular model: Two-section, 32' x 72', 3BR, 2BA, 1798 sq. ft. with 174 sq. ft. covered porch and side entry, 6/12 roof pitch, Dutch Hip 10' dormer with 9/12 roof pitch, spacious kitchen w/ prep island and adjacent morning room.
Brands/series:
BonnaVilla Homes: single and double-wide (HUD or Mod)
Golden Villa: triple-wide only (HUD or Mod)
What distinguishes brand from its competition: Better quality throughout (including finish work), stronger construction specs (e.g. better grade of lumber, double top plates, box headers all windows, 3/4" T&G decking, solid ash trim, quality cabinetry, dry wall finish (three coats)
Number of dealerships — Company owned: 3
Independents: 50
Percentage of HUD homes sold of total homes produced: 15%
In-house financing? No
In-house Insurance? No

Warranty structure and length: 1 year structural. Dealers responsible for warranty service but factory and contract service crews available for major repairs.
Web site rating: Outstanding. A model of what a web site can be: clean, uncluttered, intuitive, fast, full of information, lots of quick pdf downloads of brochures and floor plans, even a downloadable, and useful, project worksheet for tracking costs and contacts.
Comment: This is a solid well-managed company that puts out an excellent high-end home with superior construction features and a very good reputation. The exterior appearance of its homes are relatively prosaic but it more than makes up for it by its gorgeous interiors and floor plans. Few of its homes (15%) are HUD-code because so few lenders will write HUD loans, a big reason most of its Midwest dealers are opting for modular (IRC) lot models. BonnaVilla is well positioned to successfully compete with site-builders for its target customer—the mainstream home buyer.

Burlington Homes of Maine, Inc.
(privately held)
620 main Street.
Oxford, ME 04270
Ph. 207/539-4406   Fx. 207/539-2900
Web site: www.burlingtonhomes.com
Background: Privately held. Founded in the mid-1970s, this single-plant home builder is the only MH producer in Maine, producing a well-regarded product through a history of three owners, including a timely rescue about ten ago by an investor group when the company was about to go under. The new owner's group increased Burlington's capacity for modular homes, a move that restored the company to profitability and has since kept the plant busy throughout the year.
States where sold: ME, MA, NH, RI, NY (upstate), CT
Principal market niche: mid-range to high end homes for private parcels, some MH parks
Retail price range before tax (includes transportation & set-up): $48,000-$98,000
Competes against: Pine Grove, Schult, Fleetwood, Titan, Commodore
Construction rating: 8
Description of a popular model: Burlington Classic, 28 x 56, two-section, 3BR, 2BA, 1,568 sq. ft. Standard features: 4/12 roof pitch, (up to 7/12 optional), 2/6 ext. walls on 16" centers, all 1/2" dia. dry wall interiors (taped, mudded primed), insulation: R-22 roof, R-19 walls (R-38 available), forced hot air system (ready for gas or oil), vinyl siding (faux cedar clapboard), white vinyl skirting.
Base price: $78,000
Burlington's series:
Burlington Classic: the high end line in both single and multi sections, lots of options, including oak cabinetry (see Classic description, above)
Acadian Series: Single and multi-section, low end, pre-papered wallboard standard (dry wall an option but "not offered in wet areas."
Edison series: Bottom of the line, affordable housing for the entry level buyer or MH park renewal.
What distinguishes brand from its competition: Locally built, quality construction designed for rough Maine winters, good warranty service, good dealer network.
Number of dealerships — Company owned: none
Independents: 46
Percentage of HUD homes sold of total homes produced: 50%
In-house financing: No
In-house Insurance: No
Warranty structure and length: 1 year factory-backed warranty, and a 9 year limited warranty by a third party carrier. Factory-based service crews dispatched to handle anything more serious than cosmetic problems.
Web site rating: Adequate but stiff and a bit clunky. Home page is a screenful of words, with nary a "welcome" message. The Photo page is a 5x5 inch collage of tiny pictures, none clickable. Most other pictures are likewise tiny: 2-1/2"x 3/4. Lots of clickable floor plans.
Comment: By all accounts Burlington builds a good product, but, oddly, a month-long attempt to reach the company's corporate marketing and sales department was met with silence. The company's receptionist refused to even divulge the name of the person in charge of marketing. We faxed Burlington's president explaining our dilemma. No response. Finally, a third party MH professional personally conveyed our request to the president. No response. Potential buyers of Burlington homes should not be blamed if they find this behavior troubling.

Cappaert Homes (privately held)
P.O. Box 620567
Vicksburg, MS 39182
Ph. 601-636-5401   Fx. 601-636-8446
Web site: www.cappaert.org
Background: Founded in 1987 by Mike Cappaert, son of F.L. Cappaert who in the 1960s headed industry conglomerate Guerdon Industries (RVs, plastics, furniture, air conditioning, and Guerdon Homes, later spun off). With a small, seasoned team, Cappaert jr.

focused on low-cost, low-end housing, built a skilled single-factory work force of 150 and prospered from the beginning. Company handily survived MH industry's perfect storm of the late 90s and continues into 2006 operating at near capacity.

States where sold: FL, MS, LA, KY, OK, TX, AR, MO (but mostly MS, LA, TX, AR)

Principal market niche: low end to low-medium buyer of affordable housing

Retail price range before tax (includes transportation & set-up):
Single-section: $19,900 - $32,000   Double-section: 29,900 - $54,000.

Competes against: low end homes of Clayton, Southern Energy, Indies House, Giles Industries

Construction rating: 4

Description of a popular model: "The Terminator," 16'x80' Single-wide, 3BR, 2BA, vinyl-on-gypsum walls, 7' side walls, vinyl siding, 3/4" plywood subfloors, 2x8 floor joists, 2x4 exterior sidewalls 16" O.C., single-pane metal windows, 2/12 roof pitch, plastic faucet fixtures, roof: 20 yr. shingles over 1/2" OSB, plumbing: Pex lines w/ brass fittings, electrical outlets secured with drywall clips, 14 cu. ft. frost free refrigerator, R-11/11/21, 30 gal. water heater. Also popular: a monster two section (32 x 80) 2500 sq. ft. "bowling alley" house.

What distinguishes brand from its competition: Good selection of floor plans, no frills, few options, excellent dollar value, focus on basic affordable housing

Number of dealerships — Company owned: 62
Independents: 92

Percentage of HUD homes sold of total homes produced: 100%

In-house financing:? No
In-house Insurance:? No

Warranty structure and length: 1 year.

Web site rating: Unsatisfactory. A static bare bones site that lists model names, floor plans standard features and not much more. About Us link is dead. No email address or geographical address given. No dealer locator.

Comment: Cappaert is a good example of a builder of low-end affordable homes for buyers whose need for decent shelter trumps designer appeal, and who aren't expecting their home to appreciate in value. The construction rating is low but Cappaert uses 3/4" plywood subfloors, a high-end feature. Their approach: know your customer and contain costs by keeping it simple. They build a seven-foot side wall interior (take or leave it) in all homes, a 2/12 roof pitch (if you want 4/12, shop elsewhere). Simplicity yields cost savings, and consistent product. Warranty service may be less so. One major Midwest dealer reported he stopped carrying Cappaert because warranty support was lacking. So, choose your dealer carefully. Company is prosperous, well capitalized and not without a sense of humor: its latest single-wide models include the Big Foot, the Screamer and the Terminator. Asked "Are you serious?" a spokeswomen laughingly replied "As serious as sin."

Cavalier Home Builders LLC (publicly held)
P.O. Box 540, 32 Wilson Blvd. Su. 100
Addison, Alabama 35540
Ph: 256.747-9800   Fx: 256.747-3044
Web site: www.cavalier-homes.com
Brands: Inglewood by Cavalier

Background: Founded in 1984 with a single plant in Addison, Alabama, this small, well-managed company went public two years later, and used its stock appreciation to acquire small, mostly family-owned one-plant companies along the eastern seaboard, the Southern tier states, Texas and the Southwest. At one point its brands included Astro Homes, Brigadier Homes, Buccaneer Homes, Bellmont Homes, Riverchase Homes, Mansion Homes, Town & Country, Delta Homes, Bellcrest Homes, Homestead Homes and Spirit Homes. In the go-go 1990s, Cavalier took a loss following a foray into setting up a dealership network. Ended up selling most of them, whittled down its manufacturing plants (to four), retired several brands and survived intact as a strong stable builder. Offers chattel and land-home loans, including FHA Title 1 and Title II, through its wholly-owned CIS Financial Services.

States where sold: VA, NC, SC, FL, GA, AL, TN, KY, IN, IL, MO, AR, MS, LA, TX, OK, KS

Principal market niche: builds the full range, from metal-on-metal single-sections to three-section modulars, but principal niche is low end to low mid-range. Targets the first time MH buyer and those able to buy homes with more options.

Retail price range before tax (including transportation and set-up): $26,000-$30,000 at low end to a high of $135,000 (almost all models mid-price and above are in either HUD or modular codes)

Competes against: Mostly Clayton, Fleetwood and Palm Harbor, although given its range of offerings, there are few brands it does not compete against.

Construction rating: 7

Description of a popular model: 4BR, 2BA, 27'x76', two-section, 2026 sq. ft. "Power House" (a generic package house with numerous options), 3/12 roof pitch, 8' side walls w/ residential ceiling, crown molding throughout, 2x6 ext. walls, vinyl siding and shingle roof, kitchen incl. 22 cu. ft. FF refrigerator, stainless steel sink, Delta single handle faucet.

What distinguishes brand from its competition: Quality materials even in standard models, great flexibility in floor plans, proprietary "Uni-wall" wall

system that hides seams, no vinyl-on-gypsum (special proprietary wall-paper instead, which greatly reduces potential moisture/mold build-up problems), no floor registers in middle of floor, quality cabinetry.
Number of dealerships — Company owned: 4 co-owned
Independents: 240 (of which 131 sell Cavalier exclusively)
Percentage of HUD homes sold of total homes produced: 95%
In-house financing:? Yes - CIS Financial Services
In-house Insurance:? Yes - CIS Insurance Services
Warranty structure and length: 1 year. Company runs service teams out of GA, NC and AL plants. See comment below.
Web site rating: Inadequate, clunky, unsatisfying. Not a single photo of a Cavalier home anywhere on the site. Floor plans are barely readable on screen (but can be printed), short on feature/benefits list. Videos of commercials unhelpful. A lackluster reflection of a company that deserves a better presentation.
Comment: This is a solid, well-managed company with one weakness, based on anecdotal reports: poor warranty service. In 2003 one large Midwest dealership dropped the brand because buyers of Cavalier homes had to wait months for service and parts. Other Cavalier dealers who were members of a buyer's group to which the dealership belonged, reported similar delays. This shortcoming may have been resolved as this goes to press, but the concern warrants the home shopper's careful inquiry. Cavalier has managed to avoid diluting quality while growing. Its popular 2500 sq. ft. "Power House" (a package w/ a floor plan, options, and color scheme, nothing of which can be changed) now comes in four models. Quality standard construction (w/ GE, Whirlpool, Delta appliances), are strong pluses.

Buccaneer Homes
(a subsidiary of Cavalier Homes, Inc.)
Cavalier Home Builders, LLC
PO Box 1418, 330 Buccaneer St.
Hamilton, AL 35570
Ph. 800-264-2822   Fx. 205/921-7390
Web site: none
Background: One of the oldest recognizable brands in the SE (the oldest in AL), Buccaneer was founded in 1971 by Steve Logan, to serve the low end affordable housing market, first with 1200 sq. ft. Single wides, then DWs to 2400 sq. ft. The brand was acquired in the 1990s by Cavalier, then discontinued in 2000 when the market tanked. In Aug, 2005, with recovery underway, Cavalier re-introduced the brand, once again to serve the low end of the market.
States where sold: AL, MS, LA, FL, TN, AR, GA, KY
Principal market niche: low end, entry level (50-50 SWs and DWs)
Retail price range before tax (including transportation and set-up): low 30s to $39k (Single wides), $40,000-$65,000 (Double wides)
Competes against: River Birch, Fleetwood, Lexington, Southern Homes
Construction rating: 4
Brands: Buccaneer Series
Description of a popular model: B5351K, Double-wide, 3BR-2BA, 28'x48' (1344 sq.ft.), 2x4 ext. walls, 3/12 roof pitch,, 20 yr. shingles, 7' wall ht., VOG (3/8"), carpet stapled to floor, single-pane windows (w/ storm clip-ins), elec. outlets attached to wall with clips/wings, floor registers on center line, 3/4" OSB floor decking, stainless kitchen sink, 20 cu.ft. refrigerator.
What distinguishes brand from its competition: Nothing stands out except for the availability of Cem-Plank exterior siding, a fiber cement product similar to HardiBoard, instead of vinyl siding.
Number of dealerships—Company owned: none
Independents: approx. 60
Percentage of HUD code homes sold of total homes produced: 100% from this plant
In-house financing: No
In-house insurance: No
Warranty structure and length: 1 year, factory-dispatched teams from plants in AL, NC and GA, plus dealer and contracted service.
Web site rating: No web site for Buccaneer. No info on brand at Cavalier web site.
Comment: Faxes and phone calls to Buccaneer's gen. mgr., sales mgr. and Cavalier's national mktg. director requesting product information were not answered. Potential buyers of Buccaneer Homes should not be blamed if they find this behavior troubling. This brand is a low end product for the shade-and-shelter market, i.e., homebuyers whose need for affordable housing trumps aesthetics, quality construction and a home that appreciates in value. Anecdotal evidence suggests that warranty service on the Cavalier brand has been an issue (see Cavalier Comment). This problem may have been resolved but potential home buyers should make sure the dealer will go the distance on warranty service, given that low end homes statistically have more problems than high end brands

Cavco Industries, Inc. (Publicly held)
1001 N. Central Avenue, Suite 800
Phoenix, Arizona 85004
Ph. 602-256-6263   Fx. 602-256-6189
Email: info@cavco.com
Web site: www.cavco.com
Brands: Cavco Homes, SunBuilt Homes, Villager Homes, Villager Profile, Sun Villa Homes, Westcourt Homes, Litchfield Limited, Winrock Homes, Santa Fe Series, Vantage Series, Vision Series (details below)
Background: Founded in 1979 as a travel trailer builder, Cavco evolved into a dominant, well-regarded MH player in the Southwest, also producing park model homes/lofts (i.e., under-400 sq. ft.), camping cabins, and specialty structures such as camping cabins for KOA and commercial buildings. In 1997, purchased by Centex, one of the country's largest site-builders, looking for a production plant that could provide homes to its planned HUD-code subdivisions. But after several years of battling zoning problems around HUD-code homes, Centex spun Cavco off in 2003, paid off its debt and left the company healthy and flourishing. Company has three manufacturing plants.
States where sold: AZ, NM, CA, NV, UT, CO, Produces 32% of all MH in Arizona.
Principal market niche: Builds for almost every retirement community in Arizona, sells primarily to families in other states
Retail price range before tax (includes transportation & set-up): $55,000-$150,000
Competes against: Palm Harbor, Schult, Fleetwood
Construction rating: 8
Description of a popular model: Two-section, 3BR, 2BA, 1500 sq. ft. Santa Fe style, cathedral ceilings, tape & textured 1/2" drywall throughout, 4/12 roof pitch, 2x4" ext. walls 16" O.C., 90" sidewall ht., oversized dual glaze windows, wood-crafted cabinets w/ hidden hinges. Price: $68,000 (before tax).
Cavco brands: Company has a bewildering number but they fall into two general categories, depending on which plant produces them --
Cavco
SunBuilt
Village Profile
Santa Fe Series
Vantage (sold at company owned retailers only)
The above five brands/series are built at the company's Durango Division which builds mostly homes for retirement communities and subdivisions, priced in the mid- to high-end range ($60,000-$120,000). Features: lots of customization, including reverse floor plans, "stretch" homes (length additions), options. Homes can be built to either HUD or mod specs.
Villager Homes
Sun Villa Homes
Westcourt Homes
Litchfield Limited
WinRock Homes
Vision Series (available from company owned retailers only)
The above five brands/series are built at the company's Litchfield Division which focuses more on low- to mid-range homes, including single-sections, sold from retail sales centers. Less customization flexibility than Durango division. Note: Single-section homes account for only 3% total homes built.
What distinguishes brand from its competition: Southwest style architecture w/ open floor plans/ oversize windows, angled walls, plant shelves, art alcoves, lots of floor plan customization, in-house engineering staff that works closely w/ customers.
Number of dealerships — Company owned: 6
Independents: 100
Percentage of HUD homes sold of total homes produced: 90%
In-house financing:? No
In-house Insurance:? No
Warranty structure and length: 1 year, 30 day cosmetic (mandated by Arizona law)
Web site rating: Outstanding. Clean, fast, good-looking, easy-to-navigate, intuitive interface, lots of information and images, a sense of transparency, a model for the rest of the industry to imitate.
Comment: You know this is a very well run, customer-oriented company when Cavco's CEO personally calls to make sure that information requests were satisfactorily answered (they were), then explains that any Cavco homeowner with anything more than minor warranty problems can expect to hear from him directly as well. Cavco also does a flourishing business building park model vacation homes (cabins/lofts under 400 sq. ft.), camping cabins for KOA, and commercial structures. Clearly, Cavco is an industry stand out, across the board.

Champion Enterprises Inc. Publicly held
Corporate headquarters:
2701 Cambridge Court, #300
Auburn Hills, Michigan 48236
Ph. 248/340-9090   Fx. 248/340-9345
Web site: www.championhomes.net
Note: the following Champion subsidiary companies/ brands have been retired, with no further production. A few homes in the remaining inventories may still be on retail sales center lots: **Atlantic Homes, Chanduleur Homes, Homes of Legend, Champion Homes of Indiana**

Background: Historically, until Clayton Homes' recent

expansion, Champion Enterprises was the MH industry's 800 lb. gorilla, the nation's largest housing manufacturer, at one point comprising 16 HUD home brands built in 64 plants in 16 states. Founded in 1953 in Dryden, MI, Champion was an early player in both the MH and RV sectors, especially the latter. In the early 70s, the company, by now publicly held, was the nation's largest RV builder (three lines: Champion, Titan and Concord). During the go-go 90s Champion divested its RV side and went on a buying spree, acquiring other MH builders, leaving them largely free to continue business with minimal interference. In a disastrous attempt at vertical integration, Champion also purchased hundreds of retail dealerships, overpaying for them and shouldering a crushing debt burden. In the wake of the industry crash that hit in 1999 the company sold, closed or consolidated 31 plants and nearly 300 retail sales locations. Still, the company came out of the '99-'04 downturn in the black. Now the #3 HUD producer, selling 13 brands, Champion is still formidable with a strong national presence (33 plants in 18 states, 2 in Canada). Add its modular home production (15%) and it topped the 2005 list for combined HUD and Mod production. In March, 2006, Champion acquired Minnesota-based HUD/Modular builder Highland Homes for $23 million in a bid to increase its market share in the north centrual US.

States where sold: Builds home for all market segments but most brands target low to mid-range affordable housing.

Notes:
1. Except where indicated Champion's brands offer 1 year structural warranty coverage, no in-house financing or insurance.
2. Company-wide, Champion's HUD-code homes account for 85% of total production.
3. Of Champion's 12 current home brands, several are identical, differing in name only, allowing Champion to double (sometimes triple) its presence in more populous markets (i.e., competing dealerships in the same market sell different brands).

What follows is a listing for each Champion Enterprises subsidiary brand, more or less in alphabetical order:

Advantage Homes, Gateway Homes
(subsidiaries of Champion Enterprises, Inc.)
Note: Don't confuse Advantage Homes with a Champion-owned California dealer network of the same name.
These are two identical brands built at the same Guin, Alabama plant, differing only slightly in floor plans and decor, i.e., color of wallboard, drapes, carpets. Advantage is also produced in other regional plants, with somewhat different specs.
Plant location:
6440 U.S. Hwy. 43
Guin, Alabama 35563
Ph. 205/468-3191   Fx. 205/468-3336
Web site(s): none
States where sold: AL, MS, LA, GA, TN, TX, KY, SC, MO, AR, FL, OK
Principal market niche: move-up (and growing) families, mid-level range
Retail price range before tax (includes transportation & set-up): $58,000-$100,000
Competes against: Southern Energy, Indies House, Franklin Homes
Construction rating: 5
Description of a popular model: 32 x 80 two-section, 4BR, 2BA, 3/12 roof pitch, ext. walls 2x4 16" O.C., 2x6 floor joists, floor decking ¾" plywood, VOG 3/8" int. walls, porcelain commodes, plastic bath sinks, MDF cabinets, Formica countertops, single-pane windows, 18 oz. carpet on ½" 5# rebond pad
What distinguishes brand from its competition: Offers more customization, upgrades to T&T, bull nose corners on walls, counter tops, more colorful inside decor.
Number of dealerships—Company owned: none
Independents: 17
Comment: Most homes are RSOs (retail sales orders) with upgrades (T&T, dual-glazed windows, ceramic tiles, hardwood cabinetry, many sited w/ an attached garage. Probably only two or three competitors can build the 32x80 DW model (it's huge, good for growing families).

Castle Homes of Pennsylvania
(A division of the New Era Group, a subsidiary of Champion Enterprises, Inc.)
PO Box 609 Boyle Memorial Drive
Knox, PA 16232
Ph. 800/227-8533   Fx. 814/797-1186
Web site: www.castlehousing.com
Background: In 1996, a group of 18 Northeast retailers headed by Elliot Fabri, head of New Era Building Systems (mostly modular) started Castle Homes of Pennsylvania, constructing a new plant 15 minutes from the New Era factory to build HUD-code MH only, including homes at a lower price point than New Era's more pricey offerings (see New Era listing). Within a few years Castle added a modular capacity (entry level mod homes) building homes known for both high customization and "crossover" floor plans, i.e., easily converted to either HUD or

mod codes, depending on buyer preference. In 2005 Castle Homes was acquired by Champion Enterprises, Inc. as part of the latter's $41 million purchase of New Era Building Systems. Castle continues to be run by the Fabri management team as a division of the newly named New Era Group.

States where sold: CT, DE, IN, MA, MD, ME, MI, MO, NH, NJ, NY, OH, PA, RI, VA, VT, WV

Principal market niche: buyers seeking mid- to high-end homes with lots of customization. Over 70% of HUD homes purchased are placed over a basement.

Retail price range before tax (includes transportation and set-up): $42,000 -$130,000

Competes against: site built homes, Colony Homes, Commodore, Pine Grove

Construction rating: 8

Brands/series:

Castle series – mid-to high end, mostly two-sections, full finished dry wall t/o, (ready for painting), roof pitch to 12/12, Cape Cod options, many ranch models with walk-up storage under a 7/12 roof. Few triple-sections, some two-story models. Floor plans easily built to mod or HUD.

Palace series – Castle's lower-end of the line: ext. walls 2x6," 16" O.C. (double 2x6" top plates), 2x3" int. walls 24" O.C., VOG (3/8" drywall), 8' side wall height, vaulted ceiling, 2-knob kitchen faucet, 28 oz. carpet on #6 rebond carpet pad. Floor plans less adaptable than Castle series to putting in basement and/or attic stairs.

Description of a popular model: Castle Cape Cod style two section, 3BR, 2BA, 28 x 56', 9/12 roof pitch with two outside dormers, 8' flat ceiling, full finished drywall t/o, ceramic tile entry way, Corian countertops, Alloc wood veneer hardwood floor. Approx: $87,000

What distinguishes brand from its competition: The New Era reputation, highly customizable floor plans easily built to either code, high quality "heavy" construction, many optional items included as standard features, ext. elevations of many homes indistinguishable from site built.

Number of dealerships — Company owned:
none **Independents:** 103

Percentage of HUD homes sold of total homes produced: 40%

In-house financing? No

In-house Insurance? No

Warranty structure and length: 1 year top to bottom, plus 9 more years structural

Web site rating: Passable but way too limited, out of date, requires work to find information. Pros: helpful fast clickable factory tour, good floor plan search/presentation. Cons: Clunky navigation, no mention of either HUD or mod codes, no listing of standard features and/or options, no mention of the Palace and Castle series. Another example of a good company with a fairly clueless web site that likely frustrates informed home shoppers.

Comment: As Castle's background indicates, its dealer/investors wanted a mid-to high end HUD product that could meet that market yet be easily converted to an entry level modular home. Having that crossover product helped Castle survive the '99-'04 industry crash. By offering all the modular amenities in a HUD code home, Castle has encouraged many HUD home shoppers to climb the ladder up to modular products. HUD or mod, Castle Homes offers a strong product that enjoys a beneficial tie to the New Era reputation, and that of its founder Elliot Fabri.

Champion Homes
(subsidiary of Champion Enterprises, Inc.)

Note: The signature name of Champion Enterprises, this brand and **Redman Homes** are the only two that are sold in all states except Florida. Built in plants serving regional markets all around the country, construction features and floor plans vary to meet consumer needs, with plants building a number of model series for different price points.

Champion brand confusion alert: At Champion's Silverton, OR plant, which builds Redman Homes, Champion is also building two new series, the **Silvercrest Classic** and the **Silvercrest Discovery**, neither of which have any relationship to the original high end Silvercrest brand produced in California by Silvercrest Homes, itself a Champion Enterprises, Inc. subsidiary. The use of the Silvercrest name with the Classic and Discover would seem to be an effort to attach the Silvercrest luster to low end and a mid-range Champion models sold in the NW, and which have little in common with their high end name sake. The Classic line sells in the $58,000 - $75,000 range; the Discovery retails for $50,000-$58,000. It is odd that Champion Enterprises would countenance this dilution of a marquee brand. The strategy is short-sighted, confusing, and a disservice to home buyers, not to mention Silvercrest Homes.

Nationally, some Champion plants have a robust marketing presence but most don't. One that does, together with a very good web site, is the Claysburg, PA division (opened 1964) which serves the Northeast market. The information that follows is for the regional market it serves, but it provides a reliable profile of the Champion brand nationally:

Champion Home Builders, Co.
(subsidiary of Champion Enterprises, Inc.)
P.O. Box 343

Claysburg, PA 16625
Ph. 814/239-5151   Fx. 814/239-2870
Web site: www.chbclaysburg.com
States where sold: ME, NH, CT, MA, VT, RI, NJ, NY, PA, OH, MD, VA, WV, DE
Brand/Series names:
Champion – mid-price range, lots of models, incl. single wides
Sovereign series – high end of product line, many "residential features" standard
Gold Medal series – Champion plus upgrades such as fireplace, finished drywall
Advantage series – low end entry level, affordable housing for first time buyers
Principal market niche: low to mid-range affordable housing, customers with $35,000 - $60,000.
Retail price range before tax (price includes transportation & set-up): Single sections - $22,3000 to $37,000, Multi-sections: $38,600 to $83,400.
Competes against: Commodore, Colony, Castle Homes
Construction rating: 7
Description of a popular model: Gold Medal series 104G, 28 x 56, large dormer, 3/12 nominal roof pitch, 20-yr. shingles, 2x6 ext. walls 16" O.C. w/ R-19 wall insulation, vaulted ceiling throughout, ½" int. finished drywall in LR, DR, master BA, 17 c.f. FF refrigerator, stone wood burning fireplace w/ raised mantle
What distinguishes brand from its competition: Champion's brand reputation, consistent quality product
Number of dealerships — Independents (incl. developers): 150
Percentage of HUD homes sold of total homes produced at this plant: 85%
Web site rating: Very good, a stand-out among Champion Enterprises brand sites, of which there are precious few. Pros: lots of photos, incl. exteriors, excellent factory tour, clear & printable floor plants. Cons: page design is spare, a bit primitive, lacking color, captions.
Comment: Champion is the quintessential example of traditional MH product: a decent, reliable, consistent quality affordable mid-range home. The PA plant's web site puts a face on the brand, offering a lot of detailed information about the brand and how it is built.

Dutch Housing
(subsidiary of Champion Enterprises, Inc.)
1500 N. Detroit St., PO Box 258
La Grange, IN 46761
Ph. 260/463-3199   Fx. 260/463-8693
Web site: www.dutch-housing.com

Fortune Homes
(subsidiary of Champion Enterprises, Inc.)
305 W. Dutch Drive, PO Box 40
La Grange, IN 46761
Ph. 260/499-3355   Fx. 260/499-3363
Web site: www.fortune-homes.com
Note: These identical brands are considered here together, except as noted below:
Backgrounds: Dutch Housing and Fortune Homes are essentially identical brands and compete in the same markets, with Fortune Homes created several years after Dutch Housing was launched in 1991. That year, a group with long experience at Redman Homes, founded Dutch Housing in White Pigeon, MI, offering a so-called package house (no customization, only two floor plans, vanilla decor, and only two colors). The goal: offer a mid-level MH product at an entry level price point that no one could touch. The strategy was hugely successful. Champion bought the company in 1994 and during the 90s boom years, Dutch grew to 7 plants churning out 30 homes a day before competitors caught up with similar offerings. After the MH crash began in 1999, Dutch turned to more customization and survived on a smaller scale.
States where sold:
Dutch Housing: MI, OH, IN, Il, PA, IA, MO, WI (scattered availability in: CO, ND, SD, NE, KS, OK, MN, AR, KY, TN, WY, NY, VA)
Fortune Homes: MI, OH, IN, Il, PA, IA, MO, WI
Principal market niche: affordable family housing, entry level to low-mid-range, mostly land-home purchases
Retail price range before tax (price includes transportation & set-up): $39,999-$89,000
Competes against: Redman, Fortune, Commander, Four Seasons
Construction rating: 6
Dutch Housing Brands/series:
Wintergreen – entry level
Millennium – mid-range
Heritage II – high end, "residential "look
Fortune Homes has floor plans only, no names series for different price points.
Description of a popular model: Dutch: 32x80 two section, 2560 s. f., 4BR, 2BA, separate LR/family room, lg. retreat room off master BA, "Jack & Jill BA between two other BRs, lg. kitchen w/ lots of cabinetry, lg. utility room, 7-1/2' int. wall ht.,VOG decorator wallboard.
What distinguishes brands from their competition: Offers the same floor plan at all price points, company claims volume materials purchase yields

lower price for same quality.
Number of dealerships — none **Independents:** approx. 200
Percentage of HUD homes sold of total homes produced: 80%
Web site ratings:
Dutch Housing: Unsatisfactory and annoying. Typical of many MH web sites, site is hardly more than an incomplete brochure. Click on Photos and you get 8-10 images of a single model's interior, one at a time, cycling every five seconds (no pause button). Floor plans are OK but no construction features/options lists. Click on Contact Us and find no address, no phone, fax, or email address, only a fill-in-the-fields template that is designed to harvest sales leads.
Fortune Homes: Like Dutch Housing, inadequate an annoying, with one spectacular exception. On the home page, lower left corner, clicking on "Take the Tour" automatically downloads a 29 page PDF filled with outstanding photos, descriptions, construction minutiae that is hands-down the best primer on MH factory construction found anywhere on line. Tip: print this out for reference, regardless of the home being considered for purchase.
Comment: Dutch Housing and Fortune Homes are two peas in a pod in a Midwest market that is already crowded with affordable housing brands, many of them Champion Enterprises subsidiaries. Though Dutch Housing is no longer the innovative "package home" that once dazzled that market segment, the brand, along with its near-twin sister Fortune, remains viable because both are decent well-built products that fill a price point that retailers need.

Highland Manufacturing, Inc.
Highland Homes
A subsidiary of Champion Enterprises, Inc.
PO Box 427   160 Rowe Avenue
Worthington, MN 56187
Ph. 507/376-9460
Web site: www.highlandmanufacturing.com
Background: This small builder in the SW corner of Minnesota (60 miles east of Sioux Falls, SD) was founded in 1986 by a group of private investors headed by CPA Greg DeGroot (who remains Highland's president/CEO. Acquiring a struggling plant built 11 years previously, DeGroot and associates earned high praise for restoring the plant to profitability and helping the local economy. In recent years it has shifted its principal product offering from HUD-code to modular housing, expanding its distribution to an eight-state area (principally the North Central U.S.). Modular models now account for 60% of its total production. In 2000 the company was purchased by the Minneapolis-based private equity investment firm Norwest Equity Partners. Then, in March, 2006, Champion Enterprises acquired Highland for $23 million, as part of its strategy of increasing its market share of the modular housing market nationally.
States where sold: MN, IA, SD, ND, WY, CO, WI, MI
Principal market niche: low mid-range
Retail price range before tax (price includes transportation & set-up): $60,000 to $95,000
Competes against: Redman, Commander, Fortune, Dutch, Champion, Schult, Wick
Construction rating: 5
Highland Homes Series:
Classic – entry level, basic features
Stoneybrook – an upgrade, with a number of Classic options standard
Description of a popular model: Stoneybrook "Gold," 3BR, 2BA, 28x52, two-section, 3/12 roof pitch, 2x6 ext. walls 16 O.C., 2x6" floor joists 16" O.C., 7-1/2' int. walls, VOG, 25 yr. shingles, R-25/14/19 insulation, perimeter heat registers primary areas only, 18' FF refrigerator, raised oak kitchen cabinets, straight-edged Formica countertops, porcelain toilets, dual pane vinyl windows, 34" six-panel front door
What distinguishes brand from its competition: A bit more customization options and floor plans than some, able to build many HUD plans to modular standards
Number of dealerships—Company owned: none
Independents: 60-plus
Percentage of HUD homes sold of total homes produced: 40%
In-house financing? No
In-house Insurance? No
Warranty structure and length: 1 year, using factory-dispatched techs or reimbursing dealers for service performed.
Web site rating: A failure, little more than a static one-page brochure (slow loading at that) with scant information for the informed home shopper; construction features pages list only supplier brands w/ no specifics, only one floor plan shown, material seems way out of date (most photos are from a 1999 show); no dealer locator; no contact form.
Comment: Obtaining information from Highland proved challenging. Repeated requests for phone contact with senior management went unanswered, while the marketing department seemed reluctant, even unprepared, to disclose useful background on company history or provide requested additional product information. Highland certainly provides a decent, albeit lackluster, product, but the company's diffident response to a bonafide media inquiry may give some home shoppers pause. Anecdotal comments suggest that, at least in the 1990s, some dealerships in the region were unhappy with factory warranty repair

service. This issue may have been since rectified. Purchasing from a reputable dealer should lay such concerns to rest. Hopefully, Highland's acquisition by Champion will lead to needed iimprovements, particularly in transparancy and public relaltions

Homes of Merit
A subsidiary of Champion Enterprises, Inc.
Two locations:
Homes of Merit Bartow
Building 121, Bartow Air Base Executive Plaza
Bartow, FL 33830
Ph. 863/533-0593   Fx. 863/533-0310
Web site: www.homesofmerit.net

Homes of Merit Lake City
100 Hwy. 100 E
Lake City, FL 32055
Ph. 386/755-3073   Fx. 386/752-9560
Web site:
www.manufacturedhomebuilders.com
Background: Founded in Bartow (west of Jacksonville) in 1973 by MH industry veteran Charles Weeder, Homes of Merit focused on providing homes to Florida's burgeoning MH land-lease retirement communities (a market that still accounts for half its volume). In 1985, the company, at that time employee-owned and operated, opened a second facility in Lake City, FL (east of Tampa), this one almost exclusively geared to building family market housing sold through street retailers in FL, GA and SC. The two facilities operate largely independent of each other, each with its own web site.
In 1999, Champion Enterprises bought the company, its last acquisition before the MH industry tanked.
States where sold: FL, GA, SC
Market niche: working family affordable housing, retirees
Retail price range before tax (price includes transportation & set-up): $39,000 to $90,000.
Average retail price: $50,000 to $55,000.
Competes against: Skyline, Palm Harbor, Fleetwood
Construction rating: 7
Bartow location's series:
Twin Manor - standard series
Country Manor - mid-range offering
Country single wides - part of the Country Manor series, limited production
Atlantic series - most basic product, up to 32x80 family size, affordable
Lake City location's series:

Bay Manor - standard series
Forest Manor - affordable, lower cost line
Description of a popular model: Bay Manor #3233, 32x62 two section, 3BR, 2BA, ¾-width LR, 2x6 ext. walls 16. O.C., 3/12 roof pitch, 2x8" floor joists, VOG standard, 7-1/2' int. sidewalls, vaulted ceiling w/ 3" crown molding, floor decking 5/8" OSB, Ultimate Kitchen package (stainless appliances), shut-off valves all fixtures, single pane white windows, china commodes & sinks.
What distinguishes brand from its competition: good fit and finish, solid construction, and a free 2-5 year extended warranty "pledge" covering structure, plumbing, electrical and HVAC.
Number of dealerships—Company owned: none
Independents: 90
Percentage of HUD homes sold of total homes produced: 95%
Web site ratings:
Bartow site: First rate. Pros: great design values, tons of information, intelligently organized, lots of exterior photos of real homes (what a concept!), conveys a sense of company personality, even pizzazz (check out the interactive movie "coming soon). Cons: Virtual tours are out of focus and non-interactive (you can't stop or zoom) but this is a very minor shortcoming to a beguiling, impressive site.
Lake City site: Undergoing a redesign and update as this goes to press but, as it stands, it's way below the Bartow site. Construction specs are hard to find, no photos of exteriors, and too wordy. The short web movie may seem like a good idea but it's way too slow. And why two web sites for one brand? It confuses home shoppers, lowers brand recognition and splits visitor traffic. Suggestion: fold the Lake City content into the Bartow site.
Comment: Homes of Merit consistently ranks #1 or #2 in number of homes built for the Florida market and it has long enjoyed a good reputation for providing decent affordable housing for retirees and middle income working families (90% of homes sold to the latter are on private land placements w/ conventional home loans). The company's 5-year pledge warranty has been an important selling point.

Redman Homes
(subsidiary of Champion Enterprises, Inc.)
Several plant locations. For this listing:
308 Sheridan Drive, PO Box 95
Topeka, IN 46571
Ph. 260/593-2962   Fx. 260/593-2401
The three principal web sites for this brand:

www.redmanhomes-in.com (Redman Homes of Indiana)
www.redmanhomesyork.com (Redman Homes of Nebraska)
www.azchampion.com (Factory Expo Home Center)

Background: One of the industry's most established and recognized brands, the company was founded in an old pickle factory in Alma, MI in 1937 by Harold and Bill Redman, producing camping trailers before moving into MH and expanding across the Midwest, then nationwide, morphing into Redman Industries, later going public. In 1988, now highly diversified but unprofitable, the company was acquired by the investment group (and turn-around specialists) Wingate Partners. Five years later, Redman re-emerged as a profitable debt-free public company, the third-largest producer of MH, operating 16 MH plants building various brand name homes sold in 40 states. In 1996 the company was acquired by the industry's #2 MH builder, Champion Enterprises. Today, the Midwest is still Redman's principal market but the brand is very much a national presence and the look of its homes varies significantly. Its plant in Chandler, Arizona, for example builds many models with a Southwest look.

States where sold: All states except Florida

Principal market niche: low end to medium-high price point, for blue collar middle class working families, 25-44 age group

Retail price range before tax (price includes transportation & set-up): $31,000 (small single section) to $80,000. Average: low $60s (two section).

Competes against: Dutch Housing, Commander, Fairmont, Clayton

Construction rating: 6

Series: Each Redman plant creates its own series to match its market. No national series.

Description of a popular model: New Moon 28x70, 3BR, 2BA, 3/12 roof pitch, 7-1/2' sidewalls, VOG int. wallboard, vaulted ceiling (optional: 8' sidewall, flat ceilings, 4/12 pitch), floor decking 5/8' Novadek, int. walls 2x3 16" O.C., kitchen: white composite sink, single-handle faucet, perimeter heat vents, water shut-off all fixtures.

What distinguishes brand from its competition: Some flexibility in floor plan changes, able to build same home to different price points, the Redman name.

Number of dealerships —company owned: none
Independents: 180

Percentage of HUD homes sold of total homes produced: 75% at this location (4 plants)

Web site ratings:
www.redmanhomes-in.com (Redman Homes of Indiana) - Serviceable, with good floor plan presentations. Contact Us page provides, refreshingly, an email address and an 800 number instead of a template-form designed to harvest sales leads.

www.redmanhomesyork.com (Redman Homes of Nebraska) - Poor, terrible design (loud red lettering, clunky), no construction features, specs, upgrade options. Floor plans are OK, Photos acceptable but almost no exterior shots.

www.azchampion.com (Factory Expo Home Center) Outstanding. Lots of info, dozens of photos (including many exteriors of real homes, not computer generated), intuitive interface, easy navigation, virtual tours, construction features and specs on every model, a great example of what an MH site can be (and this is just a dealership).

Comment: Because it is built nationally for widely diverse markets with differing weather and demographics, a Redman home has a lot of different looks and price points. But on the whole the brand is noted for being a decent affordable home at a mid-range price, with quality and customer satisfaction dependent to a large extent on the reputation of both the dealer who sells it and the plant that makes it.

Commander Homes
(subsidiary of Champion Enterprises, Inc.)
1100 W. Lake Street, PO Box 95
Topeka, IN 46571
Ph. 260/593-2970   Fx. 260-593-2901
Web site: www.commander-housing.com

Background: This brand is almost identical to Redman above and is produced at the same plants. Commander was launched in 1997 at the height of the MH boom to penetrate Redman's market with a slightly different look but at the same price points. In recent years it has added options Redman doesn't offer, to differentiate the brand.

Retail price range before tax (price includes transportation & set-up): $40,000 to $95,000

Construction rating: 7

Commander series:
Yorkshire – entry level, low-end (some single sections)
Riverdale – low mid-range
River Ridge – mid-range, lots of options.
Spring Creek – high end, residential features, $100,000-plus

Description of a popular model: Riverdale or River Ridge two section, 3BR, 2BA, all finished dry wall, 8' side wall, 7/12 roof pitch, two-sided fireplace (hand laid rock) or Ultimate Kitchen (w/ stainless appliances).

What distinguishes brand from its competition (including Redman): optional log siding, true hand-laid ceramic tile on counters, distinctive decor, laminate sub flooring, 7/12 pitches.

Number of dealerships — none   **Independents:** 180

Percentage of HUD homes sold of total homes produced: 60%
Web site rating: A faint pulse but brain dead. Home page is two sentences of small print. Model search is primitive, floor plans but no construction specs/options. About Us page lists only a street address. Contact Us is completely blank. Commander Housing evidently has yet to grasp the importance of a robust Internet presence, or that a poor, outdated web site can actually cost them sales.
Comment: Like fellow Champion brand Fortune Homes, Commander Housing was created as a knock-off of a sister brand, in this instance Redman Homes, to increase the penetration of the same markets in which Redman was being sold by providing a different name and a slightly different look. A decently built affordable home from the Champion Enterprises stable of Midwest brands.

Moduline International, Inc. (Canada)
(subsidiary of Champion Enterprises, Inc.)
Two plants:
1175 Railway Avenue, PO Box 190
Penticton, BC V2A 6K3 CANADA
Ph. 250/493-0122   Fx. 250/4963-0500
1421 Briar Park Crescent
Medicine Hat, AB T1A 7E4 CANADA
Ph. 403/527-1555   Fx. 403/526-1724
Web site: www.moduline.ca
Background: Founded in Penticton in 1969, Moduline has quietly prospered as a well-respected Canadian HUD-code builder. Known for their high quality craftsmanship, the skilled work force averages 17 years w/ the company. Purchased by Champion in 1993.
States/provinces where sold: B.C. plant ships to: WA, ID, MT, AK. Canada: BC and Alberta. Alberta plant ships to MT, WY, ND, SD, MN
Principal market niche: mid-to high end MH, developers, mostly modular homes
Retail price range before tax (price includes transportation & set-up): $60,000 to $100,000.
Competes against: Skyline, Marlette, Champion brands
Construction rating: 8
Brands/series: Coronado series
Description of a popular model: Clifton, 27x48 two-section, 1269 sq. ft., 3BR, 2BA, 6/12 roof pitch, real cedar siding (or Hardiplank), 7-1/2' side wall, vaulted ceiling, T&T walls, rounded corners, 18 cu. ft. FF refrigerator, 50 gal. water heater, Moen faucets t/o, R-36/20/36 Super Good Cents insulation. Approx. $80,000.
What distinguishes brand from its competition: Good looking designs, superior construction, tubular steel I-beam chassis (stronger), drywall panels mounted horizontally (stronger, eliminates "proud seams"), energy efficient for harsh Canadian winters, ten year warranty (7 in Alaska), ranked #1 in Canada for warranty service.
Number of U.S. dealerships — Company owned: none   **Independents:** 8
Percentage of HUD homes sold of total homes produced for US market: 15%
Warranty structure and length: 10 years (7 in Alaska)
Web site rating: Very good, fast, intuitive, lots of information. The look is a bit pedestrian but is more than made up for by an innovative feature available with on-screen floor plans: viewers can click on any floor plan to flip it (horizontally), or mirror it (vertically) to show those available options.
Comment: Moduline, the only non-U.S. builder in this guide, builds a good solid home with lots of value (and insulation). Moreover, its popularity in the US, while limited to a few northern boarder states, until recently owed to the favorable exchange rate for US buyers. But with the Canadian dollar much stronger (worth 81 cents US at this writing), its price advantage is diminished. Transporting a home to a US site will also run more, figure around $5,300 for a two section. But with its outstanding warranty and quality construction, Moduline still has much going for it.

New Era Building Systems
(a division of the New Era Group, a subsidiary of Champion Enterprises, Inc.)
451 Southern Avenue PO Box 269
Strattanville, PA 16258
Ph. 800/678-5581   Fx. 814/764-5658
Web site: www.new-era-homes.com
Background: In 1992 when Pennsylvania HUD/mod builder Strattan Homes was about to go under, respected industry veteran Elliot Fabri, at the time Strattan's general mgr., together with a group of investors, purchased the Strattan Homes plant, and launched New Era Building Systems (w/ many Strattan employees staying on). Initially a modular only builder, company began building a HUD line (no single sections) to accommodate one of its investors, Jensen Communities, owner of 28 upscale 55+ MH communities on the eastern seaboard. Today, New Era's HUD-home production (only 12% of its total) goes almost exclusively into Jensen communities, but one can still order a HUD-code New Era home through its dealerships. Note: in

1996, Fabri, backed in part by a group of 18 retailers, started Castle Homes of Pennsylvania, constructing a new plant 15 minutes from the New Era factory to build HUD-code MH only. (See Castle Homes listing). In the years since, New Era has earned a national reputation as an innovative builder of well-constructed, custom-designed, upscale homes. Earlier this decade New Era acquired modular builder Carolina Building Solutions (Salisbury, NC). In 2005, Champion Enterprises, Inc. acquired New Era (along w/ Castle and Carolina Building Systems) for $41 million, a move that makes Champion the country's largest provider of modular homes. Fabri and his management team continue to run the company as before under the new name, the New Era Group.
States where sold: PA, NY, CT, MA, NH, VT, ME, MD, NJ, WV, DE, VA, NC, SC, MI, RI, WI, IL, IN
Principal market niche: "active adult" (55+) land/lease community developers (i.e. Jensen). Some HUD sales from other builders.
Retail price range before tax (includes all elements of a turn key home package in Jensen MH communities): $105,000 to $319,000. Average: $170,000
Competes against: Ritz-Craft (homes for pvt. property parcels outside of land/lease communities)
Construction rating: 9
Brands/series:
Spectrum series – for community developers, typically end-entry w/ attached garage
Description of a popular model: Spectrum NES018, 26x56, two-section, 1,456 sq. ft., 2BR, 2B, den, breakfast nook, end-entry, 4/12 roof pitch, 8' ext. side wall, full finished dry wall, vaulted ceiling, kitchen cabinets white maple w/ raised panels, 2-knob kitchen sink, laminate countertops, vitreous china commode, acrylic BA sinks, Shaw 25 oz. carpet, vinyl double-pane windows.
What distinguishes brand from its competition: Built heavy, much to mod specs, true customization flexibility, higher end appliances/fittings/coverings (Koehler, Whirlpool, Shaw), full finish dry wall, wood molding t/o, ten year warranty, the New Era reputation
Number of dealerships—Company owned: none
Independents: 105
Percentage of HUD homes sold of total homes produced: 12%
In-house financing? No
In-house Insurance? No
Warranty structure and length: 1 yr. top to bottom, 2 yrs. on portions of heating/electrical systems, years 2-10 limited structural provided by Residential Warranty Corp (RWC) paid for by New Era
Web site rating: Quite dreadful, clunky, difficult to navigate, out of date, geared more to dealers/builders, than informed shoppers doing research, looks like it was designed as an afterthought by construction engineers. This site is an embarrassment to a company with a deserved cutting edge reputation. Pros: with patience one can get some idea of the products. Cons: broken links (Financing, Dealers only), Company video is fine but poor screen resolution. Potential New Era customers are typically savvy Internet users and deserve much better.
Comment: This is one of the few MH builders closely associated with the name and reputation of its principal founder. Like Patriot Homes' Sam Weidner, New Era's Elliot Fabri enjoys high esteem not only for building (and standing behind) quality products, but for his leadership in working with govt. and non-profits to solve housing problems with HUD and mod engineering. Home buyers choosing a New Era HUD-code home can expect to pay more, but they'll be buying a heavily constructed, over-built home that is as good or better than comparable site-built.

Silvercrest Homes
(subsidiary of Champion Enterprises, Inc.)
Note: The Silvercrest name described here should not be confused with a series under the Champion brand in the NW: Silvercrest Classic and Silvercrest Discovery, both introduced in 2004, and both several clicks below Silvercrest. See **Champion brand confusion alert** under the **Champion Homes** listing, pg. 28
Western Homes Corporation
299 N. Smith Avenue PO Box 759
Corona, CA 92880
Ph. 951/734-6610   Fx. 951/737-9043
Web site: www.silvercrest.com
Background: Widely regarded as the Mercedes of MH, particularly in the West, Silvercrest was founded in 1969 (as Silvercrest Industries) by a southern California MH dealer unhappy with the poor quality of mobile homes then available. The company quickly earned a reputation for site-built quality, architectural flair, customization and airy, open floor plans.
In 1985 the company was sold to a large MH park developer, later merging with Western Homes which, in turn, was purchased in 1989 by Redman Industries, which itself was acquired in 1996 by Champion Enterprises, Inc. Builds out of two California plants.
States where sold: CA, southern OR, WA, NV, AZ, NM, CO
Principal market niche: mid to high end, pvt. land/home placements, MH parks, developers, move-up buyers, affluent retirees.
Retail price range before tax (price includes transportation & set-up): $60,000 to $377,000 (4 section home), Average price: $100,000.
Competes against: mainstream homes, in MH

communities: high end Palm Harbor and Skyline
Construction rating: 9
Series:
Two-story townhouse series – high end (placed on prime California lots, they're fetching up to $950,000).
Manor series – three section homes, high end, 1883 sq. ft. to 3,000 sq. ft. From $120,000.
Edgewood series – mid- to high end, large sized, for pvt. property parcels
Westwood series – mid-to-high, pvt. property placements, MH parks
Westwood Craftsman series – high end of mid-range, Craftsman style, pvt. property
New Cottage series – mid-range, cottage sized
Backyard Home series – mid-range from $60,000, 674 sq. ft. max, for guest house, detached office/studio, rental, grandmother unit, pool house. Complies with new California legislation to create more housing.
Good Neighbor series – Developer homes, ready for attached garage, for in-fills, subdivisions
Description of a popular model: Westwood W-60, 26x60, 3BR, 2BA, 1537 sq. ft., front dining room, open kitchen w/ island work center, breakfast nook w/ bay windows, approx. $85,000
What distinguishes brand from its competition: Very well built, high end materials, stylish architecture similar to site-built, flexible customization, steel-framed "super floors," excellent fit and finish, Silvercrest reputation.
Number of dealerships — Company owned: 1 (Champion-owned Advantage Homes dealerships, California)   **Independents:** 75
Percentage of HUD homes sold of total homes produced: 95%
Web site rating: Outstanding. Simple, elegant, fast, accessible, intuitive, easy to navigate, lots of images, every model has a downloadable pdf with both floor plan and features list. Refreshing extra: the Contact Us page offers a choice of an email address or a form. What a concept! A model web site.
Comment: Through repeated ownership changes, Silvercrest has maintained its reputation for top quality design, construction and finish work. Over the past decade its developer business has grown to nearly 30% while the hot California housing market, especially MH park renewals (i.e., replacing old mobile homes), has made its homes a relative bargain. Silvercrest is booming. Down side: a production delay currently running 8-10 weeks or more, plus scattered anecdotal evidence of some fall off in quality of factory warranty service on homes sited outside California.

Summit Crest Homes
(subsidiary of Champion Enterprises, Inc.)
2221 Clayton Place, P.O. Box 10
Berthoud, CO 80513
Ph. 800/818-2632   Fx. 970/532-4352
Background: Summit Crest started out in 1969 as a Champion expansion plant building Titan Homes, but during the 1980s the plant's managers grew increasingly frustrated that the brand's poor reputation in other markets as a low end home was hampering its efforts to market higher end models. In 1986, with the blessing of Champion corporate, the subsidiary changed the brand name to Summit Crest Homes to build mid- to high end homes embodying the distinctive architectural character of the Colorado Rockies.
The strategy worked. The Summit Crest plant also builds Champion's modular home line, Genesis Homes, and offers an increasingly popular option of building all of Summit Crest's HUD-code models to modular specs. Company has achieved Built Green certification, indicating compliance with environmentally sound building practices.
States where sold: CO, NM, AZ, UT, NV, ID, MT, WY, KS, NB, MO. Note: In CO buyers are people looking for a rural slice of heaven (esp. with the cabin series). In states to east: buyers seeking quality rural housing in the mid- to high end price range.
Retail price range before tax (price includes transportation & set-up): $60,000 -$130,000
Competes against: Magnolia Homes, Guerdon Homes, Karsten, BonnaVilla
Construction rating: 8
Brands/series:
Cabin series – mountain getaways, 1,000 – 1,700 sq. ft. w/ expansive covered porches. Very nice elevation.
Meadowcreek – mid-price range, single and double sections
Elite – mid- to high-end double sections, Cape Cod 2nd story option available
Legacy – mid- to mostly high-end three-section home (some w/ two furnaces, no less)
Custom Design Series – Two section models to 1,975 sq. ft. and highly customizable
Description of a popular model: Two section, 1,600 sq. ft., 3BR, 2BA, 10/12 roof pitch w/ Cape Cod 2nd. story, full T&T. Note: on all two-story & hinged roofed models, a factory set-up crew completes home installation on site.
What distinguishes brand from its competition: Great flexibility and customization, attractive homes, solid construction, excellent brand reputation

Number of dealerships — Company owned: none
Independents: 40 (about half developers)
Percentage of HUD homes sold of total homes produced: 25%
Web site rating: A disappointment, way short on content, clueless. Only one image of a home exterior! No lists of features, specs. Company has excellent printed brochures w/ lots of images and content, all of which should be put on this site. On the floor plan/ elevations page, clicking on a model number produces a clunky Multiple Listings Service-type data card with mostly blank, irrelevant fields. Floor plans, yes, but no elevations, no images. Print buttons don't function. Not a good sign of product quality for Internet-savvy home shoppers.
Comment: Summit Crest's emphasis on building its homes to modular specs helped it survive the recent MH downturn because mod-code homes enjoy acceptance for conventional home loan financing. Company builds an attractive home with distinctive touches (e.g., log wainscoting in the master BR of its cabin series). With builders hard to find in rural areas, Summit Crest, with its flexibility, features and good looks, is an excellent alternative to site-building, whether the home be HUD or modular.

Titan Homes
(subsidiary of Champion Enterprises Inc.)
Note: This brand is produced in several regions. Models differ but generallly the brand is for the low-end, low-medium markets. Here is info for two markets: NE and SE:
Titan Homes - Northeast region
PO Box 177 951 Rt. 12 South
Sangerfield, Ny 13455
Ph. 800/937-3911   Fx. 315/841-4660
Web site: none
Background: Founded in 1973 in upstate New York, Titan developed a steady presence in the Northeast with a single plant operation, much of it supplying homes to MH communities. Was purchased by Champion in the 1980s. In 1999, after Titan's plant burned to the ground, Champion, noting Titan's profitability, opted to build a new state-of-the-art plant, keeping employees on salary during the rebuild.
States where sold: NY, PA, ME, NH, VT, MA, CT
Principal market niche: entry level to low mid-range, MH communities
Retail price range before tax (price includes transportation & set-up): $33,000 to $70,000
Competes against: Commodore, Fleetwood, Colony Homes (Commodore)
Construction rating: 5
Titan series:

New England Manor (Titan's high end)
Brentwood (a click below)
Avenger (low, entry level)
Description of a popular model: Brentwood #951, 3BR, 2BA, 1386 sq. ft. Standard features: 3/12 roof pitch, 2x6 ext. walls (16" OC), 16 cu.ft. refrigerator, R-22/19/26 insulation, floor 7/16" Novadek, whole home water shut-off only, ½" int. walls VOG, dual faucets on sinks/basins
What distinguishes brand from its competition: Standard features include 7'6" side walls, 2x6 ext. walls (16 OC), Low E Thermalpane windows, 2x4 dbouble marriage wall. Good customization flexibility.
Number of dealerships: Co-owned: 25
Independents: 100 (25 of these MH communities)
Percentage of HUD homes sold of total homes produced: 65%-70%
In-house financing? No
In-house Insurance? No
Warranty structure and length: 1 year, plus free 2thru 10 year structural
Comment: Titan's average construction rating reflects the brand's long association with decent affordable housing. Nothing really stands out but it has the Champion name standing behind it.

Titan Homes Southeast region
6440 U.S. Hwy. 43
Guin, Alabama 35563
Ph. 205/468-3191   Fx. 205/468-3336
Web site(s): none
States where sold: AL, MS, LA, GA, TN, TX, KY, SC, MO, AR, FL, OK
Principal market niche: Entry level, affordable
Retail price range before tax (price includes transportation & set-up): $29,000-$69,000
Competes against: Clayton, Fleetwood, River Birch, Indies, Cappaert, Southern Energy
Construction rating: 4
Brand: Titan at various price points
Description of a popular model: 3BR, 2BA, 1500 sq. ft., 7-1/2" ext. side wall, 3/12 roof pitch, 2x4 ext. walls (16" OC), 16 cu.ft. refrigerator, 1/2" VOG, 15 yr. shingles, OSB roof sheathing, vinyl siding, water shut-off at all fixtures.
What distinguishes brand from its competition: A lower priced home with good value (most models under $40,000), no changes or customization
Number of dealerships: Company-owned: none
Independents: 55
Percentage of HUD homes sold of total homes produced: 100% at this plant.
In-house financing? No
In-house Insurance? No
Warranty structure and length: 1 year

Comment: The same facility that builds Advantage and Gateway Homes began building Titan models in early 2005 to provide a line a click or two below those brands in quality and price. About 30% are single-section homes. Champion's goal: provide dealers a home for under $40,000. The demand was there. Orders are steady.

Chariot Eagle, Inc. (Privately held) 2 Divisions
Florida location:
931 NW 37th Avenue
Ocala, FL 34475
Ph. 352/629-7007   Fx. 352/629-0026
Web site: www.charioteagle.com
Background: Founded by Bob Holliday in 1980 on a shoe string in an old building in Ocala, FL, Chariot Eagle's initial focus was building park model RVs (mini-homes up to 500 sq. ft. mostly sited in special sections of RV parks and used as seasonal get-away homes by snow birds). After FL in the mid-1980s approved HUD-code park models, Chariot Eagle began offering full-sized residential HUD-code homes on a small scale, all virtually custom-built to the buyer's design and sited on private property (often at ocean front sites, mounted on 16 foot pilings). No marketing effort, just referrals and word of mouth. These homes today account for only about 12% of the company's total production. In 1994 company established Chariot Eagle West (see separate listing below) in Phoenix to serve the SW market.
States where sold: FL
Principal market niche: Solvent snow birds and retirees, buyers who want a custom-built home and can afford the cost of custom designed and engineered plans.
Retail price range before tax (price includes transportation & set-up): $75,000 to $150,000. Average: $115,000-$125,000
Competes against: site-built vacation homes
Construction rating: 8
Brands/series: None. All homes custom designed.
Description of a popular model: 3BR, 2BA, 28 x 56 two-section, 8/12 or 9/12 roof pitch (to avoid an MH appearance), vaulted ceilings, ext. & int. walls 2x4" 16" O.C., OSB wrap, ¾" T&G plywood decking, dry wall t/o, bull nose corners, 36 oz. plush Shaw carpets, R-30/13/19, dual pane vinyl windows, Formica countertops and cabinets, with MDF cabinet doors (company reports many buyers prefer Formica over composite countertops).
What distinguishes brand from its competition: All custom designed and built (and thus more expensive), quality construction, no active marketing effort
Number of dealerships—Company owned: None
Independents: 176
Percentage of full-sized residential HUD homes sold of total homes produced: 12% (park models account for 65%, modular homes 23%
In-house financing? No
In-house Insurance? No
Warranty structure and length: 1 year top to bottom, factory dispatched crew
Web site rating: Quite serviceable for park models but nary a word about full-size HUD-code homes. Clearly the company's principal focus is on park models.
Comment: See comment following Chariot Eagle West listing below.

Chariot Eagle West (privately held)
Arizona location
8100 W. Buckeye Road
Phoenix, AZ 80543
Ph. 623/936-7545   Fx. 623/936-7012
Web site: www.charioteaglewest.com
Background: The western location was started in 1994, building a plant from scratch
States where sold: AZ, CA, CO, OR
Principal market niche: 55+ MH communities (70% of homes sold); secondary: buyers seeking vacation homes in the mountains
Retail price range before tax (price includes transportation & set-up): $75,000 - $120,000
Competes against: Cavco (Durango series), Silvercrest, Hallmark Southwest, Schult
Construction rating: 8
Brands/series: None
Description of a popular model: 3260A, 3BR, 2BA (3rd. BR serves as den), 1351 sq. ft., 4/12 roof pitch, 8' ext. side walls, vaulted ceiling, drywall w/ bull nose corners t/o, breakfast nook, cultured marble window sills t/o, Energy Master package incl. R-57 ceiling, smaller air registers for smaller rooms, wrapped water heater, Ventaline air exchange vent system for roof.
What distinguishes brand from its competition: High degree of customization (but not as much as Florida plant), cultured marble window sills t/o (makes for easy cleaning of desert dust, mountain moisture), strong track record w/ regional MH communities.
Number of dealerships — Company owned: None   **Independents:** 28 (eight street retailers, 20 MH community owner/developers)
Percentage of full-sized residential HUD homes

sold of total homes produced: 28%
In-house financing? No
In-house Insurance? No
Warranty structure and length: 1 year top-to-bottom
Web site rating: Poor, unattractive, outdated (unchanged since 2002), little more than a static brochure, no construction specs/upgrade lists, only one (dreary looking) exterior elevation image. Pros: a good listing of its energy saver features. This site needs to be redesigned w/ more pizzazz and better integrated into the company's flagship Florida site.
Comment: Clearly Chariot Eagle's market is park models (consistently ranking #1 or #2 in 11- and 12-wides) and the company has flourished in this niche. Offering full-size HUD-code homes, particularly for MH communities in the West, was a natural outgrowth. There, the company is up against formidable high end competition in the likes of Silvercrest and Cavco, both of which have generally greater curb appeal. But the company is holding its own with all the business it can handle in both in Florida and Arizona. Together with an unblemished reputation, Chariot Eagle is worth a close look, even if it's not vying for your attention.

Clayton Homes, Inc.
A subsidiary of Berkshire Hathaway, Inc.
P.O. Box 9780 5000 Clayton Road
Maryville, TN 37804
Ph. 865/380-3000   Fx. 865/380-3781
Web site: www.clayton.net
Background: Long regarded as a premier MH company, Clayton was founded in 1966 by Jim and Joe Clayton, sons of a TN cotton farmer, as an across-the-street expansion of their fledgling car dealership. Opened first MH plant in 1970, began acquiring MH communities, later started Vanderbilt Mortgage (1977) to offer in-house financing/insurance. In '82, brothers formally divided the businesses w/ Jim taking over Clayton homes, taking it public in '84, expanding company-owned dealerships, building plants and adding more MH communities. By '92 CEO Clayton joined the Forbes' list of 400 wealthiest Americans. During the go-go 90's, company steered a disciplined course, avoided lax lending standards, and sailed through the '99-'04 MH crash relatively unscathed.
By 2003, Clayton Homes was a national, vertically integrated housing giant (owning 82 MH communities), operating in 49 states and with a market cap of $1.2 billion, more than the book value of its ten nearest competitors combined. Its financial services division now included partial ownership of a second finance company, 21st Mortgage, created in 1995 to provide MH buyer financing to independent, non-Clayton-owned dealership, most in the SE and SW.

That spring, in a surprise move, Clayton announced a planned merger with Omaha-based Berkshire Hathaway, Inc, the huge holding company helmed by billionaire Warren Buffet, in exchange for $1.7 billion in cash. By year's end, just after the deal was finalized, Clayton Homes acquired all of 21st Mortgage. In 2004, abetted by Berkshire's deep pockets, Clayton Homes acquired bankrupt former MH heavyweight Oakwood Homes and the three well-regarded MH brands the latter had acquired in the late 1990s: Schult, Marlette and Golden West (plus modular builder Crest Homes). In 2005 in a period of a few weeks, Clayton acquired the prestige western brand, Karsten Homes and, from struggling Fleetwood Enterprises, Inc., that company's network of 135 Fleetwood-owned sales centers. The Clayton juggernaut continued in 2006 with the acquisition in August of Southern Energy Homes and its subsidiary Giles Industries.
As 2006 drew to a close, Berkshire Hathaway had completed a four-year strategy of mergers and acquisitions (including the purchase of MH loan portfolios worth billions) that together solidified its position as the dominant player in the MH industry. Assets include: 32 plants, 392 company-owned sales centers, more than 1,100 independent retailers, 87 MH communities, and a $17 billion loan portfolio. The impact of the "Berkshire effect" on the MH industry so far has been positive, if only because the infusion of capital, in particular to the lending sector, has increased the availability of MH loans to home buyers.
Note: Each of Clayton Homes' subsidiary home-building companies are the subject of separate listings in this guide. What follows is a breakdown for Clayton's flagship brand.
Brand: Clayton Homes.
States where sold: All states except HI
Principal market niche: Entry level to mid-range affordable housing for 25-55 yr. old buyers, working families earning $30,000-$50,000, concentrated in manufacturing, construction and service-related industries.
Retail price range before tax (price includes transportation & set-up): Single-sections $28,000 to $45,000. Multi-sections from $35,000 to $80,000. Average home sale price: $45,000
Competes against: Fleetwood, Palm Harbor, Champion Enterprises brands (e.g. Redman, Commander, Dutch Housing, Fortune, Homes of Merit), Hart, Franklin, General Housing
Construction rating: 5
Brand: Clayton
Description of a popular model: Keystone, 32x56, 1,792 sq. ft., 3BR, 2BA, 3/12 roof itch, with LR and 20x15' Family room, 2x4" ext. walls 16" O.C., 7-1/2'

side wall ht., VOG, floor decking 19/32" OSB, 18 oz. carpet on ½' rebond pad. fiberglass sinks, one-piece showers, water shutoff all fixtures, in-line floor registers. Approx. $45,000

What distinguishes brand from its competition: Because of company size, able to negotiate best prices from suppliers, thus putting more product in home at same or better price; superior factory-built cabinetry; name-brand appliances; availability of in-house financing through Vanderbilt w/ creative loan qualifying options such as land-in-lieu and construction loans w/ zero points or fees. Good warranty service.

Number of dealerships — Company owned: 392 **Independents:** more than 1,100

Percentage of HUD homes sold of total homes produced: 85%

In-house financing? Yes, through Vanderbilt Mortgage & Finance

In-house Insurance? Yes

Warranty structure and length: 1 year

Web site rating: Unsatisfactory, disjointed, poorly designed, short on specifics, broken in places, and sorely in need of an extreme makeover. Under Our Brands, the Oakwood Homes site was down for many months; the company history for the Schult subsidiary Marlette Homes is word-for-word the same as that of Schult, only the brand name is changed (sloppy at best, inexcusably misleading at worst). The impression conveyed is that Clayton is clueless about the Internet, placing it way down the list of priorities, leaving informed home shoppers decidedly unimpressed. A poor reflection on a company that does so many things right.

Comment: Even before its 2003 acquisition by Berkshire Hathaway, Clayton Homes was a shining light in the MH industry, a principled, well-managed company with no significant bad raps that stuck to its knitting during the 90s boom when so many manufacturers joined what one wag called "the industry's latest suicide binge." Despite its recent purchase of several up-market brands, the company's core business has been, and remains, affordable housing for working families, and the vast percentage of its products have the boxy, bland, low-roof-pitch appearance of a cookie-cutter "mobile home." That's just fine for a substantial number of home buyers. In sum, Clayton Homes is the Wal-Mart of manufactured housing.

Note: Like Wal-Mart, Clayton has not been immune from negative publicity. In Sept. 2005, the Associated Press reported that Clayton had settled out of court 50 Texas law suits that accused Clayton sales staff of forging signatures on false deed and lien documents involving a "land-in-lieu of" clause in financing home purchases. The first case scheduled for trial alleged, in part, that Clayton Homes agents forged several signatures giving the company a family's 893-acre farm if the buyer of a Clayton MH (who in this instance was a relative allowed to live on the acreage) defaulted. The suit claims the forged signatures were those of people who had died years earlier. Industry sources say Clayton was badly burned by a single, rogue sales manager, and paid dearly (probably many millions), but this incident is an anomaly for a principled, responsible corporation.

At the end of 2006, the company and its newly acquired subsidiaries were together the dominant industry presence with a 25% market share. Moreover, Clayton's two lending arms, Vanderbilt Mortgage & Finance and 21st. Mortgage together comprise a mini-capital market for the MH industry. It is no secret (but not widely known by the public, either) that Clayton Homes' makes far more profit from financing its homes than it does from the homes themselves. Still, Buyer's of Clayton's products can take comfort that a reputable company stands behind its many brands and will be responsive to their needs.

Giles Industries
A subsidiary of Clayton Homes, Inc.
405 South Broad Street
New Tazewell, TN 37825
Ph. 800/844.4537   Fx. 423/626-6919

Background: Founded in 1959 by businessman R.O. Giles, company grew beyond mobile homes to build office units, school rooms, even RVs, but in mid-80s, following a fizzled Knoxville Worlds Fair (taking a loss on motels and restaurants built for the event), company refocused on HUD homes only, targeting entry level to low-medium homes with competitive price points, which proved a successful strategy. Giles remains a family-held enterprise, currently headed by the founder's grandson. The company's New Taswell HQs north of Knoxville are on a 50 acre tract with two plants, one producing single-sections exclusively, the other double-sections. Interestingly, Clayton Homes dealerships are Giles' biggest customer, enabling those retailers to carry a line that's a click below Clayton in features and price points.

States where sold: TN, AL, WV, VA, NC, SC, GA, AR, KY, NY, IN, DE, OH, NY

Principal market niche: entry level affordable housing

Retail price range before tax (price includes transportation & set-up): $19,000 (single-section)

to $52,000 (two-section, 32'x80')
Competes against: Clayton, Southern Energy, Fleetwood
Construction rating: 4
Description of a popular model: Two-section, 28'x44', 3BR, 2BA. Standard features: 2x6 ext. walls, 8' foot sidewalls, flat ceiling, one-piece fiberglass tub/showers, 3/4" T&G plywood floor, PEX plumbing (brass fixtures), vinyl-on-gypsum wallboard, porcelain sinks, center-line floor registers, carpeting stapled to floor.
What distinguishes brand from its competition: Better standard features (see above), including GE appliances, 20-year shingles (no metal roofs), rolled roof insulation (not blown-in cellulose), a competitive price and excellent warranty service.
Number of dealerships — Co. owned: none
Independents: 150
Percentage of HUD homes sold of total homes produced: 100%
In-house financing? No
In-house Insurance? No
Warranty structure and length: 1 year. Giles uses factory dispatched crews and/or reimburses dealerships for warranty services performed.
Web site rating: Primitive, disappointing but with one big plus: site uses IPIX technology to offer 360 mouse-controlled views of many model interiors. But many "virtual tour" buttons don't work, no photos of home exteriors, some dead links.
Comment: Carefully managed by the founder's grandson Alan Neely, Giles Industries has found a way to build in better standard features to low end homes and maintain very competitive price points (they achieve this in part by not allowing any customization). Add an admired warranty service program that includes a factory training school for service techs from other industry builders (Clayton, for one), and homebuyers in this market have ample reason for confidence in Giles product line.

Karsten Company, Inc.
A subsidiary of Clayton Homes, Inc.
P.O. Box 9780 5000 Clayton Road
Maryville, TN 37804
Ph. 865/380-3000   Fx. 865/380-3781
Karsten home office:
9998 Old Placerville road
Sacramento, CA 95827
Ph. 916/363-2681
Web site: www.thekarstenco.com
Background: Founded in 1995 by former Golden West Homes CEO Harry Karsten, this well-regarded Western US home builder is the latest acquisition of Clayton Homes, representing a full-circle career track for founder Karsten. In 1984, Harry Karsten and a group of investors, purchased S. Cal.-based Golden West and for the next decade built quality homes for the West Coast market that competed favorably with the high end Silvercrest brand. In 1994, Oakwood Homes, Inc. bought Golden West, selling the unwanted GW plant in Sacramento, CA to Karsten, then, inexplicably, lowered the brand's construction quality (see Golden West listing). Barred for 5 yrs. from active involement in MH by his non-compete agreement, Harry Karston stayed off the radar while his brother Andy started Karsten Homes from the Sacramento plant.
In 1999, with Oakwood now struggling—and doubtless seeing a market opportunity—Karsten, now free to compete, took an active role in Karsten Homes, duplicating his successful Golden West designs, signed up many of his former Golden West dealers, and thrived.
By 2005 the Karsten Brand was available in 14 Western states from four plants (CA, OR, NM and TX), with its MH community models gaining in popularity as well. Then in June, 2005, Clayton Homes, which in 2003 had acquired Oakwood Homes, Inc., announced it was purchasing Karsten Homes and its production facilities, folding them into Clayton's manufacturing division, CMH Manufacturing, Inc. Harry Karsten continues to run the enterprise, with no reported diminution of construction quality. (See **Clayton Homes** listing for more info on what has been a major industry consolidation of this and other companies and brands.)
States where sold: WA, OR, CA, MT, ID, NV, WY, UT, AZ, CO, NM, & western regions of TX, KS, OK
Principal market niche: mid-to high end, homes with a residential look
Retail price range before tax (price includes transportation & set-up): $48,500 to $176,500. Average $65,000-$70,000
Competes against: Skyline, Silvercrest, Cavco (Durango), Hallmark Southwest, Marlette, Golden West
Construction rating: 8
Brands/series:
CA plant: **Villa 2000 Series** (two-section 20 wides, 610-1,130 sq. ft.), **Villa 2400 Series** (two-section 24 wides, 947-1,420 sq. ft.), **Villa 2700 Series** (two-section 27 wides, 1080-1,782 sq. ft.), **Castle Estate Series** (triple-wides, 40.5' wide, to 2,670 sq. ft.); **Castle Series** (triple-wides, 40.5' wide, to 2,660 sq. ft.)
OR plant: **The Excel** (high end), **Starview** (a click below Excel), **McKenzie Triple Section** and **McKenzie Double Section** (mid range prices, vaulted ceilings), **Baycrest** (low mid-range price), The **Elite** (a click above Starview, w/ energy plus package, upgraded appliances)
TX and NM plants: Numbered models at all price

points, from 1,387-2916 sq. ft.
Description of a popular model: Villa 2700, 27x56, two section, 3BR, 2BA, 1,512 sq. ft., 4/12 roof pitch, 2x6" ext. walls 16" O.C., 7-1/2' ext. side walls. T&T bull nose t/o, opt. dormer and walk-a-bay bay windows off LR, walk-in closets, lg. kitchen w/ breakfast nook. $81,000
What distinguishes brand from its competition: longitudinal floor system using 30% more steel than standard transverse floor systems, overbuilt roof system, higher insulation, well-designed exteriors, T&T walls w/ bull nose corners std., solid dealer network, one of industry's best warranties. Note: in early 2006 Karsten changed its hallmark longitudinal floor system to the industry standard transverse floor system, this to allow the building of on-frame modular homes.
Number of dealerships — Company owned: none   **Independents:** 154
Percentage of HUD homes sold of total homes produced: 75%
In-house financing? Yes (see Clayton listing)
In-house Insurance? Yes (see Clayton listing)
Warranty structure and length: 30-day cosmetic, 1 yr top-to-bottom structural, 10 years on roof, sub floor, walls, chassis.
Web site rating: Good. Straightforward, intuitive interface, useful. Pros: May be viewed in Spanish (great feature — the only other site that offers this is Palm Harbor), detailed lists of specs and upgrades, full line of clickable floor plans, a helpful site map, "Contact Us" page provides needed info w/o forcing visitors to fill out questionnaires/lead sheets. Cons: not enough ext. photos of different series, Factory Tour is a non-interactive, painfully slow, frustrating slide show (suggestion: make this tour fast and clickable or scrap it).
Comment: As this goes to press Karsten's indie dealers are holding their breath that Clayton Homes won't make the same mistake that Oakwood did in the 90s with the Golden West brand: strip its construction quality down to low end specs. Most likely they won't. Harry Karsten really knows his market and his much esteemed designer Clay Latimer (who did the orig. GW lines) has done a splendid job with the Karsten offerings. The higher end models, with attached site-built garages, are indistinguishable from site-built and compare well by almost any measure.

Norris Inc. #01 (Norris Homes)
(A subsidiary of Clayton Homes)
PO Box 96 Highway 22 West
Bean Station, TN 33708
Ph. 865/993-3343   Fx. 865/993-3141
Web site: none
Background: Started in 1965 by two local entrepreneurs, Norris Homes prospered in the region, selling a well-regarded mid-level HUD-code home. Clayton Homes acquired the company in 1982, allowing Norris to continue building and selling under its own name, both to Clayton-owned sales centers as well as indie retailers outside the Clayton universe. Norris continued modest growth, adding a second plant close to the original.
While both plants can build mod homes, one plant builds 95% HUD-code, the other 60% HUD-code. In recent years Norris has focused more on upper-end homes with 9' side walls, full dry wall and hinged roofs (to 10/12 pitch) with models configured for an attached garage and more of a site-built look.
States where sold: TN, NC, SC, VA, DE, MD, WV, KY, OH, IN, IL, MO, AL, GA, FL (panhandle)
Principal market niche: mid to upper end, reaching into off-frame modular
Retail price range before tax (price includes transportation & set-up): mid-40s to low 100s.
Competes against: Patriot, Liberty, Franklin, Southern Energy, Horton
Construction rating: 6
Brand: Norris Homes
Description of a popular model: two-section, 3BR, 2BA, 28' x60' den model, 2x4' ext. walls, 16" O.C., 8' side wall height, partial dry wall (square corners), laminate countertops, wood edged trim, MDF baseboard trim, hardwood kitchen cabinets, all china sinks/toilets, fiberglass tubs, Low E dual thermal pane windows.
What distinguishes brand from its competition: Lots of customization available, superior in-house cabinetry and doors, able to provide a site-built appearance
Number of dealerships — Company owned: none
Independents: 90 (apart from Clayton-owned sales centers)
Percentage of HUD homes sold of total homes produced: 75%
In-house financing? Yes (see Clayton Homes listing)
In-house Insurance? Yes (see Clayton Homes listing)
Warranty structure and length: 1 year
Web site rating: N/A
Comment: Clayton Homes has wisely allowed Norris Homes to maintain its own brand identity and quality of construction, serving as a kind of private label unaffected by the down market, cookie-cutter reputation of the Clayton Homes brand. While Norris builds Cape Cod homes and

so-called T&L ranch models (a triple section w/ a tag unit on the front), few of its models are true high end homes (e.g., full drywall, rounded corners, 2x6 ext. walls, Corian countertops, etc.). In all, a decent product from a small reliable Clayton-backed builder, well worth consideration.

Oakwood Homes, Corp.
A subsidiary of Clayton Homes. Inc.
500 Clayton Road, PO Box 9780
Maryville, TN 37804
Ph. 865/380-3000   Fx. 865-380-3781
Web site: None (see web site rating)
Background: This one-time Greensboro, North Carolina-based builder was, until recently, a major presence in the South, until it became the poster child of the MH industry's 1990s boom-and-bust cycle. Founded in 1946, Oakwood grew steadily as a respected builder of affordable housing for the SE market, went public in 1971, and continued to prosper. In 1985 it launched Oakwood Acceptance, an in-house financing unit, then expanded into the TX and OK markets just as recession hit those oil patch states, nearly crippling the company. By the early 90s, with the MH marketplace thriving once more, Oakwood rode the rising tide, becoming the darling of Wall St. investors as it aggressively expanded its dealer network (with an iron fist, some say) to 300 stores nationally, beefed up its production capacity, and acquired other builders and their plants. At one point its market value approached $1-1/2 billion. But by 1998 the grim slide began: Oakwood's lax, easy-credit lending standards, at sub-prime interest rates, triggered a horrendous avalanche of home repossessions, resulting in a billion dollar write-down and the loss of Wall St. investment support. Further, Oakwood had over-expanded its dealer network and overbuilt production capacity, the latter causing construction quality to plummet. To conserve cash, the company allegedly cut corners on the warranty side, which fueled a consumer backlash (including web sites created by unhappy homeowners) that badly tainted the Oakwood name, especially in its core SE market.

On the plus side Oakwood had acquired several manufacturers with brand name luster, notably upscale pioneer builder, Schult Homes (and its subsidiaries Marlette Homes and modular builder Crest homes) as well as well-regarded California-based Golden West Homes (see separate listings for these brands).

In 2003, following several CEO and management changes and after shutting down most of its plants and dealerships, once-mighty Oakwood declared Chapter 11 bankruptcy, a victim of corporate hubris, strategic blunders, wild excess and just plain greed.

Less than six months later, Clayton Homes, Inc., which itself had been purchased months earlier by Warren Buffet's Berkshire Hathaway, Inc., bought Oakwood Homes and its subsidiaries for $373 million, a bargain basement price. Clayton Homes pledged to retain substantially all of Oakwood's work force and has done so.

Some industry observers expected Clayton to retire the Oakwood brand due to its sullied reputation, but by mid-2005, the brand was still alive (with 60 Oakwood-owned sales centers) however it is no longer being marketed in the deep South and TX, once its core market. (See **Clayton Homes** listing for more info on what has been a major industry consolidation of this and other companies and brands.)
States where sold: CO, DL, ID, MO, NC, SC, NM, OH, OK, OR, PA, TN UT, VA, WA, WV
Principal market niche: entry level low-end to low mid-range
Retail price range before tax (price includes transportation & set-up): $25,000 - $90,000. Average price: $51,000
Competes against: Southern Energy, Cavalier, Liberty, Fleetwood, some Champion brands
Construction rating: 4
Brands/series:
Oakwood Classic Series – low end to low end of mid-range affordable homes
Freedom series – Identical to Oakwood Classic series, one of several private brands used to allow Oakwood dealers in the same market to compete w/o brand duplication.
Description of a popular model (SE market): Oakwood Classic 2001, 4BR, 2BA two-section. Standard features: 3/12 roof pitch, 2x4" ext. walls 16" O.C., 7' side walls, vaulted ceilings, VOG wallboard glued/stapled to studs, 2x4 int. walls 16" O.C., (non-load bearing walls 2x3" 24" O.C., single pane windows, int. doors w/ two mortised hinges, elec. outlet boxes clipped to walls, 16 oz. carpet w/ #5 rebond pad, MDF kitchen cabinets, dual knob kitchen faucet, laminate self-edged countertops, no backsplash.
What distinguishes brand from its competition: Now a part of the Clayton Homes stable, meaning reliable construction and good warranty service; buyers able to obtain in-house financing and insurance through Clayton's finance unit Vanderbilt Mortgage and Finance.
Number of dealerships—Company owned: 60
Independents: approx. 100
Percentage of HUD homes sold of total homes produced: 50%
In-house financing? Yes (see Clayton Homes listing)
In-house Insurance? Yes (see Clayton Homes listing)
Warranty structure and length: 1 year (plus a 2-5 limited extended coverage in some regions)

Web site rating: Incomplete, disappointing. Pros: models by region easily found, images OK, many links to Clayton pages; Cons: standard features list vague on specifics, last updated 3/98, annoying pdf downloads for spec lists, floor plans. See rating for Clayton web site.

Comment: To be fair, Oakwood Homes Corp. was not alone in the insane 90's rush to extend easy credit loans to uncreditworthy homebuyers, but it was the high-profile leader of the stampede, and when it went over the cliff, it took hundreds of millions of investors' money with it, wrecking the MH industry's image on Wall Street. The good news: its new owner, Clayton Homes, Inc. is now in the driver's seat, steering a disciplined course, scaling back the brand's availability (avoiding some markets where the brand had a very poor reputation), and is committed to restoring the luster of the Oakwood Homes' brand. Homebuyers can be confident that Clayton is standing behind the Oakwood product line.

Schult Homes, Inc.
A subsidiary of Clayton Homes, Inc.
P.O. Box 9780 5000 Clayton Road
Maryville, TN 37804
Ph. 865/380-3000   Fx. 865/380-3781
Web site: www.schulthomes.com

Background: The industry's oldest MH builder, Schult was launched in 1934 in Elkhart, IN by partners Wilber Schult and Walter Wells who began with house trailers (building a 50' custom rig for Egypt's King Farouk in the 40s), then pioneered the first true sectional home, used as emergency housing for the Manhattan Project during WWII. Company prospered during the 50s and 60s, introducing many advances, incl. interior plumbing, bay windows, built-in appliances, heating systems—helping turn Elkhart into the capital of MH and RV manufacturing. Schult merged with Inland Steel Corp in 1970 but in 1984, Schult's management, together with an investor group, bought the company back, reforming as Schult Homes.

In 1989, Schult acquired well-respected Marlette Homes from Coachman Industries, expanding its reach into the eastern seaboard up to New England, as well as to the NW. Both companies focused on mid- to high end homes for those requiring customization and site-built upgrades; Schult in particular earned a reputation for solid, well-built, good-looking homes built with a conscience. Company led the industry in introducing T&T dry wall, and was one of the first to peg salary bonuses to customer satisfaction ratings. In 1998 Oakwood Homes, Corp. acquired Schult and for the next six years allowed it to continue with little interference or compromise to its quality (see Oakwood Homes listing), although it did begin building Schult homes at some of its SE plants, hoping thereby to gain some of the brand's luster. With the subsequent acquisition of Oakwood by Clayton Homes in 2004, Schult became Clayton's designated up-scale national brand, now sold in 34 states. (See **Clayton Homes** listing for more info on what has been a major industry consolidation of this and other companies and brands.)

States where sold: CA, NV, AZ, UT, MT, WY, CO, NM, ND, SD, NE, KS, OK, MN, IA, MO, AR, WI, IL, MI, IN, KY, TN, OH, PA, MD, WV, VA, NC, SC, GA, AL, FL, D.C.

Principal market niche: mid- to high end, emphasis on dry wall, heavy quality construction, a site-built look

Retail price range before tax (price includes transportation & set-up): $45,000-$110,000 (Schult also builds low-mid price point homes w/ VOG)

Competes against: Patriot, Wick Building Systems, Palm Harbor, Commodore, Pine Grove, Burlington Homes

Construction rating: 8

Brands/series: The Schult brand is built in seven factories, each with series and floor plans developed for their regions. The principal model series:

Chateau Élan – High end, 8' side walls, vaulted ceiling (flat ceiling available), 5/12 hip roof, 6-panel doors, T&T drywall t/o, can look like site-built

Oasis and Sonora – both mid-range, for the SW market

Super Value Series – low end of mid-price point, VOG, conventional looking MH

Legacy – low-mid range, VOG, features upgrade extended front porch

Manor Hill, Presidential, Regal – Midwest models, low mid-range, VOG, 3/12 roof pitch

Description of a popular model: Legacy, 28x56, two-section, 3BR, 2BA, 1,549 sq. ft., basement model, 4/12 roof pitch, 8' side wall ht., flat ceiling, ½" painted drywall t/o, walk-in closet master BR, perimeter heat, raised panel oak cabinet doors, R-38/22/22, 30 yr. shingles

What distinguishes brand from its competition: Venerable brand name, loyal and well-established dealer network, high quality construction, superior warranty (5 years plus 1 mo.), home can look like site-built, high customer service rating, widely available nationally

Number of dealerships — Schult owned: 0

Independents: approx. 120
Percentage of HUD homes sold of total homes produced: 60%
In-house financing? Yes
In-house Insurance? Yes
Warranty structure and length: 1/5 year, plus 1 month. First year: top to bottom, incl. cosmetic details; years 2-5 +1 mo: structural.
Web site rating: A sub-site of the Clayton Homes umbrella site (www.clayton.net), inadequate, outdated, and annoying. Here again, clicking on a model number downloads a floor plan to your desktop, requiring one to close two windows and launch a viewing program. A simple, fast click to a printable html page would suffice. See Clayton web site rating.
Comment: This much-revered company and brand survived unscathed its acquisition by Oakwood, despite the latter's terminating all but four of Schult's 54 corporate staff. Even during Oakwood's bankruptcy, Schult did not lose a single dealership. Clayton's purchase of Oakwood was a relief, for Schult could anticipate stable, capable management that understands continued success for Schult means leaving it free to do what it has done best longer than any other builder: build good homes.

Marlette Homes, Inc.
A subsidiary of Clayton Homes, Inc.
P.O. Box 9780 5000 Clay ton Road
Maryville, TN 37804
Ph. 865/380-3000   Fx. 865/380-3781
Web site: www.marlettehomes.com
Background: Founded in 1953 in Marlette, MI by three partners, incl. Earl Swett who championed the establishment of standardized MH construction standards, Marlette earned a reputation for a solid, well-built home, comparable to Schult Homes. In 1964, company opened a second plant in PA, expanding its reach out East from VA to ME. Coachman Industries acquired Marlette in 1981, subsequently opening a third Marlette plant in OR to expand to western markets. In 1989, Schult Homes purchased Marlette from Coachman, giving Schult a needed presence both out East and out West. Marlette was a good fit since, like Schult, it boasted a seasoned work force, solid quality construction, and a well-regarded product. When Oakwood bought Schult in 1998 without tampering with the latter's construction standards, Marlette enjoyed Schult's halo of protection—until 2004 when Clayton Homes acquired Oakwood. Within months, Clayton management decreed that henceforth the Marlette line would offer fewer floor plans, less customization and fewer upgrade options—in short, still a worthy product but now a click below Schult.

(See **Clayton Homes** listing for more info on what has been a major industry consolidation of this and other companies and brands.)
States where sold: AZ, CA, CT, DL, ID, ME, MD, MA, NV, NH, NJ, NM, NY, PA, RI, VT, VA, WV
Principal market niche: low mid-range to high-end, for semi-retired, move ups, young families
Retail price range before tax (price includes transportation & set-up): $54,000 to $112,000
Competes against: Skyline, Palm Harbor, Redman, Burlington, Cavco
Construction rating: 7
Brands/series:
Signature series – From PA plant, many models covering all price points
Extra Value series – From AZ plant, many models, all price points, SW decor and floor plans
Lakeland Series – From OR plant, comprising: **Desert Manor, La Grand, Elation, Canyon Crest, River Crest, Sierra Vista, Meadow View, Columbia.** These are package houses with different options, across all price points.
First Edition – Low end to low-mid range, all price points, many models
Description of a popular model: Fm. OR plant: Meadow View, 3BR, 2BA, two-section, 1867 sq. ft., w/ 13x26' Great Room w/ fireplace/bookcases, 8x8' computer room w/ built-in desk, large util. room, sliding glass patio doors, LR box bay windows, recessed entry.
What distinguishes brand from its competition: Solid home, solid reputation (from its long association with Schult Homes), interesting floor plans well suited to regional preferences.
Number of dealerships — Marlette owned:
none   **Independents:** 300
Percentage of HUD homes sold of total homes produced: 65%
In-house financing? Yes (see Clayton Homes listing)
In-house Insurance? Yes (see Clayton Homes listing)
Warranty structure and length: 1 year
Web site rating: This is another sub-site of the Clayton Homes umbrella site (www.clayton.net). Same problems: woefully inadequate, out-dated, and annoying. Here again, clicking on a model number downloads a floor plan to your desktop, requiring one to close two windows and launch a viewing program. A simple, fast click to a printable html page would suffice. See Clayton web site rating.
Comment: Despite its parent company's decision in 2004 to reduce Marlette's options and customization choices, the brand is still worthy and well-built, although, according to some anecdotal comments, the fit and finish on homes from the OR plant in 2005 have been a bit below Marlette's usually high standards. While it boasts interesting floor plans (see Meadow

View description above), the brand's exterior elevations in general convey the distinctive, boxy, low-roof pitch, conventional look of a manufactured home. This may not be an issue for placement in an MH community, but home shoppers looking for a site-built look may find other brands more to their liking.

Golden West Homes
(A subsidiary of Clayton Homes. Inc.)
500 Clayton Road, PO Box 9780
Maryville, TN 37804
Ph. 865/380-3000   Fx. 865-380-3781
Web site: www.goldenwesthomes.com
Background: This well-known west coast builder started in 1965 in Santa Ana, CA, opening a second plant four years later in Albany, OR. The company changed hands in 1980, then again in 1986 when it was sold to a group of private investors headed by Harry Karsten, the highly regarded industry veteran. Karsten consolidated GW's three S. Cal plants into a new plant in Perris, CA purchased from RV builder Coachman Industries (who had briefly built there a motorhome to compete with Fleetwood RV's wildly successful Bounder model—and got their lunch handed to them). GW's S. Calif. plant focused on homes designed for its largest market, MH land-lease communities, while the OR facility provided homes w/ more of a site-built look (e.g., higher roof pitch, longer eves) for its market, private property placements. Note: From the beginning Golden West employed a longitudinal floor system, instead of a transverse floor system that the great majority of other builders use. Both plants built complex, high quality, heavy homes with consumer appeal and brand luster that rivaled Silvercrest.

That changed in 1994 when Oakwood Homes, on an expansion tear to become a national giant, purchased Golden West and, inexplicably, reduced the brand's construction quality to be more in line with Oakwood Homes, e.g., plastic sinks, cheaper materials, thereby undermining GW's reputation, demonstrating it had no understanding of the west coast & NW markets.

Finally, in 2000, Oakwood brought in savvy pros and gave them a freer hand to rescue Golden West. The turnaround was underway when Clayton Homes bought Oakwood in '04. Clayton mgmt. has wisely allowed GW to stay the course. Note: In 1996 GW's former CEO Harry Karsten, doubtless aware of GW's quality slide, launched his own MH brand, Karsten Homes, to duplicate his previous success with GW) (see Karsten homes listing)

States where sold: CA, AZ, ID, NV, NM, UT, OR, WA, MT, WY
Principal market niche: CA plant: retirees and others with disposable income purchasing mid-to high end homes in MH land-lease communities. OR plant: mid- to high-end homes for placement on private property
Retail price range before tax (price includes transportation & set-up): $55,000 - $130,000. Note: In CA, home purchases in MH communities are mostly turn-key packages (incl. site acquisition cost, site prep), price range: $120,000 to $150,000.
Competes against: site-built, Karsten, Silvercrest, Hallmark Southwest, Skyline, high end Fleetwood
Construction rating: 8
Brands/series:
Built in the CA plant (two-thirds of home go into MH communities):
Kingston Millennium - high end, for private property placement
Golden West Exclusive – best selling MH community model, many upgrades
Golden Pacific – Designed for MH communities only, smaller footprint, less expensive
Golden Oaks - Low mid-range w/ floor plans adapted from Oakwood Homes line no longer sold under that brand name
Built in the OR plant (85% of homes built are for private property placement):
Country Manor – high end, for private property placement, similar to Kingston Millennium. With optional 5/12 roof pitch and garage edition, identical in appearance to site-built
Golden Estate Series – mid-range, a click below Country Manor, optional tags
Classics - Package homes featuring many optional upgrades as standard specs
Custom Golden Estate series – Single sections (14 x 66) and narrow double-wides 20-24' wide, designed for MH communities, infill lots
Performer series – low mid-range, least expensive, models w/ more of a conventional MH look, 2x4" ext. walls standard
Description of a popular model: Golden West Exclusive, 3BR, 2BA, 8' side walls, vaulted ceiling, T&T t/o w/ bull nose corners, upgraded kitchen, carpets, countertops. Turn key price in MH community (incl. site acquisition cost): $130,000.
What distinguishes brand from its competition: Diverse product offering for MH communities (e.g., wide variety of home widths), availability of Clayton Homes' buying power, in-house financing/insurance.
Number of dealerships — Company owned: none
Independents: 70

Percentage of HUD homes sold of total homes produced: 100%
In-house financing? Yes (see Clayton Homes listing)
In-house Insurance? Yes (see Clayton Homes listing)
Warranty structure and length: 1 year
Web site rating: Unsatisfactory, incomplete, annoying. Aside from a few exterior elevation renderings of its high end homes, site is little more than a list of clickable model numbers under each series. Clicking on any selection triggers an annoying pdf download of the floor plan that requires you to delete two windows and launch a pdf reader like Acrobat, all totally unnecessary and dreadfully slow for those w/ a dial-up internet connection. Only one home model provided features & specs. Another clueless Clayton web site.
Comment: Since 2000 GW's management has done a fine job of regaining the brand's luster, and Clayton Homes has wisely left them alone to prosper in a challenging market. Quality is much improved at both CA and OR plants (still a click below Silvercrest, some Skyline and Karsten models) and business is strong. Heading into 2006, GW's CA plant had a 14-16 wk. backlog on orders.

Southern Energy Homes, Inc.
A subsidiary of Berkshire Hathaway, Inc
144 Corporate Way   P.O. Box 390
Addison, AL 35540
Ph. 256/747-8589   Fx. 256/747-8586
Web site: www.sehomes.com
Background: Founded in 1982 in Addison, AL, Southern Energy quickly carved out a profitable niche by offering lots of options and floor plan customization for homes retailing for as low as $15,000, on up to $100,000 (1982 prices). Customers could fax their preferences and within 24 hours receive a factory price quote. By the early 90s the company was well-established in the SE and S. Central U.S., its core market. After going public in 1993, just as the MH boom kicked in, SE's career seemed to careen from one catastrophe to another. First was a failed joint venture with a German developer to build and ship townhouses and apartments to Hanover, Germany (many units arrived damaged, SE was fired from the project and sued for $25 million). Then followed an effort to build very high end homes that proved too ambitious for factory fabrication.
Finally, in 1999, following a year-long investigation of 275 homes made from '95 to '98, HUD investigators announced they had found numerous violations (e.g., faulty wiring, plumbing vents that didn't go through the roof, walls improperly glued to studs). SE settled for a $300,000 civil fine and inspect up to an additional 600 more homes. SE also found itself saddled with 33 retail sales centers it had purchased during the go-go years; with the market tanking in '99, they were a major drain on profits.

Its reputation (and share price) on the line, SE brought in a savvy new management team that over the next few years turned the company around: closing all but two retail sales centers, redirecting SE's focus to building homes, offering a new line of package homes in the mid-tier price point and getting serious about factory quality control and warranty service. Today SE homes are much improved and the company has returned to robust profitability, so much so that in March 2006, SE acquired TN-based small low-end builder Giles Industries for $18.5 million.

Less than six months later, in August, 2006, industry powerhouse Clayton Homes agreed to acquire SE in a deal worth $110 million, bringing both SE and Giles into the Berkshire Hathaway fold. See Clayton Homes listing.
States where sold: AL, AZ, AR, CO, FL, FA, IL, IN, KS, KY, LA, MS, MO, NM, NC, OK, SC, TN, TX, VA.
Principal market niche: Low-end to mid-range affordable housing with many buyer options
Retail price range before tax (price includes transportation & set-up): $20,000 - $135,000
Competes against: Cavalier Homes, Clayton Homes, Fleetwood, Palm Harbor, Champion brands (e.g. Gateway, Advantage, Titan)
Construction rating: 4
Brands/series:
Southern Energy - top-of-the-line, multi-section (to 3,268 sq. ft.) - $38,900 - $135,000
Southern Estates - packaged homes w/ the most popular options - $45,000 - $68,000
Southern Homes - entry level homes, SW and multi-sections - $20,000 - $65,000
Southern Energy of Texas - homes across all price points, built with Southwest style floor plans and decor.
Description of a popular model: Southern Homes SS6815 The Viking, 3BR, 2BA, 28x66, 1,774 sq. ft. w/ large LR, formal DR and kitchen opening to large den, 3/12 roof pitch, ext. walls 2x4" 16" O.C., 7' side wall, int. walls 2"x3"-24" O.C., vaulted ceilings, VOG 5/8" wall board, single pane windows w/ white aluminum frames, heat/cooling registers on floor centerline, faucets plastic w/ metallic finish, kitchen cabinets MDF, porcelain toilets/bath basins, plastic shower/tub. Price: $49,000-$50,000. Most buyers add $1,500-$2,000 in options.
What distinguishes brand from its competition: Competitive price points and design engineers on staff at all plants able to provide a high degree of customization even for low end homes (moving walls, adding bay windows, sliders, flipping floor plans,

hardwood floors, hand-layered rock).
Number of dealerships—Company owned: 1
Independents: approx. 350
Percentage of HUD homes sold of total homes produced: 95%
In-house financing? No
In-house Insurance? No
Warranty structure and length: 1 year
Web site rating: Adequate but badly needs a makeover to correct design flaws. Pros: lots of information; mortgage calculator outstanding—the best of all MH sites; good selection of financial info for investors; good list of models/floor plans. Cons: Frustrating to navigate, link list is in tiny print in pastel boxes; not particularly attractive; no home page link on every page; no site map; almost no photos of exteriors (and those available are tiny).
Comment: SE has paid some heavy dues for its misadventures during the 1990s boom, not the least being correcting the reputation it earned for poor quality construction that resulted in a formal HUD recall. To its credit, the new management team brought in to clean up its act has done an excellent job, a big reason why SE and its newly acquired Giles Industries subsidiary were acquired by Clayton Homes in 2006. Company now does customer satisfaction surveys, the CEO takes an interest in helping resolve difficult warranty complaints. SE's wide range of customization and options, even with entry level home, remains a strong selling point. In sum, Southern Energy is back on track, but the home buyer should take care to choose a dealer with a solid reputation for ensuring customer satisfaction no matter who may be at fault for any warranty issues that may arise.

Commodore Corporation (privately held)
Corporate headquarters:
1423 Lincolnway East PO Box 577
Goshen, IN 46527
Ph. 574-533-7100 Fx 574-534-2716
Web site: www.commodorehomes.com
Brand names of HUD homes:
Commodore Homes of Indiana
Colony Factory Crafted Homes
Commodore Homes of Pennsylvania
Commodore Homes of Virginia
Astro Homes
Note: Company also builds modular homes: **Colony Factory Crafted, Manorwood Homes, Pennwest Homes, Commodore Homes of Indiana and Commodore Homes of Virginia**
Background: Founded in 1952, this venerable builder has been around forever (by MH standards), achieving a significant market share in the 25 states that comprise the northeast quadrant of the US. Publicly held for many years, Commodore was struggling in the late 1980s when it was purchased by a Chicago-based management company that in turn sold it to a family enterprise that took the company private and has since built the Commodore brands into a solid consistent success.
In 2002 the company purchased the entry-level Astro Homes brand from Cavalier. In early 2005 Commodore opened a new factory in Pennsylvania for the Pennwest modular brand.
States where sold: NE, KS, IA, MO, WI, IL, MI, IN, OH, KY, TN, GA, SC, NC, VA, WV, MD, DE, NJ, PA, NY, CT, RI, MA, VT, NH, ME
Principal market niche/target customer: Empty nest Boomers, move-up homebuyers, entry level home buyers. Company does not build high end multi-sectional mansions.
Description of a popular model: Products are too diverse for any one representative model. Here are descriptions of HUD homes by brand:
Commodore Homes of Indiana: multi-section homes
Colony Factory Crafted Homes: single-section to three-section homes
Commodore Homes of Pennsylvania: single-section to three-section homes
Commodore Homes of Virginia: multi-sectionals only
Astro Homes: affordable, entry level homes (single-section and multi-section) featuring vinyl-on-gypsum interior walls and similar entry-level construction features
Retail price range before tax (price includes transportation and set-up): $49,000 - $189,000. Majority are in the mid-$60,000 range.
Competes against: Patriot, Skyline, Hart Housing, Four Seasons, Fall Creek, New Era, Wick, Pine Grove, Burlington, the Champion brands, Fleetwood, Schult
Construction rating: 8
What distinguishes brand from its competition: A seasoned production staff, responsive warranty service, stand-out hearth kitchens, master BR suites and "glamour" BA designs, wide range of options and customization, and a loyal, well-established network of retailers and builders.
Number of dealerships — Company owned: none
Independents: 400
Percentage of HUD homes sold of total homes produced: 65%
In-house financing:? No
In-house Insurance:? No
Warranty structure and length: 1 year structural.

Retailers perform minor/cosmetic repairs; factory crews dispatched as needed for all other service. Extended 2-to-10 year home warranty offered through MHWC (Manufactured Home Warranty Corporation).
Web site rating: Quite good, lots of information but page design unimaginative. Like too many other MH sites, no distinction between HUD code and IBC modular is provided (if a home can be built to either spec, it should say so). Big plus: A great gallery of customer's homes, with their comments.
Comment: This is a good, solid company that builds a good product. In general, designs reflect the more prosaic, conventional look of Midwestern homes (floor plans offer few angled walls and open sight lines typical of Western and some Florida homes) but customization is easily done. Commodore's modular business is growing, largely because of easier financing. Quality construction is consistent with homes built to either spec.

Deer Valley Homes (privately held)
205 Carriage St, PO Box 310
Guin, AL 35563
Ph. 205/468-8400   Fax 205/468-9060
Web site: www.deervalleyhb.com
Background: This start-up, founded in early 2004, may be the newest HUD-code builder in the SE, but its eight investors represent both youth and decades of MH experience. The company's president, Joel Logan, the son of Steve Logan, founder of Buccaneer Homes (which evolved into Cavalier), started Pinnacle Homes at age 27, later selling that company to Patriot in 1998. The sales manager previously ran two of four divisions of Southern Energy Homes. Deer Valley's business model: offer a single line of more heavily constructed package homes (no customization allowed) featuring T&T dry wall w/ bull nose corners throughout, heavier insulation (for Zone III) and 8-foot flat ceilings as standard. The strategy worked from the outset—the builder showed two models at the 2004 Tunica Home Show and took orders for 100 homes even before its production line was even up and running. As this goes to press, Deer Valley is producing seven floors a day and has a 14 week back log. Plans are in the works to add modular homes to the product offering.
States where sold: AL, AR, FL, GA, KY, LA, MO, MS, NC, OK, SC, TN, TX, IL
Principal market niche: Educated shoppers, established cash buyers looking for a better constructed smaller affordable home in the mid-price range
Retail price range before tax (includes transportation and set-up): $59,000 to $129,000 (Deer Valley builds few triple-section homes)
Competes against: Cavalier, Southern Energy, Liberty, Franklin, Fleetwood
Construction rating: 6
Brands/series: Augustan, Blazer, Charleston — All virtually the same, with minor variances in decor, appliance packages, and floor plan offerings, at similar price points
Description of a popular model: DV 8008, 32x80, 2560 sq. ft., 4BR, 2BA, two-section, 1600 sq. ft., 2x6 ext. walls 16" O.C., 2x6" top & bottom plates, double-studded headers over windows/doors, 23/32" OSB floor decking, R-30/19/11, full finished $\frac{1}{2}$" dry wall t/o, all windows dual-glazed, lg. kitchen w/ island sink, post form countertops w/ rolled edges, dual handle brushed nickel faucet, stainless sink, 16"-square hand-laid kitchen tiles (no rolled lino), breakfast nook, 17 cu. ft. over/under refrigerator, 16 oz. carpet w/ $\frac{1}{2}$" rebond pad, porcelain BA sinks/toilet, 60" tub/shower, elec. outlet boxes secured w/ butterfly tabs, 40 gal. dual element water heater. Approx. $76,000.
What distinguishes brand from its competition: Full-finished dry wall t/o standard, heavier insulation, heavier construction, homes trimmed out by factory techs, good quality control and warranty follow up service.
Number of dealerships — Company owned: none   **Independents:** 89
Percentage of HUD homes sold of total homes produced: 100%
In-house financing? No
In-house Insurance? No
Warranty structure and length: 1 year, factory-dispatched service techs, some regional contract work, service by dealers.
Web site rating: Unsatisfactory for informed home shoppers but has potential. Pros: available in Spanish (very smart), good looking home page, straightforward navigation, decent renderings of some exteriors, good interior shots; Cons: no list of features/options, several broken links, no list of dealers by state, a feeling of general incompleteness. Note: site also has a page of inspirational "daily devotionals" which, like the pages of stock car racing content on the Manufactured Housing Enterprises site, may strike some home shoppers as irrelevant or off-putting, especially if they're looking for detailed construction specs.
Comment: In a crowded SE market where T&T dry wall is only just beginning to catch on, Deer Valley came up with a formula for offering this (and other options) as standard features. The trade-off, to keep prices competitive, is virtually no customization, smaller selection of floor plans and few models over 2200 sq. ft. The formula has worked. Deer Valley homes' exteriors reflect the boxy, unimaginative, unmistakable look of a mobile home (because of the 8' side wall height, the

roof pitch is closer to 2.5/12) but the look seems to fit comfortably with southern MH aesthetics. Likewise, some home interiors, particularly the bathrooms with tubs on pedestals framed with faux-Greek columns and avocado green walls, may strike some as pure Las Vegas kitsch. But give Deer Valley credit for knowing its market and offering something new and different. More important, this still-young company appears to have its ducks lined up and its priorities straight, especially its program of finish and trim-out by factory reps, and a commitment to good warranty service. Deer Valley will be an interesting company to watch.

Destiny Industries LLC (privately held)
250 R W Bryant Road, P.O. Box 2947 (PO Zip 31776)
Moultrie, GA 31788
Ph. 866-782-6600 Fx: 229-873-6620
Web site: www.destinyhomebuilders.com
Background: Started as Destiny Industries (building Destiny Mobile Homes) in 1978 in Moultrie, GA, by brothers Bill and Donnie Edwards and two friends, the company grew steadily, becoming the city's largest employer and, w/ nearly a quarter-billion in annual sales, a significant player in the SE market. In 1995, Oakwood Homes purchased the company, with the Edwards brothers moving into Oakwood management positions. In 1998 Oakwood, which had become the industry poster child of the boom-and-bust 90s, began to implode (see Oakwood listing).
A year later, following the resignation of Oakwood's CEO, Bill Edwards stepped in as CEO for a brief time until a replacement was found. The Edwards brothers left Oakwood, which subsequently went into Chap. 11 bankruptcy, closing the Destiny plant in 2002 as part of a restructuring effort. In June, 2003 the brothers, together with other investors, purchased from Oakwood the closed Destiny properties, including a 200,000 sq. ft., state-of-the-art plant that had been built in 1997, recruited a seasoned management team and re-launched as Destiny Industries, LLC. A year later, the first home came off the line. With the MH industry on the road to recovery, this reborn company has made a well-timed return to the MH marketplace.
States where sold: FL, GA, AL, SC, MS
Principal market niche: FL and GA, affordable housing for working families, seniors and retirees, a click above Clayton and Fleetwood
Retail price range before tax (price includes transportation & set-up): $20,000 (entry level single-section) to $150,000 (large double-section, loaded). Median price: $65,000 -$70,000.

Competes against: Homes of Merit, Palm Harbor, Horton, Jacobsen
Construction rating: 4
Brands/series:
Southern Pines – single-section and sectionals, across all price points
Description of a popular model: 32x80 (E804-02-96, in-house nickname: The Big Bubba), 2,560 sq. ft., 4 BR, 2 BA, w/ wood-burning fireplace, MBR walk-in closet, 3/12 roof pitch, 20 yr. shingles, 12" eves all around, ext. walls 2x4' 16" O.C., 2x4 int. walls, 7/16" VOG walls, 5/8" T&G plywood decking, 18 oz. plush carpet, overhead HVAC ducts, single-lever kitchen faucet w/ sprayer, island work station, self-edged Formica countertops, solid wood raised panel cabinets, 40 gal. water heater, 18 cu.ft. GE double-door refrigerator, water shut-offs t/o.
What distinguishes brand from its competition: Wood burning fireplace and 8' flat ceilings (no cathedral ceilings) standard on all sectionals, 4" crown molding, many construction specs parallel to company's mod products, new company, no long term record of customer service.
Number of dealerships — Company owned: none   **Independents:** 75
Percentage of HUD homes sold of total homes produced: 80%-85%
In-house financing? No
In-house Insurance? No
Warranty structure and length: 1-year on structural, plumbing electric, and a one time visit for cosmetic repairs during first year, plus years two through nine warranty on structure only (walls, roof, floors). Dealer may purchase an extended 2-10 warranty from third party provider, providing it at no charge or selling it at time of home purchase.
Web site rating: Satisfactory, needs more relevant content, design tweaks. Pros: Well-written history and intro to company and management (curiously, the word "Oakwood" is nowhere to be seen), helpful list of retailers w/ clickable web sites, printable floor plans; Cons: only one photo of a HUD home, barely readable list of construction specs/options, clunky interface in places, under Contact Us, no email address provided for either company or its departments. Here's a work-around: email to info@destinyhomebuilders.com and enter department/person on the subject line.
Comment: The last decade has been a wild ride for the Edwards brothers whose recent return to Moultrie, GA to wake up an MH plant was cheered by the town's business community. Clearly Destiny understands the SE HUD-code market in its core sales region (GA and FL), in particular buyers' taste for large "Big Bubba houses." Delivering such homes

at affordable prices involves lowering the construction standards (e.g., 7/16" VOG wallboard, un-mortised door hinges, acrylic kitchen sink, elec. outlet boxes screwed to the wallboard, not nailed to studs), but by including 8' flat ceilings and a fireplace in all sectionals as standard features, Destiny has found its sweet spot in the highly competitive southern market. This reborn company's customer satisfaction record is scant to date, but if it earns a solid rating with buyers, Destiny will be an interesting company to watch.

Eagle River Homes, LLC (Privately held)
P.O. Box 336 21 Groffdale Road
Leola, PA 17540
Ph. 717/656.2381   Fx. 717/656-8781
Web site: www.eagleriverhomes.net
Background: As this printing goes to press (Fall, 2006), Eagle River is the newest kid on the MH block, having just begun production and with no literature, no functioning web site, and a barely nascent dealer network. Eagle River is the second MH start-up venture involving ex-Champion Enterprises CEO Walt Young (the first was Alabama-based Platinum Homes) who in addition to investing is also serving as the company's chairman. The key managers are former Young lieutenants Jim Dunn (former Champion VP for the eastern region) and Sam Hollister, long-time sales mgr. of Champion subsidiary Redman Homes. In early 2006, when a Liberty Homes plant in Leola became available, Dunn and Hollister approached Young with a business model to provide low end homes for the Atlantic seaboard and New England region. By summer Eagle River LLC was formed, purchasing the Liberty plant in June. The first floor came off the line in late August.
States where sold: PA, NY, NJ, DE, MD, WV, VA, CT, MA, VT, NH, ME
Principal market niche: Basic low-end package homes (30% of product line to be SW's)
Retail price range before tax (including transportation and set-up): $40,000 - $150,000. SW's $40,000 and up, DW's starting at $60,000
Competes against: Redman, Fleetwood, lower end of Commodore line
Construction rating: 4
Brands: Susquehanna Series – Single wide models, 16' wide, from 60' to 80' long. Priced $40k - $90k
Hudson Series – Sectionals. Priced $60k - $150k
Description of a popular model: Hudson DW, 3BR, 2BA, 28 x 56, 1568 sq.ft. 3/12 roof pitch (5/12 optional), 2x6 ext. wall studs Grade #2 or better, 7' sidewall ht. (8' optional, w/ flat ceiling), R22/19/14 insulation, 3/8" VOG wallboard, single-pane storm windows, decking 5/8' Novadek glued & stapled to 2x6" floor joists, 14 oz. carpet, 6 lb. rebond pad stapled to floor, Kitchen counters WilsonArt self-edged Formica (no backsplash standard), dual knob faucet, stainless steel sink 7" deep, rolled lino vinyl flooring, MDF cabinets w/ hidden hinges, baseboard molding MDF.
What distinguishes brand from its competition: Lots of customization available at every price point, strong focus on quality construction, better fit & finish, superior cabinetry, stand-out decorator designs, promise of very strong customer service.
Number of dealerships—Company owned: none
   Independents: 12 and growing
Percentage of HUD code homes sold of total homes produced: 100% (No plans for mods now)
In-house financing: No
In-house insurance: No
Warranty structure and length: 1 year. All warranty service to be provided by contractors and dealers who will be reimbursed by the company for service provided.
Web site rating: None. Web site under construction.
Comment: It's too early to get a good read on this builder but any MH start-up that attracts investor interest from ex-Champion CEO Young, a very smart knowledgeable man, can claim an early advantage. Co-founder Dunn and his production manger have vowed to build home with "very very few service problems." Company plans to show models at the Spring 2007 show in Hersey, PA. Until Eagle River develops a track record, home buyers should take pains to ensure they are purchasing from a reputable dealer who will stand behind their homes.

Fairmont Homes (privately held)
P.O. Box 27, 502 S. Oakland
Nappanee, IN 46550
Ph. 574/773-7941   Fx. 574/773-2185
Web site: www.fairmonthomes.com
Background: Founded in 1971 by James Shea in Nappanee, this family-owned and operated builder has long been a strong Midwestern manufacturer, and one of northern Indiana's largest employers. Quietly dominant in their niche. Focus is on high quality upscale homes with lots of options, wide range of choice in floor plans, options. But also builds single-sections with many floor plans. Has a huge single-plant, state-of-the-art, production facility, maybe the industry's largest. Ships homes further distances than most builders.
States where sold: Indiana, Kansas, Nebraska, South Dakota, North Dakota, Minnesota, Wisconsin, Missouri, Illinois, Iowa, Kentucky, W. Virginia, Ohio, Pennsylvania, New York.
Principal market niche: Mid-range to high end with lots of choices, options.

Retail price range before tax (includes transportation & set-up): single-sections, $18,000-$20,000 and up, multi-sections (including triples) to $100,000-plus

Competes against: site-built homes (new and used), all HUD builders, including Patriot, Liberty, Champion brands.

Construction rating: 7

Description of a popular model: double-section, either 72x32 or 80x28, 3BR, 2BA, 2240 sq. ft., raised panel oak cabinetry, 5/12 roof pitch, 30-yr. shingles, 40-lb. snow load roof truss, OSB ext. sheathing, vinyl lap siding, 8 ft. side wall, flat ceiling, perimeter heat, 40 gal. water heater, china commodes

Fairmont brands: Company builds two brands, **Century** and **Friendship**, identical except for their names, allowing Fairmont to sell to multiple dealerships in the same markets.

Each brand has five series, also identical to their counterparts:

Century Homes	= Friendship Homes
Independence HUD code series)	= Foxwood (top-of-the-line
Statesman	= Celebrity (mid-range series)
Mid-American	= Westfield (mid-range
Century Villa series)	= Fairmont Villa (low-end
Innsbruck	= Bayview (single-wides only, entry level to mid-range)

What distinguishes brand from its competition: Good floor plans, "Cradle of Strength" construction (a legitimate boast), superior in-house-made cabinetry, lots of options (e.g. hutches, wet bars, entries), stone fireplace fronts, good looking exteriors.

Number of dealerships — Co. owned: 5
Independents: 200 (50-60 exclusively Fairmont)
Percentage of HUD homes sold of total homes produced: 50% (Almost all models can be built to HUD or modular code)
In-house financing: No
In-house Insurance: No
Warranty structure and length: 1 year. Fairmont sets aside (escrows) a small percentage of each home's dealer invoice amount to pay for warranty service on that home (for either factory service crews or to reimburse dealer expenses). At the end of the year, unused funds are released to the dealer. Fairly common in the industry .

Web site rating: Excellent. Fairmont was the first to introduce 360-degree IPIX inter-active imagery that puts you in the middle of a room and rotates the view through a complete circle. You can use your mouse stop, tilt the viewing angle, or zoom. Lots of exterior home photos, tons of floor plans, and a great cutaway diagram of its construction features. Visit this site to learn a lot about MH and what models look like.

Comment: Fairmont annually builds more than 2,500 homes, all from a single large plant. That puts them in the Top 10 producers, but more important, with its entire work force under one roof, Fairmont can better maintain quality control, which it does. Add above average construction standards and one can appreciate why its high end HUD and mod models can compete with site-built homes.

Falcon Luxury Homes, LLC (privately held)
Note: As this goes to press, this is the new name for Fall Creek Homes. The Fall Creek web site has been discontinued and the site for the new name is under construction. What follows is the most recent info on Fall Creek, but until full details of the new entity are available, home shoppers should call the company (all phone contact info remains the same).

The Fall Creek Home LLC (Privately held)
53850 Fall Creek Way
Elkhart, Indiana 46514
Ph. 574/523-1444   Fx. 574/522-4660
Web site: www.falconluxuryhomes.com

Background: Fall Creek was founded in 1998 at the height of the MH boom. Its timing couldn't have been worse—a year later the MH market began a grim slide. After getting off to a great start, the company spluttered, was sold to a clueless investment company who in turn sold it in Nov. 2003 to Capital First Realty, a savvy Chicago-based owner of 16 MH communities in several states that saw in Fall Creek an opportunity to acquire a good provider of homes for its communities as well as the larger MH marketplace. Today approx. 25% of Fall Creek's homes go into First Capital First Realty's MH communities.

States where sold: MN, WI, MI, IL, IN, IA, MO, OH, PA, KY, WV

Principal market niche: mid to high end, move-up buyers not looking just for price, who are also considering residential site-built (new and used). Does not build three-section HUD homes.

Retail price range before tax (includes transportation & set-up): $60,000-$80,000
Competes against: Commodore, Patriot Energymate
Construction rating: 7

Description of a popular model: 200 Series, two-section, 3BR, 2BA, 1520 sq. ft., hinged true 4/12 roof pitch, 30 yr. shake style shingles, 2x6 ext. stud walls 16" O.C., 8' side walls w/ flat ceilings, 2-1/4" crown molding at ceiling, seam tape on wall joints, R33/19/19 insulation, 18 cu. ft. frost free refrigerator
Brand: Fall Creek in various models and series
What distinguishes brand from its competition: Better floor plans, wider homes (e.g., 27'-8" vs. 26'-8" typical industry width), vinyl-on-gypsum wallboard, steel reinforced vinyl windows w/ heavy duty balance system, better balanced exterior home elevations, more & larger windows. Plus: Cape Cod roof option on every 28 wide floor plan (HUD and modular) – everything from 40-foot to 76-foot homes.
Number of dealerships — Company owned: none   **Independents:** 60
Percentage of HUD homes sold of total homes produced: 50%
In-house financing: No
In-house Insurance: No.
Warranty structure and length: 1 years. Optional 2 thru ten via 3rd. party (MHWC).
Web site rating: Very good, nothing fancy but fast, intuitive, a good start for a home shopper. Always nice to see good photos of the homes' exteriors, lacking on so many MH sites. Cons: no floor plans of model-specific spec sheets to view and print.
Comment: Fall Creek's early history of ownership and management changes made some retailers leery of carrying the line, but under the wing of Capital First the company has stabilized (in its 25 yr. history Capital First has never closed or sold any acquisition). Fall Creek has recruited some sharp veterans with innovative strategies. For one, the optional Cape Cod roof available on every 28-wide (or wider) creates an instant site-built look (3 dormers), a max interior head space of 7' and 900 sq. ft. of storage/living space. For another, company created The Village at Fall Creek, a gorgeous corporate display of its top-selling homes, fully decorated, furnished and landscaped, in a wooded residential setting. Company has lately upped its modular percentage (from 15% to 50%), because, 1., financing is easier to obtain, and 2, increased demand for modulars for subdivision developers.

Fleetwood Enterprises, Inc. (Publicly held)
3125 Myers St. PO Box 7638
Riverside, CA 92513
Ph. 909/351-3500
Web site: www.fleetwoodhomes.com
Background: The name "Fleetwood" is probably the most recognized brand nationally in both RVs and MH, and with good reason: the Riverside, California, company, started in 1950 to build travel trailers (going public in 1965) seems to have been around forever; and it builds a heck of a lot of product that leaves its factories on wheels: Fleetwood's fiscal year 2005 sales totals accounted for a hefty 15% of the overall RV market and nearly 18% of the MH market. Its 21 MH plants (in 14 states) built 23,962 homes last year, second only to Clayton Homes. Fleetwood branded homes are sold in 46 states through about 1,320 sales centers, including 135 that are company-owned (or were at the start of 2005 – see below), but its primary markets are the Southern and South Central US: Florida, Texas, California, North Carolina and Tennessee.

The past ten years have been a wild, rough ride for this Fortune 1000 company. In the late 1990s, in a stab at vertical integration, Fleetwood made a fateful move, buying up scores of retailer dealerships (244 by the end of 2000), way over-paying for them, and taking on a huge debt burden of several hundred million dollars, just before the MH industry tanked. At one point a total of 1800 dealers (company owned and independent) were selling Fleetwood homes.

During the severe downturn of 1999-2004, the company took a beating, its MH production falling by 65%, mirroring the industry's overall MH contraction. In 2001, with chattel lending drying up, Fleetwood created a subsidiary financial services company, HomeOne Credit Corp., to provide finance and insurance products to its retail operations. But the move failed to spark a return to profitability.

In the spring of 2005, with losses continuing to mount, Fleetwood abruptly changed course (and CEOs) and within months sold all but 12 of its chain of 135 company-owned retail sales centers, plus its finance company's loan portfolio, to—you guessed it—Clayton Homes. Reliable industry sources later confirmed that, in fact, Clayton had an offer on the table to buy out Fleetwood's entire MH division, but at the last minute, Fleetwood's board declined. But even if the MH division were to be sold at some future point, home buyers need not be much concerned, for the brand and its products will most likely remain intact.

While in recent years Fleetwood has introduced several interesting home series, including a number of modular designs, to appeal to the higher end of the market, by far its principal target remains its traditional customers — those seeking entry level to low-end-of-mid-range affordable housing: $20,000 to $60,000. In 2005 better than one out of every four single-section homes sold was Fleetwood made, selling for an average of $27,700.

States where sold: All states except Alaska and Hawaii, with 82% of 2004 sales going to 20 states, lead by FL, TX, CA, NC and TN

Principal market niche: low end, entry-level housing where price in the most important factor. Includes young, growing families seeking affordable housing and retirees looking to downsize and/or move into MH communities.

Retail price range before tax (price includes transportation & set-up): $20,000 to $120,000. Average single-section: $27,700. Average double-section: $52,000.

Competes against: mostly other low-end to low-mid range brands, including Clayton, Southern Energy, Giles, Liberty, General Manufactured Housing, Titan, Advantage, Gateway, Hart Housing, Cappaert. Note: Fleetwood's corporate media relations dept., when asked to name competing brands, inexplicably replied, "We decline to respond."

Construction rating: 5

Brands/series

Three principal brands nationally representing different price ranges:

Beacon Hill homes — a decent, low end, entry level home (a 3BR single section as low as $20,000) to high 30s. No frills, low construction quality, basic shelter for a growing family. Plus: a 50 gal. water heater.

Celebration (a.k.a., **Festival** in some regions) — low end of mid-range ($48,000 - $65,000), w/ tape & textured walls (round corners optional), dual plastic faucet handles, acrylic bath sinks, MDF cabinets, 2" tile backsplash, standard range (no clock, window, timer).

Barrington—Fleetwood's high end brand, not available in all markets, $65,000-$120,000.

In addition, company builds several series available in different markets. These include:

The Entertainer Home—low mid-range, with home entertainment center featuring large screen TV, DVD player, family room w/ surround sound, wood-burning fireplace. A great concept.

LifeStages Home — Generally mid-range in price, ten floor plans, ext. design closer to the site built look suited for developments (4/12 roof pitch, accepts attached garage), vaulted ceilings (but VOG walls standard), Craftsman influenced front elevation. Adding a robust list of options will put the total price close to the high end range.

The Inspiration Home — Comparable to the Barrington, high mid-to-high end price range, better construction, more features standard, higher roof pitch.

The Anniversary Home — Regionally designed homes reflecting the architectural character of their surrounding area, e.g. cape cod second stories, dormers, Savannah front porches. Generally mid-range price.

Description of a popular model: Celebration, 27x56 double-section, 1,512 sq. ft., 3BR, 2BA, ext. walls 2x6" 24" O.C., VOG int. walls, 7-1/2" ceiling, 3/12 pitch, laminate kitchen countertop w/ straight edges, opt. shut-off valves throughout, MDF cabinets, opt. single lever faucet, china commodes and deep stainless steel sink. Approx. $58,000

What distinguishes brand from its competition: The longevity of the Fleetwood name and its brand recognition, widely available nationally, competitive price points, a bit flashier in appearance, wide range of upgrade options, refreshing new models such as the Entertainer Home series.

Number of dealerships — Company owned: 25
 Independents: 1.185 Note: of these, 514 belong to the Fleetwood Pinnacle Retailer Program, under which they sell Fleetwood homes exclusively.

Percentage of HUD homes sold of total homes produced: 95%

In-house financing: No (this unit sold to Clayton Homes in July, 2005)

In-house Insurance: No.

Warranty structure and length: 1 year. Uses factory-based and dispatched tech crews for warranty service, not regional subcontractors. This structure makes sense but anecdotal evidence indicates Fleetwood's warranty service is not one of its strengths. Example, one former Fleetwood retailer commented one reason he moved to another brand was he was paying on average several hundred dollars in unreimbursed, out-of-pocket costs per home to keep his Fleetwood customers satisfied. This may be an anomaly but illustrates the importance of finding a dealer who stands behind the home and will make sure the customer is satisfied, no matter who pays for it.

Web site rating: Superficially adequate but ultimately unsatisfying, lots of puffery but way short on specifics, tone a trifle smarmy, condescending. Pros: navigation is quick and intuitive, images and general page design attractive. Cons: no detailed list of standard construction features/options for each model series (only a short generalized version), few images of exteriors, floor plans provided as annoying PDF downloads rather than straightforward click-to pages that can be easily printed.

Comment: Fleetwood is a large—some say, top-heavy—public company whose MH division mostly builds for the industry's traditional market: those seeking affordable home ownership, principally in the Southeast and Central South. It makes decent, affordable housing with a tendency for superficial flash while finding cost savings in less visible construction features (e.g., int. wall studs 24" O.C. vs. 16" O.C., using staples, not screws or nails, to attach interior walls). To its credit, Fleetwood does a better job with its choice of materials than many competing brands, and it boasts a deep pool of experienced industry pros. Unlike Champion Enterprises, Inc, with its history of acquiring MH builders and allowing them to retain both their brand identity and a high degree of autonomy, Fleetwood prefers-top-to-bottom corporate integration behind one brand, Fleetwood homes. That makes sense given the name recognition, but with so many plants and dealerships (some better or worse than others) home shoppers should make sure the dealer they buy from will really stand behind the home, particularly on warranty service.

The company's recent foray into modular code homes to get around the zoning and financing discrimination against HUD-code homes has resulted in a half-dozen of its plants building homes to both codes on the same assembly lines, a mix that can cause production problems.

Overall, given the management changes in recent years, Fleetwood appears to be struggling to find its focus and get back on track as the industry recovers. Aside: here's a worrisome sign that Fleetwood, like too many MH builders, still clings to the old auto industry model of regarding its dealers, not home buyers, as its true customers: Early in 2005 the company encouraged its retailers to stock up on lot inventories by offering points toward free trips to a grand Fleetwood celebration at Disney World. Over 1,000 retailers, their employees and their families attended. Fleetwood's subsequent press release, printed in the industry trade magazine *Automated Builder*, never mentions "retailers" or "sales" people, instead gushes about hosting its "valued customers," explaining "Its not enough to say your customer comes first, you have to mean it." To be sure, Fleetwood is not alone thinking this way; the company just happened to put it in writing.

Four Seasons Housing, Inc. (privately held)
11333 CR 2   PO Box 630
Middlebury, IN 46540
Ph. 800/547-5011   Fx. 574/825-6716
Web site: www.fourseasonshousing.com
Background: Started in 1994 by a small group of investor-backed sales professionals with strong track records at Patriot Homes and Dutch Housing, this still-young company got off to a great start offering homes very similar to Dutch Housing but with more flair in decor and colors. Though the founders excelled in setting up a retail network and selling homes, they were less skilled as business managers. In 1997, with the company foundering, one of the principal outside investors, Richard Baidas, together with his son Austin, bought out the partners. Austin Baidas took over the reins as CEO and, though a total newcomer to MH, proved a quick study, adopting a prudent management strategy, trimming model lines, skillfully positioning Four Seasons in the middle of the market with designs favored by Midwest home buyers, and expanding the retailer network into the upper Midwest and Northeast. The company today is stable, market-savvy and prosperous.

States where sold: Close to 30—throughout the Midwest and upper Midwest, as far west as WY, MT CO, up and down the eastern seaboard — New England to VA

Principal market niche: home buyers wanting a residential feel and appearance (e.g. 5/12 roof pitch, finished drywalls) in the mid-price range ($58,000 - $80,000). Company avoids the low end and the high end, offering many floor plans but relatively little customization.

Retail price range before tax (price includes transportation & set-up): High 30s (a few single-section models) to around $100,000

Competes against: Crystal Valley (Patriot Homes' high end brand), Dutch Housing, Redman, Champion, Fall Creek, Commodore

Construction rating: 7

Series: All series have Four Seasons' hallmark construction features: 100% full-finished dry wall, ext. walls 2x6" 16" O.C., 2x6" top plates and window/door headers in ext. walls, toe kick registers in kitchen and bath areas:

Limited—Pre-packaged, entry level single-section homes, plus two two-section models, starting in the high 30's.

Springdale—The basic sectional home, 3/12 nominal roof pitch, 7-1/2" side wall ht, 9.5 oz. nylon carpet, vinyl wrapped cabinet doors/drawer fronts, ABS (plastic) toilets. aluminum-framed windows, R-25/19/14 insulation, laminate countertops w/ flat edging. Approx. $58,000

Summerbrook—mid-range w/ perimeter floor registsers, gridded vinyl windows, solid ash cabinet doors, 18 cu. ft. FF refrigerator, 16 oz. carpet on ½" rebond pad. Price from the low 60's.

Autumn Manor - high end, w/ leaded glass entry door, 30 yr. shingles, deluxe stainless kitchen sink, raised panel solid ash cabinets, radius hardwood countertop edging, 20 cu. ft. FF refrigerator w/ice dispenser, 25 oz. carpet, 2" deluxe blinds, 3-arm DR chandelier.

Description of a popular model: D64-14, 3BR, 2BA, 1,605 sq. ft., 28x57 two section, w/ front kitchen and kitchen island, larger picture window above sink, lots of

upgraded cabinetry, available in both Summerbrook and Autumn Manor series. Approx. $74,000.
What distinguishes brand from its competition: Stays focused on mid-price range homes w/ standard construction features like full-finished dry wall, higher quality factory-built cabinetry and trim, less flexible on customization allows competitive pricing, carefully selected retailers, good warranty service.
Number of dealerships—Company owned: 2
Independents: 150 (approx. 18 exclusive)
Percentage of HUD homes sold of total homes produced: 100%
In-house financing: No
In-house Insurance: No
Warranty structure and length: 1 year (but, a Four Seasons exec adds, "we don't advertise it but even after the warranty has expired, if a problem shows up that's our fault, we fix it at our expense – we take care of our customers.")
Web site rating: Excellent. Pros: Clean welcoming design, simple, fast, all floor plans available as html/printable, good description of product lines, a full listing of standard features/options, clickable photos included with many model plans; Cons: not a single exterior image of a home, anywhere (!), print outs of floor plans nearly unreadable; no mention of Four Season's modular lines.
Comment: Four Seasons has in the past eight years survived a tumultuous MH industry downturn, transforming from a promising but shaky start-up that competitors had all but written off into a solid success story. Much credit is due its young CEO Austin Baidas, 35, a savvy, consumer-oriented manager who prizes good communication (he's personally visited 90% of the company's 150 sales centers).

In a region glutted with low and mid-priced MH brands, Four Seasons has found its sweet-spot niche and delivers a home with generally more features than competitors in the same price bracket. Aside: the Four Seasons annual catalog, a slick 72-page color offering with tons of information and superb graphics, is one of the best in the industry.

Franklin Homes Inc. (privately held)
10655 Highway 43
Russelville, Alabama 35653
Ph. 256/33-4510   Fx. 256/331-2203
Web site: www.franklinhomesusa.com
Background: Founded in 1968 by two brothers, Thomas and Jerry James, Franklin Homes has remained a family-run enterprise with a good reputation for design, construction and quality control, all of which has enabled them to survive cyclical downturns intact. (Aside: in 1972, Thomas James, who had a 1/3rd. ownership stake in Franklin, started nearby Indies House, reportedly to produce homes of lesser quality in greater volume. His brother Jerry became a 1/3rd owner of the new company.) All Franklin homes are produced out of a single plant complex.
States where sold: AL, ARK, FL, GA, IL, IN, KS, KY,LA, MO, NC, OH, OK, SC, TN, TX
Principal market niche: mid-range, move-up buyers
Retail price range before tax (includes transportation & set-up): $42,000 (single-section) to $179,000 (four section)
Competes against: Palm Harbor
Construction rating: 7
Description of a popular model: Benchmark 1800, two-section, 3BR, 2BA, 1800 sq. ft., 3/12 roof pitch, 2x4 ext. side walls 16" O. C, 8' flat ceiling, tape & textured int. walls, 12" fixed overhang eves all around, 18 cu. ft. FF refrigerator, stainless kitchen sink w/ dble. handle faucet and spray, residential single-hung windows with storm windows.
What distinguishes brand from its competition: Stand-out quality control program, dedicated work force, and well-built homes with higher value than more expansive competition.
Number of dealerships — Company owned: none
Independents: 75+
Percentage of HUD homes sold of total homes produced: 60%
In-house financing: No
In-house Insurance: No
Warranty structure and length: 1 year. Factory has three full-time warranty service technicians who do most of the repairs. Dealers handle the rest.
Web site rating: Marginal to unsatisfactory, a poor reflection of a worthy company. Many floor plan links don't work, few photos of home exteriors, no clear distinction between HUD code and modulars, printouts of features/spec pages are low-res and hard to read. Downloadable brochures a good idea but deserve better design, content.
Comment: Franklin Homes' president Jerry James has a reputation as a dedicated, capable executive who, together with family members (his son and daughter are engineering and sales, respectively) has maintained Franklin's image as a solid home builder. The company claims its warranty service costs are on average less than 1% of the home's price (2%-4% is average).

Fuqua Homes, Inc. Privately held
Corporate headquarters
7100 S. Cooper
Arlington, TX 76001
Ph. 817/465-3211

Background: Founded in 1970 as a division of the sprawling Fuqua Industries (lawn mowers, recreational boats, sporting goods, to name a few lines) this home builder had grown to 14 plants when it was spun off in 1985, following which its managers jettisoned all but two of its most profitable factories—in Missouri and Oregon—created separate, and very autonomous divisions around each plant, maintaining minimally staffed corporate offices in Dallas-Ft. Worth. Each division has been successful pursuing separate business models attuned to the region it serves, as follows:

Fuqua Homes of Oregon (Bend division)
PO Box 5579
Bend, Oregon 97708
Ph: 541/382-4252   800-336-0874
Web site: www.fuquahomes.com
States where sold: WA, OR, CA, NV, ID, UT, MT, westsern WY
Principal market niche: Mainstream home buyers looking for a site-built compatible home, either on an individual parcel or in a subdivision selling new turn-key homes (land included) anywhere from about $100,000 to over $1 million, but primarily in the $190,000 to $240,000 price range.
Retail price range before tax (includes transportation & set-up): under $40,000 to over $300,000. Average: $75,000-$80,000
Competes against: site builders of entry level to mid-market priced mainstream homes, Discovery Homes (HUD-version of Palm Harbor modular line)
Construction rating: 8
Description of a popular model: Star Pointe series, Willow model, two section, 64 x 28, 1335 sq. ft., 3BR, 2BA, with attached 2-car garage (built on site), optional Craftsman front porch with railings, optional 6/12 roof pitch, 12" eves all around, optional 9' interior side wall w/ flat ceilings, R-40/33/21 insulation, Super Good Cents/ Energy Star certified, stain-proof Saxony carpeting, Maytag appliances, porcelain kitchen sink w/ Moen single lever faucet, hardwood cabinet stiles, 200 amp elec. service
What distinguishes brand from its competition: Homes very similar in appearance to site built to appear to mainstream home buyers (not the affordable home market), higher quality construction and superior brand names, active partnerships with many subdivision developers.
Number of dealerships — Company owned: 4
Independents: 60-plus

Percentage of HUD homes sold of total homes produced: 99% (anticipated to be 75% in 2006)
In-house financing: No
In-house Insurance: No
Warranty structure and length: 1 year. Note: During the 1990s Fuqua burned out quite a few dealers with a frustrating, penny-pinching warranty policy that basically forced retailers to perform, and pay for, warranty work themselves. Fortunately, at the start of this decade, Fuqua corrected this misguided policy and customer service satisfaction has been high.
Web site rating: Serviceable but below potential. Site lists many models but links to photos are broken (as are some others). In general frustrating, especially given the stand-out exterior appearance of Fuqua's homes.
Comment: This is among the most innovative MH producers in the industry, with a good shot at attracting the MH industry's holy grail: the mainstream home buyer. Fuqua Oregon made a conscious decision to produce attractive models indistinguishable from site-built (and costing nearly the same), a move that has captured strong developer interest, with many selecting its homes for subdivisions around the region, because Fuqua can build homes faster and deliver them on time (thus saving money). In contrast to many MH producers who shy away from developers for fear of alienating their dealers, Fuqua encourages developers, believing subdivisions appeal to a non-competing market, i.e., buyers looking for neighborhoods, whereas dealerships offer homes for people looking for a little slice of heaven on scattered single parcels, particularly in semi-rural areas (note: in recent years more than 50% of homes purchased from dealerships have been three-sections or more). The strategy is working.

Fuqua Homes of Missouri (Boonville division)
PO Box 394
Booneville, MO 65233
Ph. 660/882-3411
Web site: www.fuquahomes.com
States where sold: WY, CO, SD, NE, KS, OK, MN, IA, MO, AR, IL, IN, WY
Principal market niche: mainstream home buyers of site-built homes
Retail price range before tax (includes transportation & set-up): $60,000 to $150,000 (4 section models)
Competes against: site built home builders, modular home builders
Construction rating: 9
Description of a popular model: Spring Creek model 2465, two section, 30 x 64, 3BR, 2BA, 5/12 roof pitch, vaulted ceilings, 9' sidewalls, tape and textured, island in kitchen with bar/veggie sink, walk-in pantry, utility room w/ computer desk, large bay windows, dormers ,

large master bath, pvt. toilet alcove, walk-in closets. Approx. $95,000.
Fuqua brands/series:
Spring Creek high end
Choice mid-to-high-end (includes Lodge homes)
Ultra mid-to-high
Celebration mid-range
Landmark mid-range
What distinguishes brand from its competition: Homes very close to site-built in appearance/construction, many mod specs in HUD versions, excellent designs, elevations
Number of dealership: Company owned: 2
Independents: 50 (8-10 sell Fuqua exclusively)
Percentage of HUD homes sold of total homes produced: 20%
In-house financing: No.
In-house Insurance: No
Warranty structure and length: 1 year/5 year program (years 2-5 cover roof/floor structures, all walls, electrical and plumbing systems
Web site rating: Excellent, lots of photos, legible floor plans, good content, intuitive interface
Comment: Fuqua of Missouri's homes are generally indistinguishable in appearance to site-built, a terrific selling point. Designs overall are excellent, with superior construction features. The division also offers its models in either HUD code or IRC/UBC modular codes, with modulars now accounting for 80% of production. Reason: financing for modular code homes is easier to obtain, less zoning restrictions, better appraisal values and better resale value.

General Manufactured Housing, Inc.
aka **General Housing, Inc.** Privately held
PO Box 1449 2255 Industrial Blvd.
Waycross, GA 31502
Web site: www.general-housing.com
Background: Founded in 1990, by MH veteran Sam Scott (see Scotbilt Homes listing) this southern Georgia builder of low end housing rode the 1990s MH boom creating a large but (anecdotal reports suggest) shaky dealership network. In 1996 GMH was acquired by RFE, a NY-based holding company that knew little about MH but was convinced the company was perfectly positioned to go public. Prior to an IPO, however, the MH market tanked, and the plan was scrapped. After 2000 company reversed course, downsized both its dealer network and its floor plans (from 300 to 55 plans) and limited distribution to six states (71% of its business derives from the Florida market). Helped by RFE's deep pockets, General survived the downturn with the help of several Fleetwood veterans in production. Currently operates two plants, built 1,504 homes in 2004.
States where sold: FL, GA, AL, MS, SC, NC.
Principal market niche: low end to low-mid-range
Retail price range before tax (includes transportation & set-up): $22,000 to $68,000
Competes against: Clayton, Fleetwood, Giles, Indies House, low end Champion brands
Construction rating: 4
Description of a popular model: Presidential, 28x80, two-section, 3BR, 2BA, 2240 sq. ft., eyebrow dormer, 3/12 roof pitch, 20-yr. shingles, 2x4 ext. walls, 2x6 floor joists, R 11/11/14 insulation, dry wall construction (vinyl covered sheetrock in kitchen and baths), porcelain water-saver toilets, single pane windows, in-line center floor registers, whole house water shut-off.
Brands/Series:
Multi Section Homes: **Presidential, Cypress Pointe, Mega, Sizzler**
Single Section homes: **Stinger, Sun Park**
Specialty series: **Woodland, Eleganza**
What distinguishes brand from its competition: Builds a consistent product, a much improved dealer network and very good warranty service
Number of dealerships — Company owned: none **Independents:** 71
Percentage of HUD homes sold of total homes produced: 100%
In-house financing: No
In-house Insurance: No
Warranty structure and length: 1 year. Service crews work out of both factories
Web site rating: OK. Gets the job done. Good details provided with printable spec sheets on each series, News page is up to date, could use more exterior photos, several clickable links don't work.
Comment: General Housing is a solid company that turns out a decent but below average product that exemplifies the unmistakable look of a no-frills manufactured home. It recently adopted decors more pleasing to the Florida market. Together with a much improved dealer network, General is on track (two plants going at full tilt). Company knows its market and business is robust.

Guerdon Homes LLC (Privately held)
5556 Federal Way
Boise, Idaho 83716
Ph. 800/473-3586   Fx. 208/336-9269
Web site: www.guerdon.com

Background: Started in Michigan in 1954 as a small division of the industry conglomerate, Guerdon Industries (RVs, plastics, furniture air conditioning and more, HQ'ed in Denver, CO), Guerdon Homes has a long history. In the 60s Guerdon grew steadily, at one point rolling out two single-section ten-wide models dubbed the Liesure-ama and the Easy-rama). Each featured a unique hinged tip-out that added 100 sq. ft. to the LR area (like a mini tag) and for awhile were all the rage. In the 70s Guerdon Homes, bent on becoming a vertically integrated national presence w/ company-owned dealerships, grew to 25 plants and dozens of sales centers before all but imploding during a sharp industry downturn.

By the early 1980s, the company was down to three plants when it was sold to CA businessman Fred Huckvale, along with a sister company, Magnolia Homes, that Guerdon Industries had launched in 1973 (see Magnolia Homes listing). In the late 1980s, Huckvale sold out to his partners who moved Guerdon Homes' corporate office from Los Angeles to Guerdon's plant in Stayton, OR. (Guerdon had a second plant in Boise, ID). In 1996, Texas high-flying American HomeStar, awash with IPO cash and on a spending spree, purchased Guerdon (and its subsidiary, Magnolia Homes), then four years later went Chap. 11. In 2001, American HomeStar's former CEO, Lad Dawson and partner Rick Murdock, both veteran builders, (together with silent investors) purchased Guerdon's Boise plant from bankruptcy, and reopened as Guerdon Homes LLC, vowing to build better looking HUD homes as well as modulars, and to court developers as well. The company has done both successfully.

States where sold: ID, WA, OR, NV, CA, UT, CO, MT, WY
Principal market niche: mainstream home buyers, mid-range to high end
Retail price range before tax (price includes transportation & set-up): $60,000 to $150,000
Competes against: new and used site-built homes, high end Nashua Homes, Fuqua
Construction rating: 9
Series: 100 Series, 200 Series, 300 Series, Cabin series
Description of a popular model: 300 Series, three-section, 3BR, 2BA, 42'x66', 2,775 sq. ft., 4/12 roof pitch, vaulted ceilings, ceramic tile entry, R-38/22/19 insulation, wood-look laminate floor in kitchen/nook, price approx. $155,000. Note: The Cabin series (w/ pine log siding, $120,000 to $160,000) also popular.
What distinguishes brand from its competition: high end homes w/ site-built look, original designs, lots of customization possible, quality workmanship, excellent fit and finish.

Number of dealerships — Company owned: none
Independents: 31 (7 exclusively Guerdon)
Percentage of HUD homes sold of total homes produced: 40%
In-house financing: No
In-house Insurance: No
Warranty structure and length: 1 year.
Web site rating: Good but missing essential content. Pros: Excellent photography, good company history, pleasing mini-bios and photos of key Guerdon execs and staff provide a nice sense of family and puts a face on the company. Cons: no list of standard features/specs; with a small page size on the screen of only 4-1/2" x 7" (vs. the standard 8"x8" + vertical scroll) impact and readability are lost; no clear ID of HUD vs. mod models/series; floor plans (even when enlarged and printed from screen) are blurry, with unreadable small print.
Comment: Since its rescue from the bankruptcy in 2001 by respected industry veteran Lad Dawson and partners, Guerdon has reinvented itself as a classy leader in systems-built homes (i.e. modular), which now accounts for 60% of production (including big developments such as 4-story condos). Expect this trend to continue. The company's effort to build HUD-code homes similar to site-built, along with creative designs and quality construction, assures purchasers of HUD-code homes an excellent product at a better price than site-built homes. Score Guerdon at the high-end of the HUD code universe.

Hallmark Southwest Corp. (privately held)
PO Box 710
Loma Linda, CA 92354
Ph. 909/796-2561   Fx. 909/796-2567
Web site: hallmarksouthwest.com
Background: Started in 1977 on an SBA loan to a family and several employees, this small boutique builder of homes on the high side of mid-range (its single plant is near Riverside in southern California), has quietly prospered without any marketing or sales staff whatsoever. Their secret: target in-fill spec builders and MH communities expanding or changing out old mobiles, offer quality construction with standard features that are options on competitor's products (e.g., garbage disposals) and rely strictly on referrals for new business.
States where sold: CA, AZ, NV(Pahrump only)
Principal market niche: mostly retired, empty nesters but some families, buyers willing to pay more for site-built value w/o paying site-built prices. Sells largely to MH communities and S. California in-fill developers. No two-story homes.

Retail price range before tax (includes transportation & set-up): $82,000-$98,000-plus
Competes against: Silvercrest, Palm Harbor, Skyline, high-end Fleetwood
Construction rating: 8
Description of a popular model: Charleston IV or Winchester IV (minor differences), two-section, 27 x 58, 1550 sq. ft., 3BR, 2BA, 4/12 roof pitch, 2x6 ext. side walls 16" O.C., 2x4 interior side walls, tape & textured drywalls, rounded corners, dual thermal pane vinyl-clad windows, 1/2 HP garbage disposal, Whirlpool appliances (incl. 21 cu. ft. FF refrigerator, washer, dryer).
What distinguishes brand from its competition: good floor plans, lots of options (incl. stucco exteriors, tile roofs) limited customization, competitive price
Number of dealerships—Company owned: none
Independents: 20 (mostly park owners)
Percentage of HUD homes sold of total homes produced: 100%
In-house financing: No
In-house Insurance: No
Warranty structure and length: 1 year. Crews work from factory, plus dealer assistance
Web site rating: Unsatisfactory, incomplete, amateur, strange, yet interesting. Pros: many ext. & int. pics (real, not renderings) provide a far better feel for homes than do many large MH company sites; Cons: poor design, many pages don't load fully, no features/spec lists, floor plans too small to read, even when printed, hokey photography.
Comment: With no marketing Hallmark Southwest Corp. is the hands down winner of the MH industry's Under-the-Radar award, and they are doing very well indeed. In 2004 they produced an astonishing 600 homes, receiving orders solely from customer referrals, set-up contractors, park owners, and word-of-mouth advertising.

With no marketing costs, they can afford to put more value in their homes and sell them at very competitive prices. Perfect for the S. California market. Very smart.

Hart Housing Group
(a division of Fall River, Inc., a subsidiary of Berkshire Hathaway, Inc.)
1025 Waterford St. PO Box 406
Wakarusa, IN 46573
Ph. 574/862-4461   Fx. 574/862-1813
Web site: www. forestriverinc.com/housing/harthousing
Background: Started in 1994 by several founders of the Dutch Housing brand (itself launched in 1991), Hart Housing took the successful Dutch Housing formula—a so-called package house (no customization, few floor plans) with mid-level quality at an entry level price point—and copied it with one addition: dry wall interiors with bull nose corners throughout (vs. Dutch Housing's VOG). The combination worked and the company prospered through the 90s, surviving the 1999-2004 downturn on the strength of its competitive entry level pricing and developing a similar models for the modular market. In June, 2004, Hart Housing was acquired by Elkhart, IN-based Forest River, Inc., the rapidly-growing RV, boat and cargo trailer manufacturer (71 plants, 5,500 employees) founded in 1996 by industry wunderkind Pete Liegl. Then, in July, 2005 Forest River itself was acquired by Berkshire Hathaway, the holding company controlled by billionaire Warren Buffet. While Hart Housing is a small component of that acquisition, it is now a part of the Berkshire's dominant stake in the MH industry (see Clayton Homes listing).
States where sold: IN, IL, OH, MI, WI, MN, SD, WY, MO, NY, PA, KY, TN
Principal market niche: low end, entry level affordable housing
Retail price range before tax (price includes transportation & set-up): $39,000 to $99,000. Note: transportation from Hart's single plant in IN to outlying states is a significant cost add-on, e.g. $10,800 to WY, $7,200 to NY.
Competes against: low end brands, e.g. Dutch Housing, Commander, Redman, Fortune, and other MH brands vying for lowest price point
Construction rating: 4
Brands: Hart Housing
Description of a popular model: Nu-Hart 110,3 BR, 2BA, 28x46, 1,280 sq. ft., two-section, 3/12 roof pitch, ext. walls. 2x6" 16" O.C., 7-1/2' int. walls 2x3" 16" O.C., dry wall/ bull nose corners throughout, Shaw Frontier 16 oz. carpet (tack strip installed, 5 lb. rebond pad), perimeter wall-mounted heat registers, 5/8" dia. Novadeck floor decking, elec. outlet boxes clipped to dry walls, plastic sinks, single lever kitchen faucet w/ sprayer, post form countertops (rounded w/ 2" backsplash), factory-built wood cabinets, Pex plumbing w/ brass and plastic fittings, main water shut-off only, 16 cu. ft. FF refrigerator, dual glazed vinyl windows.
What distinguishes brand from its competition: Competitive entry level price point, standard dry wall interiors throughout, hardwood cabinets, all trim is wood (not wrapped molding), tubs/showers fiberglass (not plastic), asphalt shingles.
Number of dealerships—Company owned: none
Independents: 120

Percentage of HUD homes sold of total homes produced: 40%
In-house financing? No.
In-house Insurance? No
Warranty structure and length: 1 year. Servicing by factory-dispatched techs, private contractors, and dealers.
Web site rating: Attractive, uncluttered but inadequate for the informed home shopper. Pros: fast, intuitive navigation, straightforward presentation, excellent graphic cutaway images of construction, floor plans also show elevation & 3D views. Cons: gallery of photos are not much larger than thumbnails even when clicked, no exterior shots, no detailed list of construction specs/ features.
Comment: In a Midwest marketplace that is cluttered with MH brands competing at every price point Hart Housing has found a way to capture its share of the entry level market by holding down price while delivering a home with standard features (e.g., dry wall interiors) a click up from the competition. The trade-off is lower construction standards elsewhere (e.g., 2x3 int. wall studs, elect. outlet boxes attached with clips), but the formula works. The acquisition by Berkshire ensures access to deep pockets. For consumers Hart represents an entry level choice worth considering.

Hi-tech Housing, Inc. (privately held)
19319 County Road 8
Bristol, IN 46507
Ph. 574/848-5851   Fx. 574/848-5851
Web site: www.hi-techhousing.com
Background: In the early 1990s Illinois landowner and developer Charles Fanaro determined to create an upscale 55+ MH community on 700 pristine acres of rural farmland about an hour's drive north of Chicago that he'd bought ten years previously. The plan: build high-end custom HUD-code homes indistinguishable from site-built, selling for around $300,000 as turn-key packages in a luxury retirement community to be named Saddlebrook Farms. Failing to find a HUD-code builder willing to make the homes he designed, Fanaro, together with a few fellow investors, started Hi-Tech Housing in 1992 at a plant near Elkhart, IN, and figured out ways to build the designs. The result is a home, usually three sections, plus an additional two or three major pieces added on-site (dormers, porches, screened decks, sun rooms, even rooms that cover the entire length of the back of the home), and built to the highest quality construction standards. Today Saddlebrook Farms is a stellar success: 1100 top-of-the-line homes, all of them appreciating in value. Along the way Hi-Tech adapted its HUD designs to mod standards and now has a flourishing business selling them to custom home builders and developers. All but a few of the HUD-code homes built are for Saddlebrook Farms, but Hi-Tech does have several HUD/mod indie dealerships repping the line.
States where sold: IL, WI, MO, KY, IN, OH, PA, NY, MI
Principal market niche: high end site-built home buyers, solvent retirees looking to cash out of their homes and move into a smaller, yet still plush home in a high-end MH community featuring lots of amenities.
Retail price range before tax (price includes transportation & set-up): low 80s to $180,000
Competes against: high end site-built homes, new and re-sell
Construction rating: 10
Models: Sage, Starlight, Sunflower, Woodfern, Foxglove, the Chelsea, The Essex, the Devon (all two sections)
Prairie, Trillium, Primrose (all three sections
Description of a popular model: Foxglove two-section, 3BR, 2BA, 28x49, 1575 sq. ft, w/ attached garage, fireplace, screened porch, walk-in closets, 5/12 roof pitch, 2x6' ext. walls 16" O.C. w/ 2x6" top and bottom plates all ext. walls, window/door headers on ext. walls made with three 2x6" lumber sandwiched on edge, 9' sidewalls throughout, "smooth" dry wall throughout (primed and painted), flush ceiling across mating wall openings (no trim, beam or header), Merillat kitchen cabinets, Moen single lever faucets, sweat-fitted copper plumbing lines/fittings at tub/shower and water heater, shut-off valves all fixtures, 33 oz. plush carpet on ½-inch 6# rebond pad.
What distinguishes brand from its competition: highest quality construction rating, great flexibility to add tags, pods, rooms, extensions (14 different room add on options), site-built design and appearance (articulated exteriors, projections, etc.), no traditional dealer network to speak of, no real effort to advertise, sells mostly to home builders.
Number of dealerships—Company owned: none
Independents: 16
Percentage of HUD homes sold of total homes produced: 65%
In-house financing: No
In-house Insurance: No
Warranty structure and length: 1 year. Note: Company reports homes are so well-constructed warranty service calls are minimal, far less than 1% of home cost.
Web site rating: Serviceable, lots to look at, designed primarily to assist builders/general contractors looking for modular products, but enough for home buyers, too. Site is best viewed in conjunction with the Saddlebrook Farms web site, www.saddlebrookfarms.n

et, to view examples of HUD-code homes. Pros: easy navigation, good list of building specs/upgrades. Cons: annoying PDF downloads of floor plans, no clear distinction between HUD and modular designs.

Comment: This company is the best-kept secret in high-end HUD housing, boasting a construction rating better than most site-built homes. It's so busy taking care of new homebuyers moving into Saddlebrook Farms, and filling orders from its regional mod home builders, that it's made no effort to expand its dealer network (although they say they'd be delighted to hear from dealers anywhere in the U.S.). Doesn't even have brochures or an ad budget. Hi-Tech's principal, Chuck Fanaro, is very low key, prefers staying out of the spotlight, yet is held in high esteem by MH builders for successfully proving a HUD-code home can be built to equal or exceed the expectations of the most demanding site-built home buyer.

Holly Park Homes (privately held)
(a division of Indiana Building Systems, LLC, owned by Pleasant Street Homes, LLC)
51700 Lovejoy Drive
Middlebury, IN 46540
Ph. 574/825-3700   Fx. 574/825-3050
Web site: www.holly-park.com
Background: Started in Shipshewana, IN in 1964, Holly Park Homes has been a recognized brand for decades in the Indiana region, even as the company went through several changes of ownership. In 1995 the builder relocated to Middlebury, IN, the same year that its current parent company, Pleasant Street Homes, LLC was launched. The latter purchased Holly Park in 2001 to add HUD-code and affordable modular homes to its product lines, making it a division of its entry level modular producer, Indiana Building Systems, launched in 2001. The factories for both companies are on the same lot.
States where sold: IN, MI, OH, IL, IA, MO, MN, WI, KY, WV
Principal market niche: affordable housing, entry level to low mid-range
Retail price range before tax (price includes transportation & set-up): high 20s to low 30s (entry level single-section) to mid-80s for sectionals
Competes against: Four Seasons, Clayton, Skyline, Champion brands (e.g., Dutch, Commander, Redman, Fortune), Southern Energy
Construction rating: 6

Brands/series:
Holly-Wood Estates – Series high-end multi-sectionals, 6/12 roof pitch, 8' side walls, finished drywall most areas.
Holly Park – sectionals, the main product offering, many floor plans, options
Holly Park single sections
Park Ridge – four package homes from the Holly Park series (multi-sectional) 1,3520 - 1976 sq. ft. w/ popular options
Pleasantview – Low end, entry level affordable singles and sectionals
Description of a popular model: 805 Malibu, 3BR, 2BA, two-section, 28' x 60' incl. 8' covered front porch w/ optional box bay windows, 1,352 sq. ft., 6/12 roof pitch, 8' side walls, finished dry wall most areas, lg. LR w/ arched opening to kitchen.
What distinguishes brand from its competition: Company is making a fresh start, floor plan flexibility, variety of attractive ext. elevations, lots of interior amenities, focused on customer appeal, strong warranty
Number of dealerships — Company owned:
none   **Independents:** 65-plus
Percentage of HUD homes sold of total homes produced: 65%
In-house financing? Yes. Holly Park's parent, Pleasant Street Homes, is part owner of TriCom Mortgage, a joint venture w/ Wells Fargo Bank (along with Commodore and Liberty) created in 2003 to specialize in home mortgage lending (but not chattel loans) to buyers of HUD and modular homes.
In-house Insurance? No.
Warranty structure and length: 1 year top to bottom, plus 4 years structural (roof, floor joists, load-bearing walls, steel frame, but not plumbing/electrical), w/ $100 deductible.
Web site rating: OK but bland, in need of a design makeover to give it more pizzazz (suggestion: lose the light avocado green and pale blue font colors). Pros: Lots of construction specs, clear description of model ranges. Cons: needs more color images, esp. exteriors, no clearly identified "Home" page icon on pages, ugly colors, poor quality 360 degree interactive images, another example of a lackluster web site that fails to excite.
Comment: Under its current ownership Holly Park Homes is seeking to expand its dealership network, advertising itself as "a fresh new manufactured housing company with a name that has roots going back to 1964." Aiming to provide quality affordable housing, Holly Park is up against a lot of competition but its combination of decent construction specs, competitive price points, one of the industry's

better warranties, flexible floor plans, and options such as box bay windows and craftsman style porches auger well for success in its niche.

The Homark Company, Inc. (privately held)
Homark Homes
100 Third Street
Red Lake Falls, MN 56750
Ph. 800/382-1154 Fx. 218/253-2116
Web site: www.homark.com
Background: Founded in 1991, Homark Homes is the result of a friendly buy-out by the 46 employees of a former MH plant that during the 1950s was the home of long-defunct Detroiter Homes. Situated 80 miles south of the Canadian border, Homark capitalized on the seasoned experience of its work force to gain a competitive niche in the mid-range marketplace, building heavier duty HUD and modular homes well-suited to Minnesota's harsh winters. Two recently introduced HUD series, both featuring cedar siding—the Hide-Away Lodge and the Cozy Cabin—have surprising successes. The company's single-plant facility currently builds about 200 homes a year (about 20 of them single-sections), including its modular line, North Country Modular.
States where sold: MN, ND, SD, IA, WI, MI.
Principal market niche: Boomers (seeking country getaways or downsizing), families seeking a mainstream home features at a mid-range price.
Retail price range before tax (price includes transportation & set-up): Homes: $50,000 (single-section) to $95,000. Cozy Cabin: from the high 20s. HideAway Lodge: $60,000-$90,000.
Competes against: Skylines, Fall Creek, Liberty, Wick, BonnaVilla, higher end Champion brands
Construction rating: 8
Brands/series:
Royal American – HUD series, from $60,000
Royal American Special Edition – includes home theatre system, big screen TV, wood fire place w/ tile surround, floor plan includes family room. Similar concept to Fleetwood's The Entertainer model.
Hide-Away Lodge – country home/mountain retreat, featuring vinyl, cedar or half-log siding, enclosed porch, 90" side walls, 3/12 roof pitch, flying gables
Cozy Cabin – similar to Hide-Away Lodge but smaller footprint (fm. 740 sq. ft.)
Description of a popular model: Royal American, two-section, 4BR, 2BA, 30x76, w/ 6/12 roof pitch, 2x6" ext. walls 16" O.C., 2x10" floor joists 16 O.C., ¾" dia. Novadek floor decking, foam-backed vinyl siding, 90" side walls, int. walls VOG, vaulted ceiling T/O, R-28/22/19, Kenmore appliances (incl. 17' FF refrigerator). Price: high 50s-plus

What distinguishes brand from its competition: High-quality construction, heavier sections, solid dealer network, good warranty service, stand-out cabin/hideaway series
Number of dealerships—Company owned: none
Independents: 25-plus (including several exclusive Homark dealers)
Percentage of HUD homes sold of total homes produced: 60%
In-house financing? No
In-house Insurance? No
Warranty structure and length: 1 year. Has factory-dispatched trucks with techs that make one-week round trips for service calls and warranty repairs; also dealer reimbursed work.
Web site rating: Outstanding, on par with the best of the larger MH builders. Pros: fast, intuitive, well-organized, lots of ext. and int. photos, lists of features/upgrades, company background, provides a nice sense of high employee morale. Cons: pdfs an annoyance (printing from the screen is faster, simpler), no lists of available upgrades, e.g., dry wall instead of VOG.
Comment: Homark is a small, well-managed enterprise (with its motivated employees owning most all of its stock) nicely positioned in a strong Minnesota economy. Its addition of the Hide-Away Lodge and Cozy Cabin lines is an inspired move, meeting the demand of upscale second-home buyers with an attractive woodsy product that faces almost no competition. Its excellent web site and media-savvy marketing department belie the fact that it is out there in the country way north of Fargo.

Homebuilders Northwest, Inc. (privately held)
1650 Salem Industrial Drive
Salem, OR 97303
Ph. 503/391-8936   Fx. 503/391-8980
Web site: www.homebuildersnorthwest.com
Background: Founded in 1994 by two veteran managers of the Guerdon Homes plant in nearby Stayton, OR, Homebuilders NW has stuck with an unusual philosophy: a slower rate of production allows for greater attention to detail and thus yields a superior quality home. The approach has paid off: despite building an average of only two sections (or floors) a day—about 1/10th the output of its major competitors, HBNW has achieved a remarkable 6% share of the MH market in Oregon alone, equal to that of Skyline and Marlette and well ahead of Silvercrest and Redman. During the 1999-04 industry slump, the company maintained one of the industry's most consistent order backlogs. HBNW keeps an intentionally low profile, benefiting from its word-of-mouth reputation as a small regional

builder whose owners-mangers are very accessible to homebuyers.
States where sold: OR, WA, ID, northern CA, western MT
Principal market niche: mid to high end homes for typically more mature buyers for whom attention to detail and finish are high priorities
Retail price range before tax (price includes transportation & set-up): from just under $40,000 to $130,000
Competes against: site-built homes, Palm Harbor, Karsten, Fuqua, Marlette, Skyline, Silvercrest, Golden West, Fleetwood
Construction rating: 8
Brands/series:
Evergreen series – Mid to high end, w/ many options standard. Includes variously named model groups: the La Casa Homes (triple-sections), 10th Anniversary homes, the Casual Elegance home
Aspen series – Mid-range price and features a click below Evergreen, w/ many upgrade options offered
Description of a popular model: Evergreen, Royal Vista, two-section, 3BR, 2BA, 27'x60' two-section, 1,537 sq. ft., w/ attached street-side 24' garage (built on site), deluxe master BA, 4/12 roof pitch, 8' ext. side walls, vaulted ceiling, Hardiplank siding, arched entryway to den and kitchen, three-window wrap-around above corner kitchen sink, opt. food prep island. Approx. $85,000
What distinguishes brand from its competition: Small builder (by choice), owners are the plant managers, accessible daily to homebuyers, in-house design/engineering offers above average customization, small volume ensures better construction/fit & finish, excellent warranty.
Number of dealerships—Company owned: 2
Independents: 18
Percentage of HUD homes sold of total homes produced: 100%
In-house financing? No
In-house Insurance? No
Warranty structure and length: 5-year structural, factory direct. "Builders Touch" program includes factory tech dispatched to every home for final finish & homeowner orientation. Every owner provided with name and contact info of a personal factory service rep responsible for follow-up service/warranty work.
Web site rating: Adequate but badly in need of a design makeover. Pros: robust gallery of photos (incl. many exteriors), extensive floor plans, full dealer listing. Cons: dated home page w/ primitive animation; confused layout w/ no obvious click points; some links broken; construction specs lack full details; no list of upgrade options.

Comment: The banner on the HBNW web site—"hard to find...worth the search"—accurately characterizes this small, well-regarded company. While not a boutique builder (no factory producer is), HBNW is prized for its personal touch (management regularly accompanies potential home buyers on plant tours), superior degree of customization and follow-through. While its homes are quality constructed, their exteriors tend to have the blah, boxy conventional look of a manufactured home (only two roof pitches are available: 3/12 and 4/12). A 4/12 roof pitch and an attached garage will works wonders to correct this. NW consumers looking for a mid- to high end home would be well-advised to include Homebuilders Northwest among the options to consider.

Horton Industries, Inc. (Privately held)
Horton Homes
Dynasty Homes
PO Box 4410 101 Industrial Blvd.
Eatonton, GA 31024
Ph. 706/485-8506   **Fx.** 706/485-5982

Web site: www.hortonhomes.com
Background: In 1970, after eight years as a site-built home builder, 36-year old Dudley Horton, inspired by the potential of MH, opened up a factory in a former chicken house, and built his first mobile home. Today, at 71 and still going strong, Horton heads a thriving enterprise (1,200 employees) on a 100 acre complex that includes a million sq. ft. of manufacturing space comprising Horton Homes (HUD and mod), Horton Vans (heavy equipment trailers, horse trailers), Horton Iron Works, Horton Iron Works Stamping Division, and Horton Components (accent moldings, door casings, base boards, etc.).
The company also owns 20 dealerships (down from 60 during the go-go 90s boom). In '98, at its peak, Horton was building 80-100 floors a day. When the MH market tanked, Horton focused on its trailer business to prevent layoffs. Currently the company produces 24 HUD-code, and five modular, floors per day,
States where sold: GA, FL, KY, NC, SC, VA, WV, TN,
Principal market niche: None. Builds MH for the whole range of buyers seeking value comparable to site-built at an affordable price
Retail price range before tax (price includes transportation & set-up): $25,000 (entry level

single-section) to around $100,000. Average: $55,000-$57,000
Competes against: Cavalier, Southern Energy (Southern Estates line), General Manufactured Housing
Construction rating: 7
Brands/series:
Horton Homes and **Dynasty Homes** – Identical brands, differing in name only to allow for distribution to dealers competing in the same market
Description of a popular model: The Boss (named after Dudley Horton's wife Helen Ruth, who designed the model), 3 BR, 2 BA, 32x68 two-section, 2006 sq. ft., 2x4 ext. walls 16" O.C., 3/12 pitch, 8' int. walls, VOG, flat ceilings, ¾" T&G OSB decking, all BRs w/ walk-in closets, spacious, open kitchen-DR area, kitchen island w/ snack shelf, wall-mounted oven and microwave, 22 cu. ft. dble-door FF refrigerator w/ ice/water, edge-rolled Formica post form countertops, fiberglass sink, single-lever Moen faucet, 25 oz. Shaw carpet, perimeter heat/AC ducts, 40 gal. water heater, shut-offs at all fixtures. Approx: $65,000.
What distinguishes brand from its competition: Reputable, 35-yr. old company, solidly built homes, exceeds HUD minimum code across the board, better standard insulation, not much customization but good selection of floor plans, superior warranty (if extended warranty purchased).
Number of dealerships—Company owned: 20
Independents: 150
Percentage of HUD homes sold of total homes produced: 80%
In-house financing? No
In-house Insurance? No
Warranty structure and length: 1-year
Web site rating: Serviceable, earnest but not enough info for informed home shoppers. Pros: straightforward design/navigation (but dated by web standards), good photos of interiors (Note: the clickable photos are huge when enlarged, requiring the viewer to scroll both ways to take it all in, but the trade-off is this allows one to see lots of detail not otherwise viewable), Cons: needs a more coherent, comprehensive list of constructions specs and options; no mention of the Dynasty Home, the pages devoted to the modular building side are incomplete, clunky, some broken links. This site would benefit from an upgrade.
Comment: Horton has long been a steady, reliable presence in the southern market with no bad raps and a reputation for homes that lack flash but are built tough. As one observer quipped, "There's nothing pretty about their models but you can drop that sucker out of an airplane and it won't break apart." Explains a company spokesman, "We build a tight house, easy to heat and cool efficiently, something that lasts. You can decorate it any way you want. We don't want to be Alabama flash, with stuff like mirrors on the ceiling, that will be out of date in a year." However, Horton is one of the very few companies who do offer an optional complete suite of rugs and furniture. One indication of Horton's confidence in its homes: home buyers can purchase a 5-year extended top-to-bottom warranty for a nominal $50.

Indies House   (privately held)
Highway 172 East, P.O. Box 190
Hackleburg, AL   35564
Ph. Web site: www.indieshouse.net
Background: Founded in 1972 by Thomas James who, together with his brother Jerry, had previously founded Franklin Homes in 1968. This small builder has long been a regional player in the core SE market, building almost exclusively HUD-code homes, garnering a reputation for customization in the low and low mid price ranges that many others don't offer. The company has also been a robust producer over the years, off and on showing up in the list of Top 25 builders in terms of number of homes built, especially single-section homes.

In 1999 Indies House was purchased by its current owner, Hugh Weeks, a successful businessman-engineer with broad experience in the foundry industry (he has a degree in metallurgy). The company struggled through the '99-'04 industry slump but as business improved, purchased a second (and larger) former MH plant in nearby Haleyville, AL, opening it in the fall of 2005 to build single-sections only, many for the Gulf coast market following Hurricane Katrina.
States where sold: IL, KY, TN, AL, FL, MS, LA, MO, AR, TX, OK
Principal market niche: Basic affordable housing for working families
Retail price range before tax (includes transportation and set-up): $43,000 (single-section) to $100,000 (two/three sections). 28x52 double-sections from $60,000.
Competes against: Fleetwood, Southern Energy, Gateway, Deer Valley, General Manufactured Housing
Construction rating: 4
Brands/series: Indies House—in all price points
Description of a popular model: Indies 32 x 80, double-section, 2,280 sq. ft., 4 BR 2BA, 3/12 roof pitch, 2x4' ext. walls 16" O.C., 8' side wall ht., int. walls VOG ½" glued and stapled to studs, ½" rebond carpet pad w/ carpet stapled to floor, floor registers on floor center line, ¾" OSB floor decking, dual glazed windows, hardwood cabinets, 40 gal. water heater.

What distinguishes brand from its competition: Been around for a long time, fills niche as a custom builder, able to build to almost any specs customer desires (8' side wall homes offer ceilings either vaulted or flat, 9' side walls are w/ flat ceilings only).
Number of dealerships—Company owned: none
Independents: approx. 50
Percentage of HUD homes sold of total homes produced: 99%
In-house financing? No
In-house Insurance? No
Warranty structure and length: 1 year. Hires subcontractors to perform warranty service
Web site rating: Unsatisfactory, little more than a page or two of contact information and a collection of home photos from the 2005 Tunica, MS home show. Pros: Photos are quite adequate, including exteriors, floor plans can be printed from screen. Cons: some picture links to enlargements don't work, no background on company history, mission, or warranty policy, no list of standard features or upgrades; a disappointment for the informed home shopper.
Comment: If unanswered faxes and unreturned weekly follow-up voice messages to Indies' sales mgr. over a six week period are any indication, Indies House is very reluctant to answer media inquiries. A sales staffer finally responded but seemed impatient to keep the conversation short. Potential buyers of Indies House homes should not be blamed if they find this behavior troubling. (A subsequent phone call to the company's president, however, was returned, and much info was cordially provided).
Indies House homes tend to be a bit pricier than their competition (the Hackleburg plant builds few floors less than $22,000 wholesale to the dealer), and their decor and accessories have a decided touch of Alabama flash, but the company has figured out a way to provide customization at a competitive price, and it delivers what its customers want.
As this goes to press, Indies has a three month back log at both plants. The company's new plant in Haleyville is building lower end cookie-cutter single-wides (at a five a day clip) w/ no customization, few floor plans, and which will retail in the low 40s. In the wake of Katrina, Indies House can expect a strong demand for these basic housing units at least through 2006.

Jacobsen Homes (privately held)
600 Packard Court PO Box 368
Safety Harbor, FL 34695
Ph. 727/726-1138   Fx. 727/726-7019
Web site: www.jachomes.com
Background: The oldest manufactured home builder in Florida (and the state's only solely owned MH builder) Jacobsen Homes was started in Safety Harbor (in the Tampa Bay area) in 1951 by Bob Jacobsen and since then has quietly and successfully ruled the Florida roost as the class act in manufactured housing. (Aside: in the mid-50s, Jacobsen also owned the Silver Dollar, an unusual MH community whose spirited residents took out the shuffleboard court and put in a skeet shooting range, thereby morphing the community into the Silver Dollar Gun Club.)
In 1981, Jacobsen's son Bobby purchased the MH business and has since steered a successful course, selling in the Florida market only, and focusing mostly on housing for the state's huge number of MH communities.
States where sold: FL
Principal market niche: custom homes for upscale seniors/retirees in Florida land-lease communities
Retail price range before tax (price includes transportation & set-up): for private property placement — $75,000 and up; for MH communities as part of turn-key package deals that include all site prep, ancillary structures (called exterior packages)— $70,000-$80,000 to $180,000-plus. In many MH communities, packages start at $120,000.
Competes against: Principally Palm Harbor (for quality) and to a lesser extent, Skyline and Homes of Merit (Bartow division).
Construction rating: 9
Brands/series:
Chancellor series – all 2BR models only, in many floor plans, customized to fit on any lot, especially the smaller sites often found in older MH communities.
Classic series – all 3BR models only, in all sizes w/ many floor plans, also customizable, the most popular series because increasingly the third room is used as a computer room/den.
Description of a popular model: Classic model CL3, 3BR, 2BA, double-section, 1,493 sq. ft.,. 2x6" ext. walls 16" O.C., 3/12 pitch, 2x3" int. wall studs, 8' int. wall height, T&T dry wall w/ bull nose corners t/o, R-30 ceiling insulation, ¾ " OSB floor decking, large kitchen w/ nook, 3 bay windows, kitchen island w/ sink and prep area, 38 oz. carpet, insulated/ducted cooling system w/ ceiling registers.
What distinguishes brand from its competition: High construction rating, great flexibility w/ customization, high customer loyalty, excellent reputation, strong dealer network, extended warranty, focuses on Florida market only.
Number of dealerships—Company owned: none

Independents: approx. 80, abut 50 of which are in MH communities
Percentage of HUD homes sold of total homes produced: 98%
In-house financing? No
In-house Insurance? No
Warranty structure and length: 1 year top-to-bottom, four additional years structural.
Web site rating: Outstanding. Pros: beautiful to look at, welcoming, clean design, uncluttered pages, fast intuitive navigation, lots of information, a sense of well-rounded completeness, a site crafted to meet the needs of informed home buyers who demand quality. Video on the 2004 hurricanes is both first rate and a powerful sell for Jacobsen and Zone III MH. Cons: list of standard construction features needs more detail, no list of options/upgrades provided.
Comment: Jacobsen is a respected, well managed company with an enviable reputation in the FL market. It remained profitable even when the MH market tanked from '99 to '04. A Jacobsen home usually beats the price of its nearest competitor, Palm Harbor, because the company doesn't have a large corporation to feed. Its quality control is highly regarded (the plant manager is a former HUD factory inspector who runs a tight ship; worker morale is high). All of which explains why the company's current back log is six to seven months (Jacobsen is still building many replacement homes for those destroyed in the 2004 hurricane season). But for Florida home buyers, especially seniors and retirees looking for a rock solid home with lots of flexibility in design and features, a Jacobsen home is worth the wait—and the money.

Kabco Builders, Inc. (Privately held)
P.O. Box 745, 1315 Industrial Blvd.
Boaz, AL 35957
Ph. 256/593-9955   Fx. 256/593-9930
Web site: www.kabcobuilders.com
Background: Started in May, 2003 by Keith Bennett, former co-owner of the defunct Homes of Legend (based in Boaz), and fellow HOE alumnus Mike Thompson. With a work force comprising a core of experienced former HOE employees, Kabco initially produced only small commercial buildings (e.g., 8' x 20' multipurpose structures), but soon shifted entirely to MH, opting to produce DWs only (28' and 32' wides, and long: 62' to 80'), keeping it simple, focusing on ten floor plans with little or no customization and targeting home buyers looking for affordable housing with as much square footage as they can afford.
States where sold: AL, MS, LA, TN, AR, GA, KY
Principal market niche: low end of medium to medium price range, "buyers with at least a 650 FICO credit score."
Retail price range before tax (including transportation and set-up): $54,000-$80,000
Competes against: Southern Energy Estate Series, Gateway, Clayton, Fleetwood
Construction rating: 4
Brands: Platinum Series (Builds 28' and 32' Double wide homes only)
Description of a popular model: Platinum KB-2801, 28'x62', 3BR, 2BA, 1736 sq.ft., nominal 4/12 roof pitch, 2x4 ext. walls, 7-1/2' side wall (vaulted ceiling to 9' t/o), 3/8" VOG walls glued and stapled to studs, ceiling fan in L/R, Thermopane windows, heat/AC registers on floor centerline, decking 5/8" plywood T&G, kitchen counters Formica self-edged, solid oak raised panel cabinet doors, stainless steel sink with dual knob goose neck faucet/sprayer, 12" sq. hand-laid tiles in kitchen and BA, 21 oz. carpet stapled to floor, R19/11/11 insulation, elec. outlet boxes secured to walls w/ wings/clips, int. door hinges surface mounted, 40 gal. water heater, 18' FF refrigerator. Approx. $54,000.
What distinguishes brand from its competition: A small young company, small product line currently building DWs only, emphasis on more square footage for the buck, competitive price points, better than average response time on warranty calls.
Number of dealerships—Company owned: none
  Independents: 48
Percentage of HUD code homes sold of total homes produced: 100% (Company has no plans to move into modular)
In-house financing: No
In-house insurance: No
Warranty structure and length: 1 year, 5 factory-dispatched teams, w/ dealers handling emergencies, e.g., electrical or plumbing problems.
Web site rating: Unsatisfactory, still under construction yet in some ways superior to many other sites. Pros: simple fast navigation, downloadable 6-pg. pdf of all floor plans w/ list of standard features (refreshing!), excellent photo gallery of click-to-enlarge images, easy to email top management; Cons: clunky design, no info for Retailers and Contact Us, no list of options/upgrades, no effort to create a sense of the company.
Comment: Kabco's focus on a small product line of spacious DW's suitable for growing families (currently only ten floorplans) may not only be a good business model, it may reflect lessons learned from Homes of Legend. HOE, acquired in '96 by Champion Enterprises, was subsequently shut down in 2001. The move was in part due to the MH market downturn, but also reportedly in part because HOE had struggled with allegations of poor construction, apparently owing to

its ambitious home designs that, according to one insider, were hard to build. Kabco management says it's committed to quality construction work and that to date they claim to have had very few service problems. Kabco's five factory-dispatched warranty service trucks is a good indication of the company's commitment to keep its home buyers satisfied.

Kit Homebuilders West LLC   (privately held)
P. O. Box 250
Caldwell, ID 83606-0250
Ph. 208/454-5000   Fx: 208/455-3274
Web site: www.kitwest.com
Background: Long a presence in SW Idaho's Boise Valley, this small company was founded in 1945 and for decades built a variety of factory-built homes and structures, principally HUD-code homes. When the MH industry slump hit in 1999, Kit struggled to survive by diversifying, building park models, developer models, high end mods, on-frame modulars, even Clayton homes, in the process losing focus, dealer loyalty—and money. In 2004 Kit was purchased (and given its new name) by two MH veterans: Miles Standish, former CEO of Oakwood who had taken that once mighty company through Chap. 11 and in 2003 sold it to Clayton Homes, and Michael Wolf, the well-regarded former manager of Marlette Homes' Hermiston, OR plant.

The new owners brought with them a focused strategy: build a quality HUD-code home in the Schult/Marlette tradition, with models across various price points in the mid-range (avoiding entry level and very high end), create a dealer network that will sell Kit homes exclusively, and provide great warranty service. Company has also returned to building HUD-code homes only for now, vowing high quality construction
States where sold: ID, OR, CA CO, MT, NV, UT, WA
Principal market niche: mid-range (no offerings in the low or very high end)
Retail price range before tax (price includes transportation & set-up): $44,000 (bare bones) to $140,000-$150,000
Competes against: Nashua, Marlette, Redman, Fleetwood, Golden West, Skyline
Construction rating: 7
Brands/series:
Cedar Canyon series - low mid-range, w/ T&T t/o, some bull nose, 3/12 roof pitch, 7-1/2' ext. side walls.
Crystal Park series - mid-range package homes w/ many options/amenities standard
Golden State series - high end, mostly three-sections w/ many options, T&T bull nose t/o, vaulted ceilings, oversized wood cabinets, kitchen islands, 9' side walls, fiber-cement lap siding.
Description of a popular model: Crystal Park #4009, 3BR, 2BA, 1,880 sq. ft., w/ sunken family room, 4/12 roof pitch, (optional 5/12), 25 yr. shingles, ceramic tile backslash/edging on kitchen counters, single lever faucet, 30 oz. carpet, orange peel textured walls/ceilings w/ radius corners. Approx. $85,000-$90,000
What distinguishes brand from its competition: All homes T&T, ridge beams concealed the full length of the house, heating/cooling ducts sealed and certified, very flexible w/ customization, OSB beneath dry wall on all marriage walls, 5 year ltd. warranty
Number of dealerships—Company owned: none
Independents: 39 (7 exclusive)
Percentage of HUD homes sold of total homes produced: 100%
In-house financing? No
In-house Insurance? No
Warranty structure and length: 1 year top to bottom, 4 years limited structural
Web site rating: Quite good but outdated, very much in need of photos. Pros: fast, straightforward, easy to navigate, full list of construction features for each series, lots of floor plans, good content about company background; Cons: No photos of exteriors, outdated company history.
Comment: Consumers can expect a much-improved Kit product. In his previous job helming the reeling Oakwood Homes (the MH industry's wild poster child of the 90s boom-and-bust) co-owner Miles Standish cleaned house and steered a no-nonsense course. Partner Mike Wolf is a skilled plant manager who can achieve results. Kit's challenge now is to revive a disaffected dealer network (and recruit new ones). It's too early to tell if the re-launched Kit Homebuilders West will succeed but the potential is certainly there. This is a good time for home shoppers to take a close look at the company's offerings.

Laurel Creek Homes LLC   (privately held)
1635 South 43rd. Avenue
Phoenix, AZ 85009
Ph. 877/369-4602   Fx. 602/272-6701

Web site: www.laurelcreekhomes.com
Background: This is the newest kid on the block. In fact, Laurel Creek won't have their HUD-code homes available for sale until well into 2006. In the fall of 2004, two MH veterans, Byron Blandin

and Al Townsend, were winding down their successful Tucson, AZ-based venture buying and refurbishing MH repos and selling them to regional dealers to remarket. Seeing the strong market rebound in the SW (and the months-long back logs that mfrs. were carrying) the two saw an opportunity to get in on the manufacturing side. Both had impeccable credentials. Blandin, the son of former Cavco CEO Bill Blandin, grew up in MH. Townsend had owned Western American Housing, a seven-store MH dealer chain in AZ that he sold to Clayton in 1995. By Spring 2005, the two had raised $13 million, recruited a seasoned management team, purchased a 243,000 sq. ft. factory on 20 acres, and by the fall were producing a line of RV park models (under 400 sq. ft.) to get a foothold in that hot sector while they tooled up their plant to build HUD-code homes. What follows is a listing based on information available going into 2006.

States where sold: AZ and CA
Principal market niche: initially, park models for MH communities and campgrounds in the SW market, then HUD-code MH in the mid-price range. Will avoid competing in high end, i.e. vs. Silvercrest, Hallmark Southwest.
Retail price range before tax (price includes transportation & set-up): Park models: $24,000 to $55,000. HUD-code MH, when available: upper 40s/ low 50s to $80,000 (including triple-sections)
Competes against: Park models: Cavco, Chariot Eagle West. HUD-code MH: Palm Harbor, Cavco, Schult, Marlette
Construction rating: HUD-code MH spec still in design stage. Park models: 9
Brands/series: Laurel Creek Park Models – including Cabin Units, Cottages and Bunkhouses.
Description of a popular model: LC-111LT, loft model w/ optional 3-window angled bay window, LR TV base, TV jacks, OH cabinets in BR, 11'-2" x 34'-5", 399 sq. ft., full dry wall T&T t/o, 25 oz. carpet, cathedral ceiling, prismatic dormer w/ window, 50" max head clearance in loft, R-33/14/11 insulation, optional dual glazed windows. Approx: $47,000.
What distinguishes brand from its competition: The company is new, HUD-code MH will have very flexible floor plans, no track record of customer service/ warranty work
Number of dealerships—Company owned: none
Independents: 18
Percentage of HUD homes sold of total homes produced: 0% as this goes to press
In-house financing? No
In-house Insurance? No
Warranty structure and length: 1-year
Web site rating: OK but still under construction. Pros: clean, good looking design, good content on mgmt. backgrounds, good Contact Us page; Cons: no list of construction specs/upgrades, annoying use of pdf downloads to provide floor plans that can easily be viewed and printed from simple html pages.
Comment: Laurel Creek shows early promise of being an interesting player in the western region, especially in the SW during the early going. With the park model market growing by 30% in 2004 and 11% in 2005 (and both Cavco and Chariot Eagle plants maxed out), Laurel Creek won't be stealing market share but serving the growing demand by delivering models w/ the same quality construction, especially to RV parks and campgrounds favored by snow birds swapping their RVs in favor of part-time rental vacation getaway cabins. On the HUD-code MH side, in addition to street retailers, expect Laurel Creek's homes to be marketed to both land-lease communities and to new subdivision developers offering land-home packages. Based on what is known so far, if their HUD MHs are available when you're shopping their competition, Laurel Creek will be well worth your consideration.

Lexington Homes, Inc. (Privately held)
PO Box 641 100 Lexington Circle
Lexington, MS 39095
Ph. 662/834-0292   Fx. 662/834-0402
Web site: www.lexington-homes.net
Background: For decades the central MS town of Lexington, pop. 2,500, was home to three Fleetwood plants but all were closed in 2000 (500 laid off) when the MH market nose dived. In 2004, a group of local businesses, hoping to jump start the town's economy, pooled their investment resources and backed a group of veteran MH managers (backgrounds included stints at Fleetwood, Guerdon and Cappaert), purchased Fleetwood Plant #1, hired 68 trained workers, and began producing low end entry level homes (no customization), keeping the prices low, making a profit on volume. The formula worked. When FEMA ordered emergency SW's after Hurricane Katrina, Lexington purchased Fleetwood Plant #2, hired more people and built 400 FEMA SW's. Revenue from those sales helped the company gain a sound financial footing. Company currently employs 325 and anticipates a gross annual revenue of $47-50 million going into 2007. Lexington is exploring conversion of Plant #2 to expensive modular homes to meet the expected Katrina rebuilding market.
States where sold: AL, MS, LA, FL, TN, AR, TX, OK
Principal market niche: low end entry level affordable homes, Wind zone 1 and 3
Retail price range before tax (including transportation and set-up): $20,000 to $55,000
Competes against: Cappaert, River Birch, Buccaneer

Construction rating: 4
Brands: Lexington Series- the main entry level products -SW's (most models metal-on-metal) and DWs, ($20,000-$50,000)

Elite Series - Single Wides, a click up, with more options (approx. $30,000-plus)

Southhampton Series - Double-wides, a click up, with more options (approx. $55,000)
Description of a popular model: Lexington Single Wide Model 5201, 16'x56', 2BR, 2BA, 2x4 ext. walls, 7' side wall ht., vaulted ceiling t/o, metal-on-metal w/ wood grain treatment, 3/8" VOG wallboard, carpet 15 oz. on 5 lb. pad attached with tack strips, single-pane storm windows, 2" wide window blinds t/o, ¾" T&G plywood decking, R14/11/11 insulation, stainless steel kitchen sink w/ single-lever faucet, MDF raised panel cabinets w/ exposed hinges, Formica self-edge countertops, 54" tub/ showers, elec. outlets attached w/ clips. Approx. $28,000.
What distinguishes brand from its competition: Young company, competitive pricing, simple designs, no customization, experienced construction work force, veteran hands-on management, strong support from local business community.
Number of dealerships—Company owned: none
  Independents: 90
Percentage of HUD code homes sold of total homes produced: 100% (but mods being considered)
In-house financing: No
In-house insurance: No
Warranty structure and length: 1 year
Web site rating: Serviceable but disappointing. Pros: straightforward navigation, floor plans list std. features and upgrades w/ each model, quality photos, good dealer listings. Cons: Dull design, no ext. photos of homes, photo gallery sparse, broken links fm. Quality page, no company history or sense of the brand and its people. A missed opportunity here to convey community pride and generate enthusiasm.
Comment: Lexington is a wonderful example of a town with a very high unemployment rate turning to its own strengths (an idle MH plant and a trained work force) to rescue its economy. The local investor group found a mgmt. team that had established relationships with MH retailers and suppliers and was able to hit the ground running. Company's unabashedly low end, no frills, entry level homes are low price leaders in a 100 mile radius (saving on transportation costs). Note: company owners are hands-on—one of them personally inspects each home before it's tagged and made ready to ship. That practice augers well for customer satisfaction. This will be an interesting company to watch.

Liberty Homes, Inc. (Publicly held)
1101 Eisenhower Drive N. PO box 35
Goshen, IN 46527
Ph. 574/533-0431   Fx. 574/533-0438
Web site: www.libertyhomesinc.com
Background: Founded by H. L. Spencer in Syracuse, IN as the Liberty Coach Company in 1941 shortly before the US entry into WWII, Liberty survived the war-time material rationing by building temporary housing for defense plants. The company struggled during the 1950s, at one point trying boat building as well as producing 8- and 10-ft single section homes, but sank deeper into debt. In 1960, Liberty's CPA, Edward Hussey, Sr., a managing partner of the Detroit firm of Anderson Accounting, purchased the company (and its $4-1/2 million debt), convinced that MH had a great future. The new owner's confidence derived in part from two of his other clients with MH involvement: Redman and Guerdon Industries. Hussey devised a smaller, simpler, more production-friendly single-wide home that soon reversed Liberty's fortunes. Over the following two decades Liberty developed a near national presence with (mostly single-section) homes in the low end affordable housing, with at one point 11 factories. In 1994, Liberty, together w/ several investors, including MH veteran Steve Logan, formed Waverlee Homes, an AL-based joint venture to build homes in the low-mid-range for the SE market (see Waverlee Homes listing).
In the latter half of the go-go 1990s, as the industry shifted more to double-section homes, Liberty began redesigning and upgrading its product lines for a more mainstream customer. During the '99-'04 industry downturn, the company mothballed four of its plants while tooling up to expand to modular homes. Today five of Liberty's seven remaining active plants build a mix of 55%/45% modular/HUD-code homes, with virtually interchangeable floor plans, largely for the mid- to high end price range. Ed Hussey's son Michael serves as Liberty's VP-Sec., but is widely acknowledged as the company's de facto CEO. Note: Liberty is part owner of TriCom Mortgage, LLC, a partnership with Wells Fargo Bank, Commodore Homes and Pleasant Street Homes to provide home loans through its participating dealerships.
States where sold: All but HI, AK, NV, AZ, southern CA
Principal market niche: mid- to high-end, mainstream home buyers looking at options
Retail price range before tax (price includes transportation & set-up): high 40s (for a single section) to $135,000 for a triple w/ many options.

Median: $65,000 - $90,000
Competes against: Patriot, Ritz-Craft, Commodore, Skyline, Wick, site builders
Construction rating: 8
Brands/series:
Liberty – many models names (five factories, ea. w/ differing model styles for each region)
Badger (also Badger Built, Wisconsin Badger) – same as Liberty, from Wisconsin factory
Waverlee – From the AL plant, serving the SE market. See **Waverlee Homes** listing.
Description of a popular model: Liberty two-section, 3BR 2BA, 1800 sq. ft., 5.5/12 roof pitch (hinged), 2x6 ext walls 16" O.C., 8' int. wall ht., 2x4 int. walls 16" O.C., 5/8" T&G Cresdek decking, T&Primed smooth dry wall t/o (attached horizontally w/ screws), bull nose corners, snack bar in kitchen, single lever kitchen faucet, stainless steel sink, ash raised panel cabinets, Formica w/ bull nose edges, ceramic tile backsplash, dual glazed thermo pane windows, vitreous china bath/sinks/toilets, R-22/19/22 insulation, 40 gal. water heater. Retail price approx. $90,000.
What distinguishes brand from its competition: Distinctive ext. designs w/ many ext options (e.g., triple peaked dormers, hip roofs, double box base), lots of customization flexibility (including 1-day turnaround on price quotes for custom floor plans), great kitchen and BA designs, solid company, in-house mortgage loan program.
Number of dealerships — Company owned: none **Independents:** 450 (about 60 of them builders for subdivisions, urban in-fills, spec rural lots)
Percentage of HUD homes sold of total homes produced: about 50%
In-house financing? Yes, through TriCom Mortgage LLC
In-house Insurance? No
Warranty structure and length: 1-year.
Web site rating: Generally OK but sterile, missing essential content. Pros: Site redesigned in the fall of 2005, much improved, excellent virtual tours, esp. the interactive set, straightforward navigation, full list of dealerships available for each region (none of this "someone will contact you" nonsense), printable floor plans from screen. Cons: design lacks warmth, no distinction between HUD and modular lines, no list of construction features/ options (broken construction features link next to each floor plan; should have link to Waverlee Homes web page, no clear instructions on how to navigate photo gallery of stills, needs more company history on About Us page, more sense of personality. But mostly a missing detailed list of construction specs/options equals a disappointment for informed shoppers.

Comment: While Liberty still builds single-sections (mostly for MH communities), and still has a lingering, albeit mistaken, reputation in some industry quarters for lower end homes, it has made a successful transition up the food chain with current product lines and price points placing it squarely in the mid- to high-end range. The company has done a good job of designing more of a site built look to the exteriors of its sectionals while providing smart kitchen designs that reflect that space's role as the home's gathering area. In addition, Liberty's ownership stake in TriCom Mortgage (which includes Wells Fargo Bank) gives its homebuyers a leg up on financing options.

Magnolia Homes, Inc. (privately held)
982 Rundell Road PO Box 657
Gering, NE 69341
Ph. 308/436-3131   Fx. 308/436-1965
Web site: www.magnoliahomes.biz
Background: Founded as a subsidiary of Denver, CO-based Guerdon Industries in 1958 in Scottsbluff, NE (in the panhandle, close to the WY and CO borders), this small builder quietly prospered, providing mobile homes for the surrounding states. In 1971, Magnolia built a new plant in Gering, a few miles south, expanding into modular homes. At the same time, a sister subsidiary, Guerdon Homes, began a considerably larger expansion (to 25 plants nationally during the 70s) before a sharp MH downturn in the early 1980s caused it to implode (see Guerdon Homes listing). At that juncture both Guerdon and Magnolia were sold to businessman Fred Huckvale, HQ'ed in Los Angeles, CA. In 1988 a four-person team of CO-based executives working for Huckvale moved to Gering to manage the Magnolia plant. Shortly thereafter, Huckvale sold out to his partners who moved the HQ to Stayton, OR.
In 1996 Magnolia changed ownership for a fourth time when then-high-flying American HomeStar, flush with IPO cash and on a shopping spree, snapped up Guerdon Homes. Five years later, American HomeStar crashed, declaring Chap. 11 bankruptcy. In early 2001, Magnolia found itself on the auction block in BK court with solvent MH heavyweights, including Palm Harbor and Clayton Homes, ready to bid.
At that juncture, in a gutsy move, Magnolia's management, the original 1988 CO team lead by John Fillingham, notified the bidders that they, too, would bid, and if they lost, they would start their own MH/modular plant nearby and directly compete with Magnolia. At that, the other bidders withdrew. Today Magnolia Homes remains quietly prosperous, building up-market homes, 90% of them constructed to the IRC modular code.

States where sold: NE, SD, WY, UT, CO, KS
Principal market niche: Home buyers looking for a HUD home built to the quality construction standards of a high end modular code home, who are more concerned about structural integrity/longevity than superficial flash.
Retail price range before tax (includes transportation and set-up): $60,000 to $150,000-plus
Competes against: BonnaVilla, Nashua, Schult (in KS), Summit Crest (in CO)
Construction rating: 9
Brands/series:
Elegant Series – high-end HUD version of the successful Paramount modular series – w/ 8' int. wall ht, flat ceilings, T&T t/o, coffered tray ceiling accents, w/ a 5/12 hinged roof std.
Radiant Series – mid-range, a click below the Elegant, a version of the Majestic modular series – 7-1/2' int. wall ht., 3/12 roof, vaulted ceiling, can upgrade to 5/12 roof pitch.
Country Cabins – based on the Radiant series, w/ prow covered front porch, redwood deck, larger front windows, cedar siding.
Description of a popular model: Elegant, 32x66, double-section, 3BR, 2BA, 2,112 sq. ft., w/ 8' covered front porch, retreat room off MBR, walk-in closets MBR and 2nd BR, open kitchen/LR/DR plan, kitchen island w/ snack bar & 3 pendant lamps, MBA w/ lounge tub/his-her china sinks, 5/12 roof pitch, copper water supply lines w/ water shut offs all fixtures, 8' ext. side walls, T&T ½" dry wall t/o w/ coffered ceilings w/ lighted ceiling fans in some areas, 16" eve and gable ends overhangs, black iron pipe gas supply system w/ shut-offs, 32 oz. carpet. About $120,000
What distinguishes brand from its competition: wide name recognition, HUD code homes built w/ mod construction quality/features (e.g., copper water plumbing), high degree of customization w/ versatile in-house engineering staff, knowledgeable builder/dealer network
Number of dealerships—Company owned: none
Independents: 36
Percentage of HUD homes sold of total homes produced: 10%
In-house financing? No
In-house Insurance? No
Warranty structure and length: 1 year, a one-time complimentary factory-dispatched visit to do punch list of needed cosmetic repairs
Web site rating: Good but missing essential content. Pros: clean design, intuitive, fast (no animation gimmicks/ annoying pdfs), excellent clickable photos, fast dealer locater listing (no attempt to harvest a service lead, just the dealers' contact into); Cons: no list of construction specs/upgrade options, no floor plans, no address/email contact info for company corp. offices in NE. For floor plans and specs, visit web site of Ft. Collins, CO dealer: www.magnoliamodularhomes.com (an excellent dealer site)
Comment: This small gem of a company has all but moved over to the mod side of factory built homes, but the HUD homes they build, being essentially modular in design and specs, are gorgeous, especially the interiors (warm and spacious, right up there with their competitor BonnaVilla).
Note: if you're looking for a basement model, you're far better off switching to mod specs. With its seasoned management going on 18 years as a team (you gotta love their successful 2001 gambit vs. the big boys to rescue Magnolia), this stable company and its dealers is well positioned to thrive in its region.

Manufactured Housing Enterprises
(privately held)
09302 U.S. Route 6
Byran, OH 43506
Ph. 419/636-4511   Fx. 419/636-6521
Web site: www.mheinc.com
Background: This long-time family-owned company in the NE corner of Ohio was started in 1965 by James Newman whose previous experience, first as a used car dealer, than as a dealer of new and used house trailers, convinced him that he could to a better job building the latter himself. The company has quietly prospered, its location on U.S. Route 6 growing from a single plant to four facilities scattered on 40 acres (one factory builds HUD single-sections only, a second HUD sectionals, a third modular homes, and a forth that builds steel chassis frames for HUD-code homes). Still solely-owned by Newman, Sr., (son James is president), MHE currently employs over 200.
States where sold: ME, NH, VT, NY, MA, CT, RI, NJ, PA, MD, DE, OH, WV, VA, KY, NC, SC, MO, MN, MO, KS, NB, IA, WI, IL, MI, IN
Principal market niche: Affordable housing for working families
Retail price range before tax (includes transportation and set-up): $20,000 (for entry single-section) to $140,000 (for a 32x80 DW, 2,300 sq. ft w/ max options). Average: $58,000-$64,000
Competes against: Fleetwood, Commander, Fortune, Dutch, Fortune, Redman, Fairmont, Four Seasons, Patriot, Skyline

Construction rating: 7
Brands/series:
Colonial Series – sectionals at all price points
Description of a popular model: Rosewood model, two-section, 28x60, 1,493 sq. ft., 3BR, 2BA, w/ 5/12 hip roof, 2'x6' ext. walls 16" O.C., 8' ext. side wall height w/ flat ceiling, T&T dry wall t/o, Novadeck 5/8" floor decking, perimeter heat, kitchen island, Formica countertop (self-edged) w/ ceramic backsplash, white acrylic sink, single lever Delta faucet, 20 cu. in. FF refrigerator. Price, approx. $70,000.
What distinguishes brand from its competition: optional hip roof in sectional series, hardwood cabinetry, all interior trim of wood (not wrapped or painted particleboard), offers a competitively priced entry-level single-section, generous extended warranty
Number of dealerships—Company owned: none
Independents: 150
Percentage of HUD homes sold of total homes produced: 84%
In-house financing? No
In-house Insurance? No
Warranty structure and length: 1 yr. structural top-to-bottom, 2-10 extended ltd. structural warranty through 3rd. party (Home Buyer's Warranty) paid by MHE.
Web site rating: Excellent. Pros: Clean design, welcoming, fast, intuitive, tons of info on features and options, well-organized, well-written content, really reflects well on the company; Cons: clickable photos too small, floor plans should be simple html pages instead of pdf files, features tables could use a better layout.
Comment: Though not well-known outside its upper Midwest region, MHE homes are sold in 27 states, mostly east of the Mississippi, down to the Carolinas. Its modest product line at competitive price points has made for a viable offering for dealers who don't balk at the higher-then-average cost of transporting homes far distances from MHE's single Ohio facility (you know you're dealing w/ modest when two of the 12 "key benefits of a Sectional Home" listed on the MHE web site are: "smoke detectors" and "exhaust fans in all bathrooms"). Prices are controlled in part by offering limited customization.
A company spokesperson explained MHE does some customization but doesn't want any more than they have "because it slows down the production line." In sum, look to MHE for decent affordable housing, with most sectionals priced a click above the pocketbooks of first-time buyers.

Modular One LLC.   (privately held)
1886 Mines Road
Pulaski, TN. 38428
Ph. 931/424-8288   Fax 931/484-8283
Web site: www.modularone.net   See also: www.meadowshomes.net
Background: In 2003, Donny Meadows, co-founder/owner of Meadows Homes, the largest independent chain of MH dealerships in Tennessee, together with two other investors, bought an idle MH factory from Oakwood Homes, Inc., which at the time was in Chap. 11 bankruptcy. The acquisition was the latest in a notable career for Meadows. In 1983 he and his wife Debi purchased a Cookeville, TN MH dealership and over the next 20 years expanded to a chain of eight sales centers, along the way creating their own in-house financing unit, HomeTown Mortgage, an insurance company, and a development division that builds apartments and townhouses. The MH factory, part of Modular One, LLC, builds both modular and HUD-code homes for both their dealership chain and regional retailers outside their market area.
States where sold: TN, KY, AL, FL (coming in 2006: MS, GA)
Principal market niche: home buyers looking for more of a site-built look in a HUD-home in the mid- to high-end price range, a click below modular cost. Very few single-sections or triple-sections but can build to order.
Retail price range before tax (price includes transportation & set-up): $60,000 to $110,000
Competes against: Clayton, Fleetwood, Southern Energy, Cavalier, Palm Harbor
Construction rating: 8
Models:
Heritage – the signature model, roomy two-section, 6/12 pitch, finished dry wall t/o
Anniversary – a higher end Heritage, more features/amenities, stainless steel appliances, 2x6 ext. walls, heavier, some tray ceilings
Description of a popular model: Heritage 30x76 double-section, 3BR, 2BA w/ den and family room, 8/12 roof pitch, 2x6" ext. walls 16" O.C., 9' ext. side walls, flat ceiling, 6" crown molding, finished drywall t/o w/ square corners, vitreous china toilets, acrylic BA sinks, HVAC ducts in ceiling, carpet 25 oz. Shaw w/ 8 lb. rebond pad, floor decking ¾" plywood T&G screwed, glued and sanded
What distinguishes brand from its competition: Exterior elevation very much like site-built, homes built heavier, much more solid, nearly identical to mod construction
Number of dealerships — Company owned: 8
Independents: 10
Percentage of HUD homes sold of total homes

produced: 50%
In-house financing? Yes, HomeTown Mortgage
In-house Insurance? Yes
Warranty structure and length: 1-year structural. Retailers responsible for cosmetic repairs
Web site rating: Unsatisfactory, primitive, a frustrating hodge-podge of incomplete info on single-family HUD and modular models (no distinctions made), and multi-family apartment buildings. Pros: a few good photos, good selection of interior detail pics; Cons: poor design, confusing, no distinction between HUD and modular, only one floor plan, no list of features/options, broken links, pages under construction, no dealer locator.
Comment: While historically quite a few MH builders got their start as retailers (Jim Clayton, for example), that path is rare these days. The Meadows have grown their enterprise carefully, staying within eastern TN and prospering. The Heritage and Anniversary HUD-code homes reflects similar care in providing models that fits perfectly in a niche just below the mod price range, with a roof pitch (6/12) and an exterior very close to site-built. These homes are quite comparable to Palm Harbor models in the same price range. This small builder could become a regional player and will be interesting to watch.

Nashua Homes of Idaho, Inc. (privately held)
5200 Federal Way, PO Box 170008
Boise, ID 83717
Ph. 800/284-6637
Web site: www.nashuahomesofidaho.com
Background: Nashua began in the early 1950s as a small Ohio builder of house trailers, then mobile homes, gradually growing in size to a dozen plants, from CA to the Midwest, including a Boise, ID facility, built in 1956. In 1971 the company was purchased by the conglomerate ConChemCo, keeping its name and brand as a subsidiary. In the late 1970s, three of the Nashua plants (including the ID facility) were sold to the Boca Raton, FL-based Zimmer Corp (sport fishing boats, van conversions, motor homes) The remaining plants were closed or sold. Through these ownership changes, Nashua's ID operation, being relatively remote, was left alone to pursue its own course. In 1987, when the Zimmer Corp. went bankrupt, one of Nashua's ID execs, Milton Barningham, together w/ Boise investor/entrepreneur Ron Yanke, purchase the ID plant and all rights to the Nashua Homes name W. of the Mississippi (aside: Palm Harbor's Lee Posey purchased all rights to the E. of the river, along with Nashua's OH plant, converting the latter into a PH plant and shelving the Nashua Homes name). Since then, Nashua has steadily evolved its product lines, still providing a full range, from singles to triples, but increasingly focusing on the regional market for large doubles placed in scattered rural and mountain settings, particularly second home mountain retreats. Nashua's president Milt Barningham continues active management of the company, overseeing planned growth on the company's modular side.
States where sold: ID, OR, WA, MT, WY, CO, UT, NV, northern CA
Principal market niche: Big two-section houses (1800-2200 sq. ft.) for upscale, Internet-savvy, over 40 professionals and solvent boomers who already own land and who looking for second homes, mountain getaways in the $85,000 - $100,000-plus range.
Retail price range before tax (price includes transportation & set-up): High 40's (single sections) to $130,000
Competes against: Silvercrest, Golden West (medium to high end price range), some Marlette models
Construction rating: 8
Brands/series:
Mountain Retreat Plus – High end two-section w/ prow panoramic front porch
Mountain Retreat – single-section or two section, many plans/options, incl. porches
Nashua Classic 24 – two-sections, 24-wide, to 56' and 64' lengths
Spring Manor – two-sections, 3-4BR, 30'- and 32' wide, lengths 52' to 75'
Villa Series – two-sections, to 4 BR, 26'- and 28' wide, lengths to 68' (incl. Super Villa, w/ 4/12 pitch, 9' flat ceilings, many options)
Spring Manor single-wide – 14-wide, to 67'
Super Triple Wide – triple sections to 2,754
Description of a popular model: Mountain Retreat, #230, two-section, 26'x70', 3BR, 2BA, 1,784 sq. ft. (perimeter frame blocking mandatory) w/ 8' covered prow panoramic porch, steel metal roof w/ 100 lb. snow load, 4/12 roof pitch, 2x6 ext. walls 16" O.C., log siding all around w/ OSB underlayment, 12" eves, vaulted ceiling t/o, T&T dry wall w/ bull nose t/o, R-38/19/22, ¾" Cresdek decking glued and screwed w/ ring shank nails, kitchen island prep station, lg. kitchen window w/ tile ledge, knotty Alder hardwood interior doors, 40 gal. water heater, 19 cu. ft. Whirlpool FF refrigerator, 17 KW elec. furnace, perimeter heat registers (in toe kicks in wet areas)

What distinguishes brand from its competition: Builds no "economy" models, excellent designs and construction, strong consumer orientation, good warranty service.
Number of dealerships—Company owned: none
Independents: 45
Percentage of HUD homes sold of total homes produced: 96%
In-house financing? No
In-house Insurance? No
Warranty structure and length: 1-year. Factory-dispatched techs, cosmetic repairs done by dealer, billed back to factory
Web site rating: Barely adequate, frustrating, badly in need of a complete makeover. Pros: some photos of most models, OK list of construction features, virtual tours fairly helpful, full dealer list accessible, floor plans available, Cons: dreadful design, home page w/ few options, counter-intuitive navigation, no "home" buttons available on pages, annoying use of PDF downloads to view/print enlarged floor plans, no list of options, no explanation of different series, no sense of the company/history/personality.
Comment: This small, well-managed MH builder has done a good job of staying on top of its regional market, correctly anticipating what consumers want and responding quickly to its dealer network's needs for design changes. Case in point: several years ago Nashua introduced a single-section 14-wide 1BR, 1BA mountain cabin getaway that quickly evolved into a gorgeous cedar-sided 1800 sq. ft. full T&T drywall two-section Mountain Retreat with a steel roof (100 lb. snow load), luxury interior and a covered "prow" front porch that retails for $100,000-plus—and the line has become hugely popular, the company's sweet spot. Elsewhere, models with a decidedly site-built look are attracting buyers who would never dream of setting foot on a "mobile home" sales lot. Add to this a solid warranty service record and Nashua easily qualifies for anyone's short list.

Nobility Homes, Inc.   (publicly held)
PO Box 1659   3741 S.W. 7th. St.
Ocala, FL 34478
Ph. 352/732-5157   Fx. 352/732-4203
Web site: www.nobilityhomes.com
Background: Founded in 1967 in Ocala, FL, by Terry Trexler, Nobility Homes got in early on Florida's burgeoning MH sector, focusing on low- to mid-price range affordable housing for first-time home buyers and retirees. The company was profitable from the beginning, went public in 1971, and continued to grow, adding a second plant south of Ocala, and becoming a dominant presence in central and northern FL. In 1994, Nobility acquired the Prestige Home Centers dealership chain to market its homes exclusively, subsequently expanding the chain to 19 company-owned "model centers" operating under the names Prestige Home Centers or Majestic Homes, both advertising the benefits of "factory direct" sales. In 1997 Nobility entered into a joint venture w/ Clayton Homes' financial subsidiary, 21st. Mortgage Corp. to offer in-house financing to home buyers.
Together with its wholly-owned insurance subsidiary, Mountain Financial, Inc., Nobility became a fully vertically integrated MH company, succeeding where other major MH players failed. Nobility also sells homes to about 60 MH land-lease communities and community operators. One of the latter, Mobile Home Lifestyles, accounted for about 13% of Nobility's 2004 sales. In total homes sold yearly in FL, Nobility ranks fifth.
In 2005, Nobility continued its strong growth, reporting remarkable quarterly net revenue increases of 37%. Future plans call for up to 30 sales centers, with plans currently afoot to open two in coastal areas hardest hit by the 2004 hurricanes. Company is also building single-section homes for FEMA following the 2005 Gulf Coast hurricanes.
States where sold: FL, southern GA
Principal market niche: Entry level low end to low mid-range, working families and seniors in MH communities
Retail price range before tax (price includes transportation & set-up): $20,000 to $80,000
Competes against: Fleetwood, Champion, General Manufactured Housing, Clayton, Cavalier
Construction rating: 4
Brands/series: About 100 floor plans and models (incl. Sonny & Cher and Elvis Plus)
Series names: Kingswood, Springwood, Richwood, Springwood Special, Tropic Isle Special, Regency Manor Special, Special Edition.
Description of a popular model: Rosey, 3BR, 2BA, 56x28', 1,378 sq. ft., 2x4" ext. walls. 16" O.C., 3/12 roof pitch, 20-yrs. shingles, int. non-load-bearing walls 2x3" 24" O.C., 7' ext. side wall height, 5/16" dia. wall board covered w/ paper or vinyl, walk-in closets all BRs, 8' covered porch off dining room, dual-knob kitchen faucet, 14 cu. ft. refrigerator, 30 gal. water heater, self-edge Formica-type laminate-on-particleboard countertops, electrical outlet boxes attached to drywall with wing screws.
What distinguishes brand from its competition: The only vertically integrated company located in FL, offers in-house financing/insurance, large selection of floor models, little customization, competitively priced
Number of dealerships—Company owned: 19
Independents: 60 (mostly MH communities)

Percentage of HUD homes sold of total homes produced: 100%
In-house financing? Yes, through Nobility/21
In-house Insurance? Yes, through Mountain Financial, Inc. subsidiary
Warranty structure and length: 1-year, service from factory dispatched crews and regional contracted providers
Web site rating: Unsatisfactory, barely a brochure. Pros: straight-forward navigation, uncluttered, on-line loan and insurance quote applications provided, printable floor plans; Cons: almost no pics of exteriors/interiors, no meaningful list of standard construction specs and upgrades.
Comment: Following multiple faxes and phone messages over a more than two-week period to senior management requesting to speak with anyone, a Nobility staffer called to advise that management had declined the request. Potential buyers of a Nobility home should not be blamed if they find this behavior troubling. Unquestionably, Nobility is a business success story: debt free, $23 million in cash reserves, booming. Founder Terry Trexler is ranked 14th. on Forbes Small Business list of the 25 Richest Executives, owning Nobility stock worth $43.1 million (Trexler and his son Thomas, the company's exec. VP, together own nearly two-thirds of Nobility's stock).

While Nobility touts the advantages of buying "factory direct" from its "model centers," be aware that there is no inherent savings over comparable brands purchased at independent sales centers; Nobility 's sales centers generate 70% of the company's profit. If a call to one Prestige Sales Center is any indication, home shoppers may have their work cut out obtaining reliable product information. The salesman there incorrectly answered four out of five simple questions on standard construction (e.g. 9' ext. side wall ht. instead of 7'), had no idea what VOG or OSB is, and proclaimed that every home, once it leaves the factory, is taken out and subjected to a wind test equivalent to a Category 3 hurricane.

Oak Creek Homes
(A division of American HomeStar, Corp
(privately held)
4805 E. Loop 820 South
Fort Worth, Texas 76119
888/850-9988
Web site: www.oakcreekhomes.com

Background: One of the shooting stars of the 90s ("the Jim Morrison of MH", one wag quipped), American HomeStar began as a merger in 1983 of Texas MH builder Oak Creek Homes and a large area dealership, with the intent of becoming a large, vertically integrated national MH builder (an objective that at the time was music Wall St.'s ears). The company went public in 1994 and became a high flyer. Flush with IPO cash, American HomeStar went on a shopping spree, buying OR-based Guerdon Homes (along with its Nebraska subsidiary, Magnolia Homes), R-Anell Custom Homes of NC, purchased or opened 107 sales centers, opened several more plants (it operated ten at its peak), and continued a steady growth-by-acquisition strategy that pleased stockholders until 1999 when the MH industry abruptly tanked.

So did American HomeStar, declaring Chap. 11 bankruptcy in early 2001. What's left is now privately held and steering a conservative course, with a focus on quality, marketing to its core Southwest buyer base in both MH and modular. Footnote: American HomeStar's well-regarded CEO during its go-go years, Lad Dawson, together with investors, later plucked Guerdon Home's Boise, ID plant from the wreckage, rescuing the Guerdon name and re-launching as Guerdon Homes LLC.

States where sold: TX, OK, CO, NM, KS, AR, LA
Principal market niche: Low end to the very high end, principally in Texas and adjacent states
Retail price range before tax (includes transportation & set-up): $24,000 - $108,000
Competes against: Clayton, Fleetwood, Patriot, Palm Harbor
Construction rating: 8
Description of a popular model: Mid-range: An Oak Creek two section, 3BR, 2BA, 1990 sq. ft., 28' to 32' width, 56' to 64' length, 4/12 roof pitch, tape & texture interiors, Energy Star rated. Base price: approx. $58,000. Low end: the Super Value series single-wide, approx. $24,000.
Oak Creek Series:

Horizon – High end two- and three- sections homes, retailing at $100,000-plus
Meridian —Identical to Horizon, different in name only
Southern Star Limited – Medium price range, average price $58,000
Texas 36 Wide — Medium price range, emphasis on space, to 2310 sq. ft.
Hallmark – Entry level to low medium range.
Galaxy — Same as Hallmark, different in name only
Galaxy Super Value Series – 5 models, single-wide and small double-wides, from $24,000 to $41,000

What distinguishes brand from its competition: Generally better construction features than most competing brands, a seven year warranty, high warranty service level, high end models comparable to site-built.
Number of dealerships—Company owned: 30
Independents: 20
Oak Creek also has display homes at 35 MH community parks.
Percentage of HUD homes sold of total homes produced: 75%
In-house financing: Yes. Can provide construction as well as permanent loans, including conforming mortgage loans
In-house insurance: Yes. Provides own policies as well as writes with all major MH carriers
Warranty structure and length: 7 years: year 1 by the manufacturer, years 2 through 7 by a third party carrier. Warranty is fully transferable if home sold during warranty period.
Web site rating: Excellent. Shopper can pull a lot of information from this site. Well organized.
Comment: This considerably downsized company focuses on the full spectrum of homes from basic entry level homes, up to the highest end homes in market, 80% of them multi-section (up to $108,000), operating two plants. Also produces about half of the modular homes made in Texas. Company enjoys a good reputation, with a good product at a competitive price for its target market of affordable home buyers, principally in Texas. The products produced at the Fort Worth plant are recognized as some of the best built (and higher priced) homes in this market.

Palm Harbor Homes, Inc. Publicly held
15303 Dallas Parkway, Suite 800
Addison, TX 75001
Ph. 972/991-2422   Fx. 972/991-5949
Web site: www.palmharbor.com
Background: One of the most innovative MH companies, Palm Harbor was founded in 1977 by MH veteran Lee Posey (one of the industry's brightest minds) who pioneered the concept of attractive, landscaped model displays directly adjacent to factory locations (which offered tours to the public). Avoiding the low end of the market, Palm Harbor from the outset pursued a strategy of vertical integration—manufacturing, retailing, financing and insuring—and has succeeded where other major builders (e.g. Fleetwood, Champion) failed. Starting in 1992, company built a network of 121 retail "superstores" in 32 states that featured trapped entrances, a landscaped neighborhood ambiance and, until recently, a selling strategy that met with great success as well as criticism for being manipulative and high-pressure (see comments). The company went public in 1995. Palm Harbor also sells through approx. 375 independent retailers, including builders and developers. By resisting involvement in the easy-credit frenzy of the 90s MH boom Palm Harbor survived intact the severe MH downturn of 1999-2004 and remains a strong, stable growing company with a 23% market share. Over 60% of its current loans to home buyers are conforming mortgages, with less than 30% personal property, or chattel, loans (average FICO score, 713). In 2004 company moved into modular production by acquiring Nationwide Homes, subsequently adding mod production capacity to eight of its 18 plants (located in eight states). By the end of 2005, Palm Harbor's modular home production accounted for 18% of the total homes built.
States where sold: FL, NC, SC, AL, GA, MS, TN, VA, WV, MD, CT, DL, TX, OK, AR, LA, NM, AZ, CA, CO, OR, WA, MT, NV,ID,OH,MI,IN, KY, IL, PA, MO. No sales centers in the upper Midwest and New England markets.
Principal market niche: mid-range to high end, Sun Belt working families and retirees (FL and TX together account for 24% of company's annual revenue). Company builds no low-end entry level homes.
Retail price range before tax (price includes transportation & set-up): $50,000-$135,000 (Single-section homes account for only 5%-6% of sales). Average: $73,000.
Competes against: Patriot, Skyline, Commodore, Silvercrest, Cavalier, Jacobsen, Schult, Fuqua of Oregon
Construction rating: 8
Brands/series:
Each of the 18 plants produces at least two series and/or brands designed specifically for that region. Design and features vary. Company web site shows model numbers only. Brand names include:
Palm Harbor, Keystone, River Bend, CountryPlace, Windsor Homes, Masterpiece and Discovery. Of these, the **Discovery** brand is noteworthy:
This home is a HUD-code version of the company's modular brand, **Discovery Custom Homes** and was first made in 2004 by the Oregon factory, targeting two markets: mainstream home buyers and developers looking for site-built homes in the $250,000 - $350,000 price range (including land). Built in three or four sections, 30' wide. Since a variety of architectural structures must be installed on-site, the Discovery requires a special HUD letter authorizing completion on site (vs. at the factory). This series shows great promise. The **Buckeye** model is gorgeous: 6/12 pitch, wrapped porch, articulated exterior, 9' sidewalls, full tape and textured int. walls, stained

marble countertops, island cook top kitchen, huge walk-in pantry. Price. approx. $144,000 delivered to your foundation. States where available: OR, WA, MT, ID, northern CA, Reno, NV area. Look for availability in other regions in 2006.
Description of a popular model: PHT356F4, Blanco, 3BR, 2BA two-section, 28x56, 1736 sq. ft., 3/12 roof pitch, ext. walls 2x6 16" O.C., int. walls VOG, cathedral ceiling, stainless kitchen sink w/ Moen single lever faucet, breakfast nook, walk-in pantry, utility room w/ freezer space, master BR walk-in closet, large master BA. Approx. $70,000.
What distinguishes brand from its competition: the most popular MH brand, generally pricier, better quality standard features, all homes finished out on site by factory-dispatched PH crews, highly customizable, some models indistinguishable from site-built, solid warranty service, top-to-bottom corporate focus on customer satisfaction.
Number of dealerships — Company owned: 135   **Independents:** 375 (including builders, developers w/o sales centers)
Percentage of HUD homes sold of total homes produced: 82%
In-house financing: Yes. Chattel and non-conforming land/home loans offered through PH's 80% owned subsidiary, CountryPlace Mortgage. Conforming and non-conforming HUD real estate mortgage financing available from PH's wholly owned BSM (BankSource Mortgage)
In-house Insurance:? Yes, through PH owned subsidiary, Standard Casualty Company, property and casualty insurance.
Warranty structure and length: Five year "Gold Key Care" covering structure (incl. fireplaces, doors and windows) plumbing system, electrical system and air distribution system.
Web site rating: Excellent, among the best. Pros: well organized, intuitive, attractive, optional viewing in either English or Spanish, good photos/floor plans, robust information on investor relations pages. Cons: no detailed lists of standard construction features and options, little or no information offered on principal brands and series (and where available).
Comment: Attempts to contact Palm Harbor's VP in charge of marketing (fax, email, voice messages) to obtain assistance were not answered, possibly owing to displeasure over the mention in **The Grissim Buyer's Guide to Manufactured Homes and Land** of anecdotal reports, well-known in the MH industry, of over-the-top pressure tactics at many Palm Harbor-owned sales centers. To its credit, Palm Harbor appears to have gotten the message. In 2004, the company reportedly introduced a revamped sales program—Fair Exchange of Information—in training classes at many of its sales centers, designed to tone down its once highly-scripted sales pitch, to make it less structured, less stressful for the buyer. Palm Harbor even deployed teams of phantom shoppers with hidden video cameras to record the performance of its sales associates, later screening the videos at sales training sessions.

Such a concerted effort to correct sales abuses typifies Palm Harbor's close attention to getting it right, across the board. There's certainly no arguing with a 23% MH market share, but in comparison to the rest of the industry, Palm Harbor is something of a culture unto itself.

Still, this is a fair-minded public company that is serious about quality and customer satisfaction: salary compensation is partially pegged to consumer satisfaction ratings (94% approval at last report); any factory assembly worker can stop the production line if a reoccurring problem is spotted; every house in the field, once the installer is through, is trimmed out and finished by a factory-dispatched employee whose bonus is based on the customer rating after move in. Palm Harbor claims that 61% of its home sales derive from customer referrals. A Palm Harbor home tends to be more expensive than comparably featured homes (this is a large corporation to feed) but given the stand-out quality, warranty service, customization and excellent designs (especially exteriors) the extra cost is worth the investment. As for Palm Harbor's sales techniques, doubtless they are improved, but home shoppers concerned about any lingering issues should not hesitate to call a PH sales center to negotiate the terms of their visit.

Patriot Homes, Inc.   Privately held
307 South Main St. #200
Elkhart, IN 46516
Ph. 574/524-8600   Fx. 574/524-8638
Web site: www.patriothomes.com
Background: One of the larger MH builders still privately held, Patriot was founded in 1972 by Sam Weidner, a well-liked and respected industry figure who built the company into a major player in the Great Lakes region (its core market), then expanded to other regions, notably Texas and the Southeast. Owns ten plants (eight currently active). Carefully managed while avoiding the entry level end of the market, Patriot developed a wide range of product lines across all price points, adopted new design and engineering advances as they became available, and cultivated a loyal dealer

network. Company has also been a leader in working with developers and subdivision builders (including some 700-home subdivisions), adapting its designs to their needs, which now accounts for 25% of its homes produced in 2005. All of which enabled the company to maintain stability, and even post modest growth, during the severe '99-'04 market downturn.

States where sold: AL, AR, CO, DE, FA, IL, IN, IO, KS, KY, LA, ME, MI, MN, MS, MO, MT, NE, NH ,NM, NY, OH ,OK, PA, SD, TN, TX, VT, VA, WV, WI, WY

Principal market niche: mid-range to high end in all regions where sold

Retail price range before tax (price includes transportation & set-up): $45,000 - $120,000 Average: $65,000-$70,000

Competes against: Midwest: Champion brands (e.g., Redman, Dutch Housing, Commander, Fortune, Champion), Commodore Homes, Four Seasons. Texas: Palm Harbor, Oak Creek, lower end tract homes built by Pulte, K&B, Centex. Alabama/Florida: Southern Energy, Cavalier, some mid-level Fleetwood

Construction rating: 8

Brands/series:

From Patriot's Midwest plants:

Crystal Valley - Patriot's flagship model, high end, award-winning design, 8' sidewalls, flat ceiling, finished drywall t/o

Heritage American Wakefield series - low end of mid-price range ($45,000+), 8' side wall, finished drywall t/o

Heritage American - High mid- to high-end, 5/12 to 9/12 roof pitch, aver. retail price $70,000+

Lincoln Park Homes - a series w/ low to mid-price points

Independence - single-section homes, VOG wall board, economy features

Ultimate Value - sectional homes, VOG wallboard, 7-1/2' sidewalls, vaulted ceiling

Villa Ridge - Top of this series, 8' sidewalls, VOG wallboard, flat ceilings, hardwood cabinet doors, wrapped wood moldings t/o

Victorian series - From Indiana plant, middle-of-the-line, higher than Lincoln Park and a click below Crystal Valley Homes.

Built in the Alabama plant:

Pinnacle Homes - high end HUD model w/ features a click below Heritage American and a different look for the southern market.

Floridian Series - Also from Alabama plant, same as Pinnacle except quite different in appearance, for the Gulf Coast market: lots of white, open floor plans, more glass.

Southridge Homes - From Alabama plant, similar to Lincoln Park Homes, incl. single-section homes

From the Texas plant (all series designed with southwest look and decor):

Bluebonnet Series - Very high end, 5/12 roof pitch, 9' flat ceilings w/ ceiling air registers, high end features/appliances/trim t/o

Alamo Series - similar to Heritage American Wakefield, 3/12 roof pitch, full T&T walls with square corners t/o, low end of mid-price range

Mission Series - a click or two up from Alamo, 4/12 roof pitch, 30 yr. shingles

Longhorn Series and **Lonestar Series** - both mid-range priced, similar features, Longhorn a click better (5/12 roof pitch, 30 yr. architectural shingles)

Description of a popular model: Heritage American, Arlington Falls, 3BR, 2BA, two-section, 30x70, 2014 sq. ft., 5/12 roof pitch, w/ inset porch, prep island in kitchen, morning room, finished drywall t/o (bull nose corners), 9' sidewall, flat ceilings, vinyl siding w/ lifetime warranty, low E dual pane windows, perimeter heat, cultured marble window sills. Approx. $74,000.

What distinguishes brand from its competition: Excellent quality construction, large selection, many models w/ site-built appearance, well-established retail network, responsive management, strong commitment to customer satisfaction.

Number of dealerships — Company owned: 10 (co-owned) **Independents:** 600 (120 selling exclusively Patriot exclusively

Percentage of HUD homes sold of total homes produced: 75%

In-house financing? Yes, through Patriot Acceptance Corp, licensed in IN, KY, MI, MO, NE, SD, TN, TX, WY

In-house Insurance? Yes, through Global Asset Protection, licensed in 38 states

Warranty structure and length: 1 year bumper-to-bumper, 5 year structural & plumbing. Company takes customer satisfaction seriously. Unresolved warranty problems end up on the desk of a senior V.P. who does not hesitate to personally meet with the concerned homeowner, regardless of the travel distance involved.

Web site rating: Outstanding, everything an MH builder's web site should be for the informed home shopper. Patriot did a complete site redesign/relaunch in 2005. Pros: Click on a state and all homes available are listed with a color illustration of exterior elevation; clicking on image brings up a window providing floor plan, full construction specs, all printable. Tons of info on financing, insurance, company history, top execs, a site map, plus a developer's channel (under construction). Cons: use of Macromedia Flash files requires Flash player, can render page loading from a dial-up connection slow as molasses.

Comment: Patriot is a classy, well-run enterprise that has earned an enviable industry reputation. There is a personal imprint of founder Sam Weidner,Sr. behind this company that has generated a high comfort level. Dealers know when they deal with a plant, they won't be treated in a cold corporate way. They know Sam is there and will step into resolve issues. Home buyers in turn benefit.

Pine Grove Manufactured Homes, Inc.
(privately held)
2 Pleasant Valley Road, PO Box 128
Pine Grove, PA 17963
Ph. 570/345-2011   Fx. 570/345-2676
Web site: www.pinegrovehomes.com
Background: In 1981 the Fanelli family, owners of Riverview Homes, a successful western PA-based chain of eight MH sales centers, launched Pine Grove Homes in eastern PA to build for the state's anticipated influx of retirees taking up residence in MH communities (fact: PA is second only to FL in the number of retirees living there). The Fanellli's subsequently started a nearby sister company, Pleasant Valley Modular Homes. Pine Grove grew steadily, developing a 15-state market presence throughout the NE and the Atlantic region. In recent years the company has drawn raves (and awards) for its gorgeous kitchen and master bath designs, including a French bistro style hearth wall kitchen, an Italian flavored brick oven wall kitchen, and its Venetian master bath (visit their web site). Most of the company's retailers have moved into builder/turn-key providers, with many Pine Grove models sited on private parcels and looking indistinguishable from site built homes.
States where sold: PA, eastern OH, northern VA, WV, DE, MD, NY, NJ, CT, RI, MA, VT, NH, ME
Principal market niche: Two markets: older mom-and-pop MH communities that order 2-3 homes a year, and solvent second and third-time home buyers looking for a substantially constructed high-end MH home that looks like site-built for private property placement, working with a turn-key Pine Grove builder/retailer.
Retail price range before tax (price includes transportation & set-up): $45,000 (small single-section) to $140,000. Note: No triple-section models will be offered in 2006.
Competes against: in MH communities: Ritz-Craft, Marlette. At street sales centers: site-built, high end Commodore (Brookwood series), some high-end Colony Factory Crafted Homes (owned by Commodore)
Construction rating: 8
Brands/series: Pine Grove, models across all designs and price points. For MH communities, offers small 12-, 14-, and 16-wides from 36', and two sections from 20-wide (fm. 36' length). No triple sections, no Capes, but does offer a popular attic model (7/12 pitch, stairs, w/ optional dry wall attic enclosure).
Description of a popular model: #1896, two-section, 3BR, 2BA, 28x60, 1,680 sq. ft., w/ Hearth wall kitchen (w/ hand-laid brick around range area), and Venetian Spa master BA w/ 32 sq. ft. shower, 6-jet whirlpool tub, and extensive wood cabinetry/display shelving, ½" dry wall t/o, T&T, w/ square corners, 2x6 ext. walls, 5/12 roof pitch, 8' int. wall height, flat ceilings, 18 cu. ft. FF refrigerator, 40 gal. water heater, laminate countertops w/ ceramic edge, 25 oz. std. carpet w/ 5-1/2 lb. re-bond pad.
What distinguishes brand from its competition: Base home standard features are upgrades for competitors, designer kitchens and baths unequalled in the industry, retail network largely adapted to builder/turn-key providers, many models indistinguishable from site-built, great flexibility to build smaller models to accommodate older MH community renewals, very good warranty service
Number of dealerships - Company owned: none
Independents: 175 (including MH community owners w/ retail licenses)
Percentage of HUD homes sold of total homes produced: 100%
In-house financing? No
In-house Insurance? No
Warranty structure and length: 1-year w/ option to buy an extended 2 thru ten structural warranty sold by the retailer.
Web site rating: Excellent. Web sites designed by a family relative rarely come up to scratch, but this site, designed by Mathew Fanelli, son of the company president Wayne Fanelli, is one of the MH industry's best. Pros: good design, straightforward, intuitive navigation, larger type is a boon for Boomers needing glasses to read web pages, plenty of content, lots of photos, plenty of feature/option lists; Cons: web pages are 12" wide (vs. industry standard 9"), necessitating hoz. scrolling for many monitor sizes.
Comment: Pine Grove may be the only independently owned HUD-code builder east of the Mississippi (north of the Mason Dixon Line), and they have wisely capitalized on the resources of a skilled work force (paying their employees and families full medical benefits). Company also guessed correctly that the enormous number of solvent retirees moving to PA, and the surge in new MH communities, would create a strong demand for its up-market homes. Pine Grove's highly original designer kitchen and bath options are a knock-out (a must-see on their web site), easily besting competitors like Champion's Ultimate Kitchen. An added plus: many

Pine Grove retailers have learned how to do land-home project and can offer a turn-key home package.

Platinum Homes, LLC (Privately held)
155 county Road 351
Lynn, AL 35575
Ph. 877/557-2469   **Fx.** 205/893-5178
Web site: www.platinumhomes-llc.com
Background: Launched in early 2006 by three well-regarded industry veterans, all recently with Champion Enterprises—Jerry Cummings, Richard Brugge and former Champion CEO Walt Young—Platinum purchased the former American HomeStar plant, a sprawling (170,000 sq. ft., 33 work stations) factory that had been completely remodeled, including overhead cranes for building modulars, just before shutting down when the market tanked in '99. Platinum introduced five model homes at the Tunica Home Show in March, signed up 50 dealers and were off and running. A surprising number of initial orders were for single-wides.
States where sold: AL, MS, LA, FL, TN, AR, GA, KY, MO, TX, OK
Principal market niche: medium to high end, both HUD code and modulars
Retail price range before tax (including transportation and set-up): Single wides: $30,000 - $45,000. Double-wides: $55,000 - $140,000. No triple-wide models yet.
Competes against: Palm Harbor, Deer Valley, Patriot, Fleetwood, Southern Energy
Construction rating: 6
Brands: Platinum Series
Description of a popular model: Platinum P-601 DW, 32x58, 1740 sq.ft., 3 BR, 2BA, 4.25/12 roof pitch, 2x4 ext. & int. walls 16" O.C., ½" dry wall t/o T&T, 8' flat ceilings (9' optional), overhead AC/heat registers, 19 oz. carpet (tack strip secured), 7lb. rebond pad, floor decking ¾" plywood glued and nailed, elect. outlet boxes secured by wing tabs, hand-laid vinyl tile (12" squares), hinges on int. doors surface mounted, GE appliances, kitchen cabinets MDF w/ hidden hinges, single lever faucet, Formica counters w/ ceramic edge trim/backsplash. Approx: $63,000, incl. factory trim-out.
What distinguishes brand from its competition: many upgrade features are standard, (e.g., T&T w/ 8' and 9' ceilings, ceiling mounted registers), optional factory trim-out package ($3k), high degree of factory quality control, veteran mgmt. (500 years combined ind. experience), commitment to customer satisfaction, new company, no warranty track record.
Number of dealerships—Company owned: none
 Independents: 50+
Percentage of HUD code homes sold of total homes produced: 95% (but modulars will increase by 2007)
In-house financing: No
In-house insurance: No
Warranty structure and length: 1 year, 3 factory-dispatched teams, plus contract providers in the region.
Web site rating: Unsatisfactory. Pros: crisp clickable floor plans of all models, full dealer listings by state, useful mortgage calculator. Cons: Woefully incomplete, unattractive design, no list of standard features and/or upgrades, About Us page blank, few photos (and those are too small, out of focus, unprofessional), several broken links.
Comment: In the highly competitive Southeast MH market, Platinum sees its competitive niche in offering T&T dry wall w/ bull nose corners (in single wides as well), 8' and 9' flat ceilings, overhead AC and heat registers standard, hand-laid tiles and a 4/12 to 6/12 roof pitch, all at competitive price points. Company plans to move into modulars to meet the post-Katrina rebuilding demand. With a state-of-the-art plant, Cummings' decades of plant management and Young's proven corporate savvy, this start-up can be expected to deliver a well-made product and be responsive on warranty service. Note: Ex-Champion CEO Young is also an investor in (and board chair of) PA-based start-up Eagle River Homes, a builder of low end entry-level homes.

R-Anell Housing Group, LLC   (privately held)
3549 N. Highway 16 PO Box 428
Denver, NC 28037
Ph. 800/951.5511   **Fx.** 704/483-5674
Web site: www.r-anell.com
Background: Note: While R-Anell was a HUD-code home builder for much of its history, today its products are more than 98% modular, but it can build a home to HUD-code requirements if desired. Hence its inclusion in this guide. Builder and entrepreneur Rollan Jones founded R-Anell in 1971 in Denver, NC, west of Charlotte, and gradually became a strong presence in the region with two plants on the Denver, NC property, then opening a third plant 25 miles away in Cherryville. During the 1990s, R-Anell began expanding into the modular field. In 1999, just as the MH market was about to tank, the company was sold to American HomeStar which was on the tail end of an acquisition spree that plunged it into bankruptcy a year later. In 2001, the Jones family purchased R-Anell back from American HomeStar. Throughout this period, R-Anell never missed a beat and prospered, largely due to its shift to the modular home market, and its strong growth continues.
Trivia item: The name R-Anell is a semi-phonetic spelling of the first two initials of Rollan L. Jones'

name. "How about "R and L Housing?" he had asked his then-wife Marilyn. "Great," she replied. "R-Anell it is."
States where sold: AL, FL, GA, NC, SC, TN, VA, WV
Principal market niche: modular home buyers, from 1,000 sq. ft. to 6,000 sq. ft., 3-11 box homes
Retail price range (HUD only) before tax (price includes transportation & set-up): $115,000 - $140,000 (for a 3-box)
Competes against: site built homes
Construction rating: 9
Brands/series: Note: All HUD-code models are basically modular homes built on an open web design floor truss (a 10" floor, in modular speak), then mounted on a permanent steel chassis to conform w/ HUD code.
R-Anell series - high end, in ranch, cape or craftsman configuration. Approx. $140,000
Gold Medal line - a click below R-Anell series, usually two sections w/ a tag, approx. 2,100 sq. ft. approx. $115,000 - $120,000
Description of a popular model: Gold Medal, 2-section + a tag on back, 3BR, 2BA w/ family room/den, 6/12 hinged roof, 2x6 ext. walls 16" O.C., 9' int. wall ht., flat ceilings t/o, T&T dry wall w/ bull nose corners t/o, sweated copper fittings, island in kitchen, bar kitchen (opening separating kitchen from living), 18 cu. ft. FF refrigerator, rounded edge laminate countertops w/ ceramic backsplash, decking ¾" OSB glued and nailed w/ ring shank nails, 40 gal. water heater. ext. siding PolarWall (foam-backed vinyl, w/ R-4 value), 25 oz. carpet. About $118,000.
What distinguishes brand from its competition: Excellent customer service t/o the entire process, continuous quality improvement program, competitive price, good builder network
Number of dealerships—Company owned: none
Independents: 60 (most are general contractors and developers, many who also do site-built projects)
Percentage of HUD homes sold of total homes produced: 2% (less than 20 HUD homes per year)
In-house financing? No
In-house Insurance? No
Warranty structure and length: 1-year factory serviced, plus a 2-10 Homebuyers warranty paid by R-Anell
Web site rating: OK but disappointing for the informed home shopper. Pros: Good straightforward design (even has a site map), good illustrations of model exteriors, easily viewed floor plans printable from screen; Cons: no listing of construction specs/options; no listing of dealers, some buttons don't work, About R-Anell and History pages have identical text and no history beyond the 1971 founding year, site in general lacks personality, depth. The site feels one-way, not inter-active, as though it were there primarily to harvest sales leads from visitors, not deliver meaningful content to educated buyers. Example: No way can you see a list of builders in your area; you submit info and one will contact you. Similarly, the Contact Us page is primarily geared as a sales lead generator. In sum, not customer friendly.
Comment: As mentioned above, R-Anell is almost entirely a modular builder but deserves a listing here because it can build a heck of a HUD-conforming home if specifically ordered. Its recent award wining model, the Preston, is a 3BR 2BA charmer worth a web site visit. If there is an R-Anell builder in your area (ask on the web site), it may be worth your while to explore the possibilities of moving over to modular, especially given the availability of conventional financing.

Ritz-Craft Corp. of Pennsylvania
(privately held)
15 Industrial Park Road, PO Box 70
Mifflinburg, PA 17844
Ph. 570/966-1053   Fx. 570/966-9248
Web site: www.ritz-craft.com
Background: Founded in 1954 in Argos, IN as a modest builder of "mobile homes," Ritz-craft grew steadily before merging in the early 1970s with the Wickes Corp., the sprawling Michigan-based supplier of lumber & building materials (the Wickes Lumber chain). The move allowed Ritz-Craft to expand facilities to offer modular homes. In 1976 four of Ritz-Craft's original managers together bought the company from Wickes, relocating its HQ to a single plant in Mifflinburg, PA. Since then the company has grown as a major factory home builder (mostly mods) with five plants (in PA, MI and NC), 1,000 employees, and over $100 million in annual sales revenue. Its HUD-code homes, all built in the PA plant, are almost all destined for land-lease communities and today represent only about 20% of its total home production.
States where sold: PA, NY, NJ, MI, ME, NH, VT, MA, CT, RI, MD, DE, VA, OH, IN, IL, WI, NC, WV, KY, MO, TN, SC, GA, FL
Principal market niche: Upscale seniors/retirees moving into high end 55+ land/lease communities.
Retail price range before tax (includes transportation and set-up): $100,000 to

$185,000, with the average high end price around $145,000-$150,000.
Competes against: Pine Grove, Skyline, New Era
Construction rating: 8
Brands/series: the LXE II sectional models
Description of a popular model: Ranch model 2511, 3BR, 2BA, 1,640 sq. ft., 28x60, 5/12 roof pitch, w/ front porch (white vinyl porch posts/railings, composite lumber porch decking), 8' ext. side walls, full finish painted dry wall (& ceiling) t/o, bull nose corners, flat ceiling, plush 30 oz. carpet throughout (excluding wet areas), oak panel cabinets (drawer over doors in kitchen), Corian countertops, Moen faucets t/o, 2"x6" headers over doors/windows, 17 cu. ft. FF refrigerator, window grids between dual pane Low E vinyl windows, 40 gal. water heater, sub floor 5/8" thick OSB in 14' sheets.
What distinguishes brand from its competition: Lots of customization, outstanding engineering staff, most home elevations indistinguishable from site-built (introduced optional hip roof packages in 2005), strong training program to "follow the customer, not the competition," high quality construction, a stable growing company and seasoned builder network.
Number of dealerships—Company owned: none
Independents: less than 15
Percentage of HUD homes sold of total homes produced: 25%
In-house financing? No
In-house Insurance? No
Warranty structure and length: 1 year top-to-bottom, years 2 through 9 limited structural, provided through third party insurer, paid for by Ritz-Craft.
Web site rating: Outstanding, among the very best. Pros: Clean, well-thought out design, fast and intuitive navigation, tons of information. Excellent use of multi-media: corporate video, slide shows (esp. the construction photo tour) and well-produced QuickTime virtual tours. Cons: HUD code homes not properly identified (LXE II sectional series nowhere to be seen), some photos missing, needs more HUD model names in place of blah numbered floor plans.
Comment: In an industry recently characterized by a great deal of consolidation by the largest players (e.g., Champion Enterprises, Clayton Homes), Ritz-Craft is one of the few remaining small, privately held builders of high end factory-built homes (it's ranked tenth as a mod builder)—and it really has its act together. Its business model is not based on a traditional dealer network. Instead, about 80% of its HUD-code models are sold to upscale 55+ buyers moving into exclusive land-lease communities in the NE and Mid-Atlantic states where the homes are part of turn-key packages ranging from $100,000 to as high as $425,000. With less than 15 sales centers selling the MH product, home shoppers should go to the Ritz-Craft web site and submit an online request for a dealer-builder in their area, and/or visit one of the company's three corporate models centers (in PA, MI, and NC).

River Birch Homes, Inc. (privately held)
400 River Birch Drive
Hackleburg, AL 35564
Ph. 888/760-3314   Fx. 205/935-3567
Web site: www.riverbirchhomes.com
Background: Founded in 1997 by a pair of industry veterans, Delmo Payne and Gerald Terrell (Payne is a former protégé of Steve Logan, founder of Buccaneer Homes, which evolved into Cavalier), River Birch in many ways exemplifies an old school builder: produce low end homes with no customization and a limited number of floor plans (SW's, 28' wides, 32-wides only) During the industry down turn ('99-'04), the company struggled, as did most SE builders, but efficient management and a seasoned sales force enabled it to survive. With over 100 dealers in ten SE states, River Birch has found a profitable niche in the highly competitive tier of low end affordable housing.
States where sold: LA, MS, GA, KY, MO, SC, TN , FL, AR, OK,
Principal market niche: low end to low-mid range affordable housing
Retail price range before tax (price includes transportation & set-up): $39,900 to $68,000
Competes against: Liberty, Waverlee, Titan, Fleetwood, Giles, Cappaert
Construction rating: 4
Series: Stonebirch—single-section and double-section. Singles from 1,088 sq. ft. to 1,216 sq. ft. Doubles 1,080 sq. ft. to 2,280 (3 to 5 BR)
Description of a popular model: Model 4027, 64x28, 3BR, 2BA, 1,560 sq. ft., 3/12 roof pitch, ext. walls 2x4" 16" O.C., int. wall ht. 7', VOG 3/8" dia., wrapped molding, 5/8" particleboard sub floor, HVAC ducts in floor median line, single pane windows, kitchen island w/ stainless sink, walk-in closet from master BA, 30 gal. water heater
What distinguishes brand from its competition: Fewer floor plans, no customization, fewer options, a competitive price point
Number of dealerships—Company owned: none
Independents: 100-plus
Percentage of HUD homes sold of total homes produced: 100%
In-house financing? No
In-house Insurance? No
Warranty structure and length: 1-year
Web site rating: Good - still a work in progress but quite useful. Pros: well-organized, intuitive navigation,

good photos (incl. exteriors), all floor plans listed for viewing, good on-line warranty service forms; Cons: some unfinished pages, not enough detail on std. features lists, annoying clunky use of large PDF files for download floor plan/features when a simple, printable html page would suffice, no dealer list or dealer locator,

Comment: Multiple faxes and voice mail messages over a two week period to River Birch's sales and marketing director were not answered. For a company that boasts on its web site that the three basic "C"s of its success are "communication, cooperation and commitment," prospective buyers of River Birch's homes should not be blamed if they find such behavior troubling. The company may be clueless about media inquiries but give it credit for providing basic affordable housing, especially single-section homes, at competitive price points. In the SE there is a market for these products. Note: in the aftermath of hurricanes Katrina and Rita the company built single-section homes for FEMA for temporary housing in the Gulf area.

ScotBilt Homes, Inc. (privately held)
2888 Fulford Road, PO Box 1189
Waycross, GA 31502
Ph. 912/490-7268   Fx. 912/490-7276

Web site: www.scotbilt.com

Background: In business just over a year, ScotBilt Homes is the third MH company founded by veteran industry pro Sam Scott who got his start in the 1970s working for Nobility Homes. In the early 1980s he launched Scott Housing Systems, building exclusively HUD-code homes, growing the enterprise to ten plants before selling his interest. In 1990 Scott founded General Manufactured Housing, also HQ'ed in Waycross, focused on low-end homes, taking the company into the MH boom years and selling it in 1996 to a deep pockets NY investment group that was all set to take the company public when the MH market tanked. Following a nine-year hiatus (which Scott could easily afford; he made many millions on the sale), he has once again returned to the marketplace, this time with a management team comprised of former execs at General Housing, including his son Greg Scott. Eschewing single-sections and triples, ScotBilt's market distinction is affordable housing with a 4/12 roof pitch, 8' int. wall height, flat ceilings, and VOG w/o batten strips as standard features.

States where sold: GA, FL, SC, NC, AL, MS, LA

Principal market niche: low end to low end of mid-range double-sections, principally GA, FL

Retail price range before tax (price includes transportation & set-up): $35,000 to $65,000

Competes against: Cavalier, Southern Energy, Homes of Merit

Construction rating: 4

Brands/series:

Cape Coral - 2 BR only, double-sections, principally for retirees in MH communities

Legend - A larger house, offering 3 to 5 BRs, to 28' wide

Heritage - The 32-wide series, up to 32x77, 2,225 sq. ft.

Description of a popular model: Legend, 28x44, 3BR, 2 BA w/ front entry into kitchen/dining area, angled bay windows, optional overhead HVAC ducting, kitchen island sink (acrylic, w/ single lever faucet), MBR walk-in closet, 4/12 roof pitch, 20-yr. shingles, ext. walls 2x4 16" O.C., 8' int. wall ht., 2x4 int. walls 24" O.C., flat ceilings (pop corn on wall board), 5/8" VOG t/o, w/ straight corners, no batten strips (tape is used), 5/8" plywood floor decking, R-11/13/21 insulation, 9 over 9 single pane windows, cultured marble window sills, 16 oz. Shaw carpet, self-edged Formica countertops w/ 4" ceramic backsplash, 18' refrigerator, 40 gal. water heater.

What distinguishes brand from its competition: New company, 8' int. sidewalls, flat ceiling, 4/12 pitch standard, VOG w/ tape instead of batten strips on panel seams, "marble" window sills on some models, a guaranteed service call w/in 12 days of a request, a 12 yr. limited structural warranty, scant customer service track record.

Number of dealerships—Company owned: none
Independents: 91

Percentage of HUD homes sold of total homes produced: 100%

In-house financing? No
In-house Insurance? No

Warranty structure and length: 1-year, plus a 2-through-12 year limited structural warranty (roof, floor, walls only) at no cost to consumer, from Manufacturer's Guardian, Inc.

Web site rating: So so, but incomplete, leaves the informed shopper wanting more. Pros: simple, straightforward layout, good content on management's background, printable floor plans from the screen, list of standard features a start, good Contact Us page w/ email addresses of principals; Cons: photos too small (unclickable to enlarge), confusing use of term "special standard features" (which appear to be options for certain models), no list of options/upgrades, warranty link

downloads a one-page certificate stating only that Scotbilt has qualified for a 12 yr. coverage but no description provided and no contact info on insurer (not even Google helped!), dealer locator is useless, listing only towns, not names/contact info of dealers.
Comment: In the crowded, highly competitive low end of the SE market (which in many ways is a universe unto itself), Scotbilt is a new product launch attempting to differentiate its brand from competing lines, in this case offering as standard features: a 4/12 roof, an 8' side wall, flat ceilings, and VOG w/ no battens, and optional "marble" window sills—all good selling points. The homes generally are nice looking, but a closer look discloses examples of poor construction quality: 2x4 ext. walls, int. walls 24" O.C., single pane windows, floor mounted center-line HVAC ducts, no water shut-offs at water fixtures, acrylic kitchen sink, 24" deep countertops, 16 oz. carpet, and electrical outlet boxes attached to the wallboard w/ clips. This said, many home buyers may feel these shortcomings are outweighed by the price points, the floor plan and other intangibles, in which case Scotbilt is worth their consideration.

Shamrock Homes (privately held)
1201 W. Markley Road
Plymouth, IN 46563
Ph. 574/935-5111   Fx. 574/935-4015
Web site: www.shamrock-homes.com
Background: In 1969 Patrick Flynn, a veteran MH exec who had worked for several builders, including Boise Cascade (which at one point owned an MH subsidiary), struck out on his own, founding Shamrock Homes, convinced there was a niche for a regional builder of high end MH constructed on par with conventional site-built homes. He was right. Shamrock homes early on developed a rep for a quality product, even its single-section homes for MH communities. In 1995 the company added modulars to its mix, offering the ability to build almost any of its models to either code. By design, this family-owned company has stayed small, avoiding the worst of the MH industry's recent down turn and maintaining a level of quality control that has earned the company high marks.
States where sold: IL, IN, MA, MI, MO, NJ, NY, OH, PA, RI, WI
Principal market niche: high-end HUD homes with lots of customization, but models across all price points
Retail price range before tax (price includes transportation & set-up): $22,000 (for a very small single-section, for an MH community) to $330,000 (for a loaded triple-section – As a Shamrock spokesman quipped, "If it costs more than a quarter-million, it's no longer a house trailer.")
Competes against: site-built, Ritz-Craft, Rochester Homes, Hi-Tech Housing, Wick Building Systems
Construction rating: 9
Brands/series:
Shamrock single-wides and tag units – 12, 14 & 16 ft. wide designs, 44' to 80" (your floor plan or theirs), 10' wides available on special request; tag units 8x28', 36', 40' and 44.' 10- & 12-wide tags available.
Regency Park – sectionals at mid-price point and up, 720 sq. ft. to 1,722 sq. ft.
Residential – High end sectionals: package homes and customized
Description of a popular model: Residential, two-section, 28x60, 1,493 sq. ft., 3BR, 2BA, w/ morning room, ext. walls 2x6" 16" O.C., 7/12 roof pitch, 30-yr. shingles, 90" ext. side wall ht., ½" finished, painted dry wall t/o, Low E vinyl thermal windows, 39 oz. carpet, residential draperies, fireplace w/ stone front, 40 gal. water heater, furnace compartment dry wall finished w/ auto sprinkler safety system, ¾" T&G plywood decking, two 32'x32' skylights, Delta single-lever faucets at sinks, tubs/showers, R-30/19/19 insulation, Wilsonart "quarry finish" laminate kitchen countertops, closed heating/return air system w/ perimeter ducts.
What distinguishes brand from its competition: Residential construction quality, high degree of customization (incl. handicap accessible), closed heating/return air system, superior in-house made cabinetry, quality fit and finish, residential look and feel, excellent warranty service.
Number of dealerships—Company owned: none
Independents: 60
Percentage of HUD homes sold of total homes produced: 70%
In-house financing? No
In-house Insurance? No
Warranty structure and length: 1-year, lifetime on many appliances/fixtures, "but," added a spokesman, "pretty much as long as you're kind to us, we'll take care of you."
Web site rating: Good, but needs work. Site is undergoing revision/construction. Pros: Good organization, straightforward navigation, good photo selection of exteriors; Cons: no specs/options listed for Residential series, no text/icon link to home page from other pages, dated design and layout.
Comment: This small company (55 employees, building on average a floor a day) has quietly prospered by sticking to its business model and capitalizing on its ability to highly customize floor plans, including the creative use of tag additions. Add to this what may be the MH industry's only closed heating system with dedicated return air ducting (even in single-sections) and an in-house cabinet shop that Shamrock maintains

is the finest in the industry, and the result is a HUD home that ranks with the top high end builders in the region. This company deserves to be on the short list for home buyers desiring a residential look and feel, along with a cost savings over site-built.

Silver Creek Homes, Inc. (privately held)
P.O. Box 150
Henrietta, TX 76365
Ph. 940/538-6600
Web site: www.silvercreekhomestexas.com
Background: This small, exclusively HUD-code builder near the Okalahoma border 90 miles north of Dallas-Fort Worth, was founded in 1998 by MH veteran David Silvertooth, whose early career was with Texas builder, Sunrizon Homes, followed by a stint as sales manager for Mississippi low-end builder Cappaert Homes. In the early 90s, Silvertooth left Cappaert, returning to Texas to start his own company, Crest Ridge Homes, which several years later he sold to Champion Enterprises, Inc. when the latter was buying up independent builders left and right (Champion subsequently closed Crest Ridge when the MH market tanked). Like Cappaert's products, Silver Creek's homes are entry level low end with the bland, boxy exterior of a "mobile home," but the company claims it has built over 7,000 of them so the demand, particularly in Texas (Silver Creek's principal market) is certainly there, particularly for those wanting as much home as possible for a growing family.
States where sold: TX, AK, CO, KS, OK, NM
Principal market niche: entry level to low mid-range, affordable housing
Retail price range before tax (price includes transportation & set-up): $39,000 to $78,000
Competes against: Fleetwood, Cavalier, Southern Energy, River Birch, Waverlee
Construction rating: 4
Series:
Silver Creek II – single-section and double-section homes in more than 50 floor plans, with some flexibility for customization.
Description of a popular model: SC II 3768, 4BR, 3 BA, 30x76 2,280 sq. ft. 3/12 roof pitch, 2x4 ext. walls 16" O.C., int. wall ht. 7-1/2', VOG 3/8" dry wall, large family room, adjoining BA between BR 3 & 4, retreat room off master BR, island work station in kitchen, self-edge Formica countertops, R-14/11/11, 30 gal water heater. A lot of house for a growing family but a 4 construction rating suggests home may not appreciate in value.
What distinguishes brand from its competition: Nothing special but company's north Texas location allows lower transport costs to regional dealerships, resulting in a competitive price. Company has no brochures and scant literature to either dealers or potential customers.
Number of dealerships — Company owned: none
Independents: 61 (36 of them in Texas)
Percentage of HUD homes sold of total homes produced: 100%
In-house financing? No
In-house Insurance? No
Warranty structure and length: 1 year structural
Web site rating: Poor, minimal, unsatisfactory for informed home shoppers. Pros: good selection of interior photos (and even a couple of exteriors), floor plans are crisp, printable html pages, ea. w/ an architect's drawing of ext. elevations; Cons: no listing of features and specs, options, photos too small, site in general is little more than an incomplete brochure.
Comment: Multiple faxes and voice mail messages over a two week period requesting to speak to any Silver Creek spokesperson were not answered. Potential buyers of Silver Creek homes should not be blamed if they find such behavior troubling. Silver Creek, like a comparable low end builder, Alabama-based River Birch, has found its niche producing a line of mostly entry-level affordable housing for its regional market, in this case, the south central US. If you're mostly price-driven, homes in this series have more features for their price than models in the Silver Creek II series. Anecdotally, there were some construction shortcomings reported on a delivered home, but to its credit Silver Creek eventually came through and made the customer happy.

Skyline Corporation (publicly held)
PO Box 743 2520 By-Pass Road
Elkhart, IN 46515
Ph. 574/294-6521   Fx. 574/293-7574
Web site: www.skylinehomes.com
Background: In 1951 several partners, including co-founder Arthur Decio, took over an Elkhart, IN house trailer factory shut down by its previous owners, and launched Skyline. The company was soon building structures more akin to mobile homes to meet the growing demand for affordable permanent housing. Skyline thrived, went public in 1959, and a year later opened its first travel trailer plant. By 1965 Decio's face (along w/ four others) appeared on the cover of a Time magazine story on America's most successful under-40 entrepreneurs.

Today Skyline produces ten brands of towed RVs (e.g., Nomad, Aljo, Layton, Forest Brook) and builds its extensive model line of homes under the Skyline Homes brand (the latter representing 74% of the company's $454 million annual sales). Known for its conservative management (occasionally autocratic, some observers say), Skyline early on invested part of its earnings in US Treasury Bills (in 2005 valued at $138 million)—earning the sobriquet "the bankers" among its dealers—a prudent strategy for cushioning the inevitable down turns in two historically cyclic industries. In its 54 years, Skyline has never had a losing quarter, is debt-free, and is highly regarded in the MH and RV industry.

States where sold: All except HI and AK
Principal market niche: mid- to high-end, but models across all price points
Retail price range before tax (price includes transportation & set-up): high 20s (Single sections) to $110,000
Competes against: Silvercrest, Karsten, Palm Harbor, Fuqua, Commodore, Valley, Hallmark Southwest, Burlington, Nashua, Castle, Fleetwood (with some lower priced models)
Construction rating: 8
Brands/series: Skyline's 16 MH plants around the country each build several series of homes with floor plans and ext. elevations reflecting regional tastes and market demographics. See company's web site for extensive photos by region. Here's a breakdown of principal series:
Kensington Park – High end models, larger windows, expansive floor plans, many upgrade features standard
Lexington and the **Lexington Park** – a click below but still high end two- and three-section homes, different floor plans
The Silver series – package homes at the mid-price range, including **The Ramada** model, with entertainment options (e.g., HDTV) to compete with Fleetwood's "The Entertainer" model
The Greenbrier – mid- range, many floor plans, w/ upgrades comparable to Lexington models
Below this tier are several series in the entry level and low end price range. Examples:
Springview – comparable to Fleetwood's low end Beacon Hill, e.g., a 5 BR, 3 BA, 28x80 for $60,000
The Hampshire – Two section, low end, a 4 BR model in the low 50s
Greenbrier Ltd – low end, mostly single-section models
Skyview, Chapparall – low end series
Description of a popular model: Greenbrier 6329 (for retirement living), 2BR, 2BA, two-section, 27x60 1,314 sq. ft., w/ covered porches on both ends, recessed can porch lights, 4/12 roof pitch, cathedral ceiling throughout, 7-1/2' int. wall ht., T&T dry wall t/o, retreat room, walk-in closet MBR, skylights in kitchen and MBA, 50 gal. water heater, pendent lights over kitchen snack bar, graduated fiberglass heat ducts, upgrade carpet. Price as optioned: $76,300
What distinguishes brand from its competition: Excellent construction in well-run factories, superior finish work, stable well-capitalized company, well-established reputable dealer network, superior warranty, not much customization flexibility (and not at all plants)
Number of dealerships—Company owned: none
Independents: 440
Percentage of HUD homes sold of total homes produced: 81%
In-house financing? No
In-house Insurance? No
Warranty structure and length: 15 months full warranty, backed by a corporate service department and an extensive field service system.
Web site rating: OK but ultimately short on the specifics that informed home shoppers need. Pros: good design/navigation, outstanding factory tour (the best of any MH web site, well worth the time to view – could any factory possibly be cleaner?), excellent photo collection of homes by regional shows (lots of exteriors, for a change); Cons: no mention of modular homes/models/descriptions (while claiming to build both), no lists of construction features, specs, or options.
Comment: Multiple faxes and phone messages over a more than two-week period to Skyline's senior executive VP in charge of marketing & sales, requesting to speak with him or anyone he designated, were unanswered. Potential buyers of a Skyline home should not be blamed if they find this behavior troubling. This said, Skyline is an industry stand-out, conservatively managed, deep pockets, stable, makes a fine MH, has a strong national network of reputable independent dealers (during the 90s go-go years, company wisely avoided acquiring dealerships) and gets high marks for prompt warranty service and a customer satisfaction ratings program that keeps dealers on their toes. Its plants are clean, efficient and well run, building homes that are solid but not particularly imaginative (a creative home buyer can largely remedy this with options). Dealers love Skyline because it is rock solid, reliable, and responsive. Skyline's low-profile founder, 76-year old Arthur Decio, Skyline's board chairman and a prominent philanthropist (and a respected legend in Elkhart) is no longer active as a day-to-day executive but still jogs each morning before starting his day. With a 17% ownership in the company, he remains very much a presence behind the Skyline brands, both on the MH and RV sides. Footnote: In the aftermath of

Hurricane Katrina, when FEMA contacted Skyline to place a large order of single-section homes, Skyline refused to profit by back dooring its dealer network, instead advising the agency to place orders through its dealers so that they could share in any profits. That's class.

Solitaire Homes, Inc. (privately held)
7605 Nickles Road
Duncan, OK 73533
Ph. 580/252-6060   Fx. 580/252-6072
Web site: www.solitairehomes.com
Background: Founded in 1965 by Jerry and Helen Elliott, this regional builder has operated quietly out of the limelight, avoiding the temptation to over expand during boom times (not even into modulars), instead opting to stay within its five-state market and enlarging its footprint. In 1985, years before the last cyclical upturn of the early 1990s, Solitaire began a strategy of vertical integration, acquiring established dealerships and building new ones in a five state market, and building new production facilities.
By the late 1990s the company had five plants in operation (four of which it had built, and one acquired – the old Signal Homes facility in Big Springs, TX, which had been operating for only two years). Early this decade, Solitaire partnered with Origin Financial to create Solitaire Financial Services to provide in-house financing for home purchases. Solitaire-owned dealerships also offer several homeowner insurance packages through a third party provider. The Elliott's have retired from active management. Solitaire currently owns 27 dealerships, and is producing homes at four of its five plants, all 100% HUD code.
States where sold: OK, TX, NM, AZ, LA, MS, KS, AR
Principal market niche: low mid-range, retirees, professionals, Boomers, second-time MH buyers
Retail price range before tax (includes transportation and set-up): $35,000-$110,000
Competes against: Clayton, Fleetwood, Oak Creek, Skyline, Palm Harbor, Cavco
Construction rating: 7
Brands/series:
Imperial series – mid- to high-end, T&Painted dry wall t/o, square corners (rounded corners optional), 8' flat ceiling, $55,000-$90,000
R-Series – A click below Imperial series, 2x6" ext. walls (2x4" for SW's), vaulted ceiling, 7-1/2' side wall ht, T&Painted ½" dry wall, 18 oz. carpet stapled to floor, $35,000 to $70,000
Lancer series - Solitaire's brand for its independent dealers, essentially the same as the Imperial and R-Series, w/ a few changes in floor plans, features.
Description of a popular model: Imperial series, two-section, 4BR, 2-1/2BA, two living areas, recessed entry, walk-in closets all BRs, brkfst. nook w/ angled bay windows,
What distinguishes brand from its competition: Many standard features are upgrades for competitors, vertically integrated company (but homes also sold by independent dealers), offers in-house financing/insurance, stays within its regional market, high customer satisfaction.
Number of dealerships—Company owned: 27
Independents: 15-20
Percentage of HUD homes sold of total homes produced: 100%
In-house financing? Yes.
In-house Insurance? Yes.
Warranty structure and length: 1-year covering structural and cosmetic repairs. Factory-dispatched techs do most warranty service, but dealer and contract service as well. See comment.
Web site rating: OK, but leaves out specifics that informed home shoppers need. Pros: Generally good design, intuitive navigation, excellent interior photos, virtual tours, lots of content, good over all intro to first-time MH buyers Cons: Outdated, not a single photo of a home exterior, very annoying use of pdf downloads for floor plans (requires closing of two windows and launching Acrobat – a frustrating, clueless use of technology), no "Home" icon on every page requires time-consuming back clicks to return to Solitaire home page, no company history to speak of, Dealer locator not-functioning.
Comment: Solitaire has been a conservative presence in its carefully defined market, but it stuck to its knitting during the 90's go-go years and thus continued to operate at a profit during the '99-'04 downturn (perhaps alone among companies in its region). The company has also found ways to build a quality, affordable home with construction specs generally a click above average (e.g., a 22 cu. ft. FF refrigerator std., a Solitaire "exclusive feature:" adding atop the floor joists a grid of 2x3"s running the length and width of the floor, enabling the use of slightly thinner plywood decking [5/8"] without loss of structural strength.) Also helping to keep the price points competitive: only 19 floor plans and minimal customization. Noteworthy: In a 2002 Consumers Union study of consumer complaints in Texas, Solitaire had the least number of complaints (.4% per 100 homes titled) of the 14

largest manufacturers selling there. That amounts to just 8 complaints on 1,820 homes built over four years, a remarkable indication of high customer satisfaction.

Sunshine Homes, Inc. (privately held)
100 Sunshine Avenue, P.O. Box 507
Red Bay, AL 35582
Ph. 256/4427 Fx. 256/352-8250
Web site: www.sunshinehomes-inc.com
Background: In 1971 Fred Bostick, owner of Sunshine Meals, a successful dog and cat food company in the small northeast AL town of Red Bay (named after the tree) was troubled that a next door MH plant owned by Commodore was closing. Motivated in part to save jobs, he bought the facility and launched Sunshine Homes. His thinking: dog food sales are slow in the summer and brisk in the winter, just the opposite of the MH business, so one company would always be busy. Sunshine not only prospered from the outset, but in a brilliant bit of marketing, Bostick had a bag of Sunshine dog food placed beneath the kitchen sink of every new Sunshine Home, which made both brands famous throughout the region (the practice continues to this day).

Bostick's son John now runs the company which prides itself on being a mom-and-pop business that sells only through a mom-and-pop dealer base (no chains), using its own trucks to transport its homes, and its own fleet of 12 service trucks to do warranty work. With a majority of its business deriving from steady customer referrals, Sunshine handily weathered the '99-'04 downturn, abetted by a savvy decision to not to abandon the single-section market even as many other builders did.

States where sold: AL, MS, GA, FL, IA, KS, OK, TX, MO, KY, AR, LA, NC, SC, IL
Principal market niche: Mid-range price points, customers from all demographics
Retail price range before tax (price includes transportation & set-up): low 30s (entry single-section) to $100,000 (triple sections)
Competes against: SE market: Cavalier, Southern Energy, Indies House, River Birch (w/ Georgetown series); Midwest market: Commodore, Four Seasons, Dutch Housing, Fortune.
Construction rating: 6
Brands/series:
Grand Bay series - top of the line, triple-sections only, up to $100,000-plus
Sunshine series - the principal line, double-sections only, across all price points
Brookwood series - single-section homes, mid-price range
Georgetown series - single-section low end starter homes (from low- to mid-30s)
Description of the #1 selling model: Sunshine double-section, 32x70, 2,240 sq. ft., 3BR, 2BA, w/ corner covered front porch, angled bay windows, vinyl lap siding, 3/12 roof, 2x4" ext. walls 16" O.C., 2x2 int. walls, 2x8 floor joists 24" O.C., OSB decking glued and nailed, 8' ext. side wall hit, flat ceilings, finished out (paint ready), ½" VOG, perimeter HVAC registers, 25 oz. carpet, Formica kitchen countertops w/rolled edges, raised panel oak cabinets (hidden hinges), single lever faucet, water shut-offs t/o, 40 gal. water heater, vitreous china BA sinks, toilet, elec. outlet boxes secured to sheetrock w/ wing tabs
What distinguishes brand from its competition: Homes solidly built, excellent quality control reputation, high customer referral rate, outstanding warranty service, homes delivered by own trucks, loyal dealer network, bag of dog food under kitchen sink of every new home (even sales center models).
Number of dealerships — Companyowned: none
Independents: 100
Percentage of HUD homes sold of total homes produced: 95%
In-house financing? No
In-house Insurance? No
Warranty structure and length: 1-year. Company authorizes dealers to do emergency plumbing and electrical repairs but otherwise uses a team of 15 uniformed factory dispatched service techs in a dozen Sunshine vans to perform all other service, incl. cosmetic repairs, promises a 30 day response time, and does whatever it takes to make the customer happy.
Web site rating: Good but missing essential content. Pros: clean, functional, fast, good clickable photos, good description of the product lines and key staff people, conveys a sense of an approachable customer-oriented company; Cons: no listing of constructions specs and/or options (Construction page shows a cut-away illustration but no text, no list of features), site not maximized to load properly with some browsers (e.g., Safari)
Comment: Sunshine Homes' belief in providing outrageous customer service has paid handsome dividends, garnering a reputation that by all accounts (even those of a former HUD factory inspector) is unblemished, hence a better than average construction rating despite less-than-average construction features. A company manager explained, "We're a bit weird—if we can't fix a problem, we'll ask the customer to go to the state, and whatever the state tells us to do, we'll do." That, plus building home models well-suited to

its market (with some interesting floor plans using tags that are worth a look) explain why Sunshine is consistently among the top 20 MH producers.

Superior Homes, LLC (privately held)
715 21st. Street SW
Watertown, SD 57201
Ph. 866/773-5055 Fx. 509/773-5077
Web site: www.superiorhomesllc.com
Background: From the late 1940s until recently this small MH builder serving the upper Midwest and mountain west regions was a family-owned enterprise that produced homes under successively different brands, most recently as Medallion Homes, a well-regarded product noted for lots of customization. In 2003, a local group of investors with no MH building experience purchased the company, keeping the Medallion name and its dealer network, while expanding production of modular homes (currently 60% of output) to take advantage of the better financing options available. Superior has benefited from both an improving economy and an MH marketplace that in 2005 finally emerged from the industry downturn.
States where sold: SD, ND, WI, MN, IA, NE, WY, CO, MT
Principal market niche: mid-to high-end price range, for buyers desiring a lot of customization
Retail price range before tax (price includes transportation & set-up): $55,000 (single-section) to low $100s (no triple sections).
Competes against: Schult, Nashua, Kit Homebuilders West, Wick
Construction rating: 8
Brands/series:
Medallion Platinum – double-sections, 24-, 28-, 32- wide, from $58,000 - $100,000-plus
Medallion Gold – single sections (only half dozen per yr. but heavily built for winter and as big as 18x80, "as big as a highway off ramp," quipped a company spokesman)
Description of a popular model: CH2865-13, 3BR, 2BA, 1,640 sq. ft., 5/12 roof pitch, 2x6 ext. walls 16", 2x4 int. walls, all 16" O.C., T&T bull nose dry wall t/o, opt. 8" ext. side wall ht, (7-1/2' std.), flat ceilings, ¾" Novadek decking glued/nailed, perimeter heat registers, 25 oz. carpet on 7 oz. rebond pad, 19 cu. ft. refrigerator, Formica beveled edge countertops, ceramic backsplash, single lever faucet, stainless sink, factory-made oak cabinets, R-38/22/19, dual thermo pane windows, vitreous china BA sinks/toilets.
What distinguishes brand from its competition: Great flexibility of customization, a lot of work done by hand (esp. cabinetry) by seasoned joiners/carpenters
Number of dealerships—Company owned: none
Independents: 18
Percentage of HUD homes sold of total homes produced: 40%
In-house financing? No
In-house Insurance? No
Warranty structure and length: 1-year. Beyond that, company endeavors to keep customers happy, handling problems on a case by case basis.
Web site rating: Fairly dreadful, minimally serviceable. Untutored, hokey design, frustrating for the informed home shopper. Pros: good selection of photos (some amateurish) w/ a few exteriors, OK Contact Us page, printable floor plans; Cons: primitive design, a terrible pair of useless videos of a kitchen that are impossibly dark (and take forever to load), annoying background texture makes lists hard to read; lists of features/options lack detail, incomplete dealer list.
Comment: Being in the heart of the western upper Midwest (200 miles from the closest MH competitor), Superior Homes is well-positioned to deliver its products to a region where brutal winters demand strong, well-built homes. By offering great flexibility in custom work (from a napkin drawing to borrowing from any other floor plan), and touches like cedar siding for large cabins, Superior should be on the list of any home shopper in the region looking for a HUD home in mid- to high price range.

Town Homes, LLC (Privately held)
133 SE Newell Drive
Lake City, FL 32056
Ph. 386/719-5598 Fx. 386/752-9291
Web site: www.groups.msn.com/TownHomesLLC/
Background: Florida's newest MH builder, Town Homes was launched in early 2005 in Lake City (east of Tampa) by a group of seven investors that include Homes of Merit founder Chuck Weeder and MH retailer mogul Wayne Fryer (32 dealerships variously named Wayne Fryer Home Center, Family Home Center, Ironwood Homes). Managed by Gary Towns, a 20-yr. veteran with Homes of Merit (Bartow division), the plant (a converted lumber milling operation) got a jump start by building 150 emergency SWs for FEMA after Hurricane Katrina. By the fall of '06 total homes were over 500, almost all sold through street dealerships (not MH park dealers). Company moving into modular series for the post-Katrina rebuild market.
States where sold: FL, GA, MS but mostly FL

Principal market niche: medium to low side of high end
Retail price range before tax (including transportation and set-up): $55,000 - $95,000
Competes against: Fleetwood, Homes of Merit, Palm Harbor, Jacobsen
Construction rating: 5
Brands: Town Home Series
Description of a popular model: DW, Model 2801, 28 x 56, 3BR, 2BA, 2x6 ext. walls, int. walls, 4/12 roof pitch, 2x4 24" O.C., 3/8" VOG, MDF baseboard molding, floor decking 5/8" OSB T&G glued/stapled to 2x6" joists, single pane windows, kitchen counters 24" deep, Formica self-edged, stainless steel sink w/ single lever metal faucet/sprayer, 20 cu.ft. refrigerator, 30 gal. water heater, 18 oz. carpet secured by tack strips, elec. outlet boxes nailed to studs (wall rocker switches wing tab secured). Retail price: $61,000-$65,000.
What distinguishes brand from its competition: New company, investors with lots of MH ind. experience, lots of customization allowed (even to custom build from customer's drawings), no track record of warranty service
Number of dealerships—Company owned: none
  Independents: 40
Percentage of HUD code homes sold of total homes produced: 98% but increasing the mod side by 2007
In-house financing: No
In-house insurance: No
Warranty structure and length: 1 year, 3 factory-dispatched teams, plus contract providers in the region.
Web site rating: Unsatisfactory, still under construction. Pros: some good int. photos. Cons: not a stand-alone site (currently part of an MSN interest group), floor plans are unreadable even when printed, no dealer list, no list of features/options, no About Us. Hardly a web site at all.
Comment: In Florida's crowded MH market, with so many choices, Town Homes boasts no obvious competitive edge beyond its willingness to customize its models, but its offering of ceiling registers as standard and 8' flat ceilings in 24' and 28' wides (9-1/2' vaulted in 32' wides) even with VOG walls (batten seams) is certainly a click up from the cramped 7' wall height of its VOG competition. Still, the floor plans are boxy, boring and unimaginative. Management's Homes of Merit pedigree is a plus, especially as its mod product ramps up. Town Homes' plant g.m. Garry Towns has experience building mods for Homes of Merit as part of the latter's participation in Champion's Genesis Homes modular program after HOM was acquired by Champion in '99. If the company can really deliver on customer satisfaction, it should prosper.

Valley Quality Homes (dealership chain)
Valley Manufactured Housing, Inc.
(privately held)
1830 S. 1st. Street
Yakama, WA 98903
Ph. 509/453-8937   Fx. 509/575-7702
Web site:
www.valleymanufacturedhousing.com
Background: In 1989, after 13 years as a successful central WA retailer (five sales centers), and disenchanted with the construction quality of even the higher end brands he sold, owner Art Berger and his family built their own MH plant in Yakima, vowing to build HUD-code homes equal in construction quality to site-built (example: copper water lines w/ sweated fittings). The resulting product line, Valley homes (which appeared inspired by the up-market Silvercrest brand that Berger had previously sold), was an instant hit with homebuyers throughout the region (WA, eastern OR, ID and northwestern MT).
Valley Homes are still sold only from the Valley Quality Homes' dealerships. The company does its own set-ups, sending salaried company crews to the home site to complete installation, finish and trim out. Similarly, a salaried warranty service crew operates out of each dealership.
States where sold: WA (to buyers in WA, eastern OR, ID, northwestern MT)
Principal market niche: mid- to high-end homes to home buyers demanding site-built construction quality and a wide choice in options/upgrades
Retail price range before tax (price includes transportation & set-up): $48,000 to $125,700
Competes against: site-built, Palm Harbor, Homebuilders Northwest, Nashua, Fuqua, high end Marlette
Construction rating: 9
Brands/series:
Valley Mansion series – high end triple sections, $96,000 to $125,700, loaded w/ features
Valley Manor series - high end double-sections, all priced at $88,000
Country Cottage series – mid-range double-sections, $48,000 to $82,000
Note: all homes are built to same construction specs, differing only in size and options.
Description of a popular model: Valley Manor #2821, 28x66, 1,778 sq. ft., 3BR, 2BA w/ LR and family room, walk-in closets in MBR and BR#2, 2x6 ext. walls 16" O.C., ½" siding w/ 3/8" plywood double wall exterior, insulation all rolled fiberglass (R-38/21/33), all copper water lines, metal risers and shut-off valves, full T&T drywall t/o, 5/8" Cresdek decking stapled, glued & screwed, low E dual pane windows 1/8th thick (argon insulated); kitchen w/ raised panel oak cabinets, upper

& lower lazy susans, rolled laminate post form countertops w/ seamless backsplash, recessed track and florescent lighting, deep sink laundry tub, snack bar and kitchen planning desk, 50 gal. dual element water heater.
What distinguishes brand from its competition: High construction rating w/ many site-built features, small vertically integrated, very accessible family-run company, factory dispatched installation crews, all homes meet Super Good Cents energy efficiency standard.
Number of dealerships — Company owned: 5
Independents: none
Percentage of HUD homes sold of total homes produced: 100%
In-house financing? No
In-house Insurance? No
Warranty structure and length: 1-year, w/ salaried service crews operating out of company dealerships.
Web site rating: Very good, nothing fancy but serviceable, plenty of relevant content for the informed home shopper. An extensive list of features and specs. Pros: intuitive fast navigation, good ext. photos, printable floor plans, dealer locations, well written; Cons: blah look to the design, few interior photos (and too small, amateurish)
Comment: This small, savvy builder has found a successful business model one could call micro-vertical integration: one plant, five sales centers with low-key sales staffs, selling one line exclusively, no independent retailers, transport and installation by factory crews, factory-dispatched warranty service — and it's operated comfortably in the black since day one. Company's average weekly out put: ten floors. A remarkable story.
Valley Homes are well-suited to the open spaces of the western region where rural sitings are common, but home buyers seeking an appearance indistinguishable from a site built home may be concerned with a roof pitch limited to either 3/12 or 4/14, a 7-1/2' inside wall height, and the unmistakable, dated exterior look of a manufactured home. In general, the homes don't possess the design flair and stylish, contemporary taste of say, comparable Palm Harbor models. If this is not a significant issue, however, a Valley Quality Home should be on the short list of every shopper in the region looking for homes in its price range.

Virginia Homes Manufacturing Corp.
(Privately held)
P.O. Box 410
Boydton, VA 23917
Ph. 434/738-6107   Fx. 434/738-6926
Web site: www.virginiahomesmfg.com

Background: Started in 1969, this small builder in southern Virginia has focused largely on modular homes (85%-90% of total homes built), with almost all its HUD-code homes destined for MH land-lease retirement communities in New England. (see comment). Builds no single section or triple section MH.
States where sold: VA, NC, DE, MA, MD, NJ, NY, PA, RI, NH, SC
Principal market niche: for HUD-code double-sections - low-mid range, MH retirement communities
Retail price range before tax (price includes transportation & set-up): $48,000- $90,000
Competes against: Redman, Champion, Horton, Marlette, Commodore Homes of VA
Construction rating: 6
Brands/series:
Bristol, Petersburg, Brentwood II — all three equal in features and price point, from 1,475 sq. ft. to 1,580, 3BR, 2BA double section models.
Description of an MH model: The Bristol, 28x60, two-section, 1,580, 3BR, 2BA, w/ den area off DR, 2.5/12 roof pitch, ext. walls 2x4" 16" O.C., int. wall ht. 7-1/2', walls ½" smooth finished dry wall w/ wood molding, R-19/11/11, stainless steel kitchen sink w/ single lever faucet, BA sinks cultured marble sinks, oak cabinets,
What distinguishes brand from its competition: Nothing stands out. Based on limited information available, company appears to make little or no effort to market its MH brands.
Number of dealerships — Company owned: none
Independents: Unknown-dealers are located in 11 states but how many sell the MH lines is not known (see Comment)
Percentage of HUD homes sold of total homes produced: 15%
In-house financing? No
In-house Insurance? No
Warranty structure and length: 1 year
Web site rating: Failure, unsatisfactory for the informed MH home shopper. Pros: fairly complete list of standard specs on MH brands; Cons: primitive clunky design, floor plans too small to read, no ext. elevations, almost no photos, no interior shots, no dealer list, no warranty info, no company background. Another lifeless web site created as an afterthought, nothing more than a static unattractive brochure
Comment: A more than three-week effort to obtain an interview and product information was unsuccessful. The company's president did ask for a call-back but several subsequent attempts were unanswered. A member of the sales staff, who knew

little of the company's background, provided the name of a nearby dealer who carried the MH line, but the dealer sold modular products only. Potential buyers of Virginia Homes Manufacturing homes should not be blamed if they find this behavior troubling. Clearly, with its company slogan, "Excellence in modular housing since 1969," VHM's focus is on its modular lines of ranches, multi-section ranches, two stories, salt boxes and Cape Cods. Photos and elevations of the mod lines reflect a robust building ability, but the MH products by comparison come across as poor relations.

Waverlee Homes, Inc. (privately held)
A joint venture w/ Liberty Homes, Inc
(see Liberty listing)
2039 Bexar Avenue East, Bedford Industrial Park
PO Box 1887
Hamilton, AL 35570
Ph. 205/921-1887   Fx. 205/921-1888
Web site: www.waverleehomesinc.com
Background: In 1994, veteran MH executive Steve Logan, together with several other investors, formed a joint venture with Goshen, IN-based Liberty Homes, Inc. to create Waverlee Homes, establishing a factory in Hamilton, in NW Alabama, an MH industry hot bed (a half dozen or more other MH plants are within a 30 mile radius). Named after Waverlee (old English spelling), a mid-19th century settlement/plantation on the nearby Tombigbee River, the company at the outset built affordable single-section homes before moving into sectionals in 1996, opening a second plant a year later in Muscle Shoals (the facility was mothballed in 2001 during the industry downturn). Currently double-section models account for 85% of Waverlee's annual production, which is largely distributed to the 10 state SE market.
States where sold: AL, AR, FL, GA, KY, LA, MS, MO, OK, TN, TX
Principal market niche: low end of the mid-range price point for working families
Retail price range before tax (includes transportation and set-up): $58,000-$75,000
Competes against: Cavalier, Sunshine, Patriot, Indies, Gateway, Deer Valley
Construction rating: 4
Brands/series:
Elite series – higher end, mostly sectionals, all with 3/12 roof pitch, 8" int. wall ht., flat ceilings, T&T t/o, 32x62 to 32x80, 12 floor plans
Country Classic series – a click below, single-sections and sectionals, 3/12 roof pitch std, 8' int. wall ht., flat ceilings (single sectionals vaulted ceilings), VOG t/o, 28x52 to 32x80, twelve floor plans
Description of a popular model: Country Classic, 32x80, 2,560 sq. ft. two-section, 4BR, 2BA, 3/12 roof pitch, ext. walls 2x4" 16" O.C. (std), 2x3" int. walls 16" O.C., 8' int. wall ht, flat ceilings, VOG walls glued and nailed, ¾" Novadek floor decking (std), windows white vinyl dual glazed, stainless steel appliance package incl. 22 cu. ft. FF refrigerators w/ side-by-side doors/water/ice, hand-laid ceramic kitchen countertops w/ wood edging, drawer-over-door base cabinets, oak w/ raised stiles, dual knob gooseneck metal faucet, stainless steel sink, 19 oz. Saxony carpet stapled and tack stripped to 6 lb. ½-inch rebond pad, elect. outlet boxes secured to wall w/ clips; 50 gal. water heater, vitreous china toilets, BA sinks one-piece cultured marble. Approx. $75,000.
What distinguishes brand from its competition: Final trim out/inspection by factory techs, modular box cabinets, more T&T bull nose walls, more contemporary int. appearance, competitive price points, in-house financing, stable backing of venture partner Liberty Homes, Inc.
Number of dealerships — Company owned: none
Independents: 120
Percentage of HUD homes sold of total homes produced: 99%
In-house financing? Yes, TriCom Mortgage, LLC
In-house Insurance? No
Warranty structure and length: 1 year
Web site rating: Good, but missing essential content. Pros: good layout and navigation, excellent selection of photos and gallery navigation, floor plans printable from screen, avoids use of gimmicky animation/applets; Cons: no triple-section floor plans, no list of construction specs and options, no description of model series, no meaningful company history, no mention of TriCom Mortgage in-house financing.

Comment: Waverlee faces tough competition in a crowded market niche (the $60k-$70k median price point) but it has taken a page from Palm Harbor, sending out factory techs to perform final finish and trim outs, including making sure homes are set up properly and conducting a customer walk-through. Doing so is in part a necessary response to the lack of qualified sheet rock contractors (textured and/or painted dry wall is really catching on in the SE market), but Waverlee benefits from a dramatically reduced service costs during the warranty period—and happy customers. Add to this access to in-house loan programs from TriCom Mortgage, LLC (See Liberty listing), and Waverlee can expect to remain competitive.

Wick Building Systems Inc. (privately held)
PO Box 490 404 Walter Road
Mazomanie, WI 53560
Ph. 608/795-4281   Fx. 608/795-2740
Web site: www.wickmarshfield.com

Background: This venerable builder, long dominant in the upper Midwest, was founded in 1954 as Marshfield Homes, in Marshfield, WI, by John Wick and Elmer Frye, the latter a mobile home builder, inventor and pioneer who developed the first ten-wide and 14-wide mobile homes, ushering in the era of the true manufactured home. By the mid-1960s Wick bought out Frye, changed the company name to Wick Building Systems, and expanded. At one point in the 70s, the company owned plants in 12 cities across the US, each building one of three Wick brands: Marshfield, Artcraft or Rollohome (the latter a brand acquired in 1975).

In the early 80s, when the US economy tanked, Wick sold all the plants except the original Marshfield facility, vowing to focus on the Wisconsin region market. The strategy worked, and the company became very strong, in time commanding an enviable market share of more than 40% in the upper Midwest. Along the way Wick launched a modular homes division (1988), a panelized home division, and a buildings division (large structures, churches, barns, offices). The company is currently headed by Wick's son Jeff, a highly regarded MH industry leader. Unique among MH builders, the company runs a closed union shop—all 500 of its production workers belong to the United Brotherhood of Carpenters and Joiners.

States where sold: WI, IL, IA, MI, MN, MO, MT, NE, ND, SD, WY

Principal market niche: Mid to high end, principally to retirees/seniors and growing families, almost all homes going on private property sites, most w/ basements.

Retail price range before tax (includes transportation and set-up): High 30s (single sections) to $145,000.

Competes against: site-built homes, Skyline, Fairmont, Friendship, Liberty, some Patriot, some Champion brands (e.g., Dutch Housing)

Construction rating: 9

Brands:

Marshfield Homes, Artcraft Homes, Rollohomes — all virtually identical, in models across all price points, with some variation in floor plans and decor. The three brands allow for selling through several retailer/builders in large, metro markets. **Note:** Though not a brand, the Wick name is often used to distinguish the brands from the competition—i.e. "It's a Wick home."

Description of a popular model: Two-section, 28x60, 3BR, 2BA basement model, w/ attached garage, lg. family room, lg. master BR suite, 2x6 ext. walls 16" O.C., 6/12 roof pitch, 40# snow load, R-44 ceiling, R-19 walls, T&T dry wall t/o, (except 2' deep closets are VOG), 8' side wall, flat ceiling, factory-made oak cabinetry, kitchen island, laminate countertop w/ ceramic backslash (available option: 1" thick granite w/ rounded edge), 30 oz. carpet w/ 7# rebond pad. Price, around. $135,000 (incl. garage, approx. $15,000)

What distinguishes brand from its competition: Many models have a site-built look, more heavily constructed w/ more lumber/materials (average section weighs 6,000 lbs. more than comparable brands), great flexibility in customization, strong retail network with dealers more like builders (offering turn key homes) and regarded as such by Wick.

Number of dealerships — Companyowned: none
Independents: 100 (about 12 exclusive)
Percentage of HUD homes sold of total homes produced: 35%
In-house financing? No
In-house Insurance? No
Warranty structure and length:
Web site rating: Nice looking but at bottom unsatisfactory, very short on content for the informed home shopper. Pros: clean, well-organized. uncluttered, well-written, fast, intuitive navigation, useful site map, slick IPIX virtual tours, helpful dealer locator. Cons: No lists of specifications and options, very few images of ext. elevations, few floor plans. Add these and the site is a winner.

Comment: Very few MH brands are notable for carrying the personal imprint of the person who heads the company that makes them. Patriot's Sam Weidner and New Era's Elliot Fabri are two; and Wick Building System's CEO Jeff Wick is a third. A conscientious builder who stands behind his products, Wick is highly regarded for both his leadership and for being one of the industry's most thoughtful minds. A Wick home will on average cost more than its nearest competition (few builders offer a single-section with full finished dry wall t/o), but homebuyers who can afford to consider all options would do well to include a Wick HUD-code choice in the mix, especially given the high degree of customization available.

The #1 best selling book on buying manufactured homes and purchasing land or leasing a home site

If you have *the Grissim Ratings Guide to Manufctured Homes*, you already know that today's manufactured homes are truly the best-kept secret in American housing. Yet for all their advances, manufactured homes are still sold like cars: through street dealerships, most of them still focused on selling lower end models to consumers unable to qualify for conventional home loans. Along the way the industry has attracted more than its share of predatory dealers and finance companies. Historically, shady dealings, fraud and misrepresentation have been all too common.

Most retailers are reputable but until now no comprehensive resource guide has been available to consumers that explains just how the manufactured home industry operates, how to find a dealer worthy of your trust, how to make the right home selection, and, as important, how to be informed, empowered, and swindle-proof. *The Grissim Buyer's Guide to Manufactured Homes and Land* is that resource—and it could save you thousands of dollars.

Exhaustively researched, and with extensive input from both industry insiders and consumer advocates, this guide contains much information that retailers, even the good guys, don't want you to know.

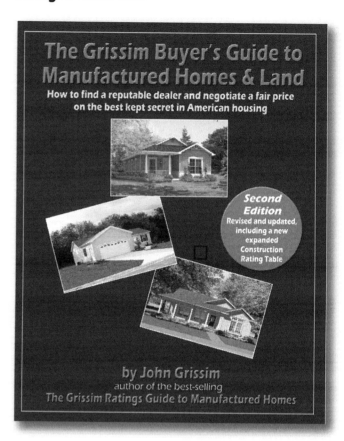

Rainshadow Publications, 192 pages, 66 illustrations
$29.95 + S&H (print), $19.95 digital PDF edition
ISBN 0-9725436-1-9

Topics include:

- Pros and cons of manufactured homes
- The 19 warning signs of an untrustworthy dealer
- The 19 encouraging signs of a reputable dealer
- How buyers get fleeced: a worst case scenario
- Checking out a dealer, getting the local lowdown
- Obtaining your own credit score before you shop
- How dealers determine their retail prices
- Guidelines for checking out lot models
- Repossessed homes: pros, cons, dangers
- Handling high-pressure sales techniques
- Tips to get the best effort out of your Realtor
- Construction loans—protecting your interests
- How to determine the fair price of a home
- Smart negotiating tactics, what not to disclose
- Deal terms—what to insist be in writing
- Questions to ask land-lease communities
- Preventive steps to avoid contractor rip-offs
- Site-prep and installation—spotting trouble
- How to get prompt warranty service
- Handling high-pressure sales techniques
- Tips to get the best effort out of your Realtor
- Construction loans—protecting your interests
- How to determine the fair price of a home
- Smart negotiating tactics, what not to disclose
- Deal terms—what to insist be in writing
- Questions to ask land-lease communities
- Preventive steps to avoid contractor rip-offs
- Site-prep and installation—spotting trouble
- How to get prompt warranty service

Price $29.95 plus $5.95 S&H (by Priority Mail)
To order, visit www.grissimguides.com or call toll-free (800) 304-6650.
Or buy the digital edition online for just $19.95 and be reading the book within seconds.
Orders usually ship within 24 hours. If you're not completely satisfied, simply return the book and your money will be cheerfully refunded. The book may also be ordered from any book store.

What others are saying about *The Grissim Buyer's Guide to Manufactred Homes and Land*

Some excerpts from book reviews:

"...a soup-to-nuts, definitive buying guide to manufactured homes, a comprehensive work."
Marin Independent Journal

"This is a guide no manufactured home buyer should be without....John Grissim has performed a fine public service in writing this guide ....[Readers] will gain a lot of good information that will help them make a financially sound purchase."
Carson City Appeal

"Finally, consumers have a detailed map of the manufactured home marketplace....Presents a huge amount of sophisticated information about financing, land-home packages, construction quality, leasehold communities and, above all, negotiating a fair deal....Extensive and up-to-date information about the industry....Grissim's advice on developing sites is especially welcome....He also hopes a new breed of 'swindle-proof' consumers will force [industry] change. With this solid book, they have their tool." *Shelterforce magazine*

"....Offers detailed information on every aspect of planning for, purchasing and situating a manufactured home, plus information about the top 25 manufacturers in the country." *Sequim Gazette*

"...Outstanding research...jam-packed with information and advice...Fair and balanced....Will save money, time, effort and frustration."
St. Petersburg Times

"From locating a reputable dealer and negotiating a fair price to understanding the pros and cons of the manufactured home...packs in ratings of top manufacturers, insights on the importance of trustworthy dealers, and guidelines for checking out models, land, and construction loans. Everything you need to buy and build one of these homes is here in one handy place." *Midwest Book Review*

"...Delves into issues that could save buyers thousands of dollars and many headaches."
Reno Gazette-Journal

From home buyers who purchased the book:

"Without John's book, we would not have known how to conduct our search, nor been aware of some 'unpleasant' dealer practices which we were able to avoid because we were forewarned....We were able to buy the right house at the right price and avoid almost all the pitfalls that await the unwary or uninformed. We cannot recommend John's book too highly." Gary and Linda Zerbst, Lopez Island, WA

"I just moved into my manufactured home after months of planning. This book got me started, then saw me through the adventure with invaluable tips and information....The journey was long and sometimes difficult, but thank goodness I had this guide. It was my personal consultant in a way that no other source could have been. In the end, it saved me several thousand dollars and countless headaches." John Edmonds, Cloudcroft, NM

"As a manufactured home owner who recently began shopping for a move up home, I thought I knew all I needed to know about manufactured homes, until I read John's book. It's without a doubt the best book out there. I consider it the consumer's 'Bible.' You'll be learning from someone who not only has done it, but has taken the time to thoroughly research every aspect." Joseph Rafalo, Petaluma, CA

"This is without a doubt the best and most authoritative guide I've found, especially for the first time manufactured home buyer (which I was). It offers a feast of essential information about buying and setting up a manufactured home that I found enormously helpful."
Josiah Thompson Bolinas, CA

"I loved this book. I had no idea of the colossal details that go into investing in a manufactured home....I was extremely pleased and surprised at how much fabulous information was in this book. I used it as a workbook and have recommended this book already to friends. Outstanding information!"
Tammy Bridenbeck, Biloxi, MS

Notes